Francis Bacon, Thomas Tenison, Francis Fulford

Baconiana;

Or, Certain genuine remains of Sr. Francis Bacon. In arguments civil and moral, natural, medical, theological, and bibliographical; now the first time published

Francis Bacon, Thomas Tenison, Francis Fulford

Baconiana;

Or, Certain genuine remains of Sr. Francis Bacon. In arguments civil and moral, natural, medical, theological, and bibliographical; now the first time published

ISBN/EAN: 9783337724399

Printed in Europe, USA, Canada, Australia, Japan

Cover: Foto ©ninafisch / pixelio.de

More available books at **www.hansebooks.com**

BACONIANA.

Or Certain Genuine

REMAINS

OF

S^{R.} Francis Bacon,

Baron of VERULAM,

AND

Viscount of St. ALBANS;

In Arguments *Civil* and *Moral*, *Natural*, *Medical*, *Theological*, and *Bibliographical*; Now the First time faithfully Published.

An ACCOUNT of these *Remains*, and of all his *Lordship's* other *Works*, is given by the Publisher, in a Discourse by way of INTRODUCTION.

LONDON,

Printed by *J. D.* for *Richard Chiswell*, at the Rose and Crown in St. *Paul's* Church-Yard, 1679.

A DISCOURSE,

BY WAY OF INTRODUCTION,

In which the Publisher endeavoureth an Account of the PHILOSOPHY, MECHANIC INVENTIONS, and WRITINGS, of Sir *FRANCIS BACON*, Baron of *Verulam*, and Viscount of St. *Albans*; And particularly of these REMAINS now set forth by him under the Title of BACONIANA.

LONDON,

Printed for R. C. at the Rose and Crown in St. Paul's Church-yard, 1679.

AN ACCOUNT

Of all the

Lord BACON'S

WORKS.

IT is my purpose to give a true and plain Account, of the Designs and Labours of a very great Philosopher amongst us; and to offer to the World, in some tollerable Method, those *Remains* of his, which to that end, were put into my Hands.

Something of this hath been done already by his Lordship himself; and something further hath been added by the Reverend Dr. *Rawley*: But their Remarks lay scattered in divers Places; and here they are put under one View, and have received very ample Enlargements.

In this last and most comprehensive Account, I have, on purpose, used a loose and *Asiatic* Style, and wilfully committed that venial fault with which the *Laconian* (in *Boccalini*) is merrily taxed, who had said that in *three words*, which he might possibly have express'd in *two*. I hop'd, by this means, to serve the more effectually, *ordinary Readers*, who stand chiefly in need of this Introduction; and whose Capacities can be no more reach'd by a close and strict Discourse, than Game can be taken by a Net unspread.

For any praise upon the account of this small Performance, it is not worth the while to be solicitous about it. Yet sometimes, mean Men get a stock of Reputation, by gathering up the *Fragments of the Learned*; as Beggars (they say) have gotten Estates by saving together the *Alms of the Rich*. If that falls not out here where it is not expected, it will be abundantly enough to me if the Inferiour Reader may have Benefit, and any Honour may be done to the Memory of his Lordship, whose more *General Encomium* I shall first set down, and then annex *a particular Narrative* of those Designs and Labours of his, which may be said,

said, not only to merit, but even to exceed all my Commendations.

I begin (as I said) with his Lordship's Praise, in a more general way. And here I affirm, with good assurance (for Truth is bold) that amongst those few, who by the strength of their private Reason, have resisted popular Errors, and avanced real and useful Learning; there has not arisen a more Eminent Person, than the *Lord High Chancellor Bacon*. Such great Wits, are not the common Births of Time: And they, surely, intended to signifie so much who said of the Phœnix (though in Hyperbole as well as Metaphor) that Nature gives the World that *Individual Species*, but once in five hundred Years.

It is true, There lived in part of the last, and this, Century, many memorable Advancers of Philosophical Knowledg. I mean not here such as *Patricius*, or *Telesius*, *Brunus*, *Severinus* the *Dane*, or *Campanella*. These, indeed, departed from some Errors of the Ancients, but they did not frame any solid *Hypothesis* of their own. They only spun new Cobwebs, where they had brush'd down the old. Nay, I intend not, in this place, either *de Chart*, or *Gassendi*. They were, certainly, great Men, but they appeared somewhat later, and descended into

into the depths of Philosophy, after the Ice had been broken by others. And those I take to have been chiefly *Copernicus, Father Paul* the *Venetian, Galileo, Harvey, Gilbert,* and the Philosopher before-remembred, Sir *Francis Bacon,* who, if all his Circumstances be duly weigh'd, may seem to excel them all. He was by *Profession*, a common Lawyer; by *Office*, in the *Queen's* time, one of the *Clerks* of the Council; in the Reign of King *James*, one of the *King's Counsel* Learned, then *Solicitor* General, and one of the *Judges* in the Knight-Marshals Court; then *Attorney* General, and one of the King's *Privy-Council*; then *Lord-Keeper* of the Great Seal, and during the Kings absence in *Scotland, Lord Protector*: And last of all, *Lord High Chancellor of England.* So that in such a Life as his, so thickly set with Business of such Height, it is a Miracle that all Seeds of Philosophy were not daily overdropped, and in a short time, quite choaked; and that any one of them sprung up to Maturity. And yet his prosper'd beyond those of the Philosophers before-mentioned, though they were not pressed on with such a crowd of secular Business.

For *Copernicus*, he concern'd himself especially in the Revolutions of the Heavenly Bodies,

Bodies, in reviving and perfecting the obsolete Doctrine of *Philolaus*, touching the motion of the Earth, and in setting free the Planets from those many Epicycles, Eccentrics, and Concentrics, in which *Ptolomy*, and others had entrangled them. And he well understood the Course of the Stars, though he did not much study that natural motive Power which carries them about in their several *Elliptics*. The like Remark may be made concerning Mr. *Gilbert*, who applied himself particularly to the consideration of Magnetic Powers; as also concerning Dr. *Harvey*, who inquired principally into the Generation of Animals, and the motion of the Heart: Subjects in which he made great progress, though into the former, the help of Microscopes, would have given him further insight (a); and in both, he rather pursued the proofs of his Hypotheses, than the nature of the Mechanic force, which produced those great Effects.

Father Paul, was a more general Philosopher, and the Head of a *Meeting of Vertuosi* in *Venice*. He excelled in *Mechanics*, in *Mathematics* of all kinds, in *Philological* Learning, in *Anatomy*. In his Anatomical Studies, he exercis'd such Sagacity, that he made further discoveries in the fabrick of

(a) *See* Dr. Highmore, *of* Generation, p. 70, 71.

the Eye, and taught *Aqua-pendente*, those new Speculations which he publish'd on that Subject; he found out (saith *Fulgentio*) the *Valvulæ in the Veins*, and began the Doctrine of the Circulation of the Blood: Though there is reason to believe, that he receiv'd the hints of it from Sir *Henry Wotton*, who himself had taken them from Dr. *Harvey* (a). But, the present state of the Affairs of *Venice* so requiring, Father *Paul* bent his Studies to Ecclesiastical Polity, and chiefly employ'd his Pen in detecting the Usurpations and Corruptions of the *Papacy:* Endeavouring (so far as Books could do it) to preserve the Neck of that Republick, from the Bondage of *Paul the Fifth*, who attempted to set his Foot upon it.

(a) Cartes *diss. de Methodo*. p. 46. Herveo *laus hæc tribuenda est quòd primam in istâ materiâ glaciem fregerit*, &c.

Galileo further improv'd the Doctrine of *Copernicus*; discover'd by Telescopes, new Stars in the Heavens; wrote *Dialogues* concerning the *System of the World*, and touching *Local Motion*; which latter is the Key that openeth Nature. But he descended not to the several Classes of Bodies in Nature, and the particulars contained in them, and their respective Motions, and Uses. Neither did he publish any thing till many Years

Years had pass'd, since Mr. *Bacon* had form'd and modelled in his thoughts, his larger Idea of Experimental Knowledg. His *Sidereus Nuncius*, came not forth till towards the midst of the Reign of King *James*. And King *Charles* had sate some Years on his Throne, er'e he publish'd his Dialogue of the System of the World. Whereas Mr. *Bacon* had not only publish'd two Books of his *Advancement*, in the beginning of K. *James*'s Reign, but early in the *Queen*'s time, (as from his Letter to *Fulgentio*, plainly appeareth) he had written his *Temporis Partus Maximus*. That Book (pompous in its Title, but solid in its Matter; like a great Feather put sometimes on a good Headpiece) contained in it, though in imperfect manner, and so far as the greenness of his Years permitted, the principal Rudiments of his *Instauration*. The work therefore of the *Instauration*, was an Original; and a Work so vast and comprehensive in its design, that though others in that Age, might hew out this, or the other *Pillar*; yet of him alone it seemeth true, that he fram'd the *whole Model* of the *House of Wisdom*.

In those days in which he began his Studies, *Aristotle* was, in effect, the Pope in Philosophy. The Lectures, both in his private

private College, and in the publick Schools, were generally Expositions upon *Aristotle*'s Text. And every Opinion, wrote by him as his own, was esteem'd as Authentick, as if it had been given under the *Seal of the Fisher*. It was, therefore, a very singular Felicity in a young Gentleman to see further into Nature, than that celebrated Philosopher, at whose feet he was plac'd. And it was as happy as it was extraordinary, that he took distaste betimes at the Vulgar Physicks. Use and Custome in that way, might have reconciled it to him, as it had done to others of great Learning. For a Philosopher is like a Vine, of which they say, It must be set of a Plant, and not of a Tree.

But, though there was bred in Mr. *Bacon* so early a dislike of the Physiologie of *Aristotle*, yet he did not despise him with that Pride and Haughtiness, with which Youth is wont to be puffed up. He had a just esteem of that great Master in Learning (c), and greater than that which *Aristotle* himself expressed towards the Philosophers that went before him. For he endeavour'd (some say) to stifle all their Labours; designing to himself an universal Monarchy over

(c) *De Augm. Scient.* l. 3. c. 4. *Caterum, de viro tam Eximio certè, &, ob acumen Ingenii, mirabili,* Aristotele, *&c:*

Opinions, as his Patron *Alexander* did over Men. Our Heröe owned what was excellent in him; but, in his Inquiries into Nature, he proceeded not upon his Principles. He began the Work a-new, and laid the foundation of Philosophick Theory in numerous Experiments.

By this Theory is not (as I conceive) so much to be understood, that most abstracted, and more narrow one, of the meer nature and definition of Matter, Motion, Place, Figure, Sight, Quantity, and the like, which a Man's Reason may find out, by a few common and daily Appearances in Nature, or Operations of Art: But we are to understand by it, a truer and fuller Knowledg, of the Systeme of the World, of the several Actions and Passions of Bodies in it, and of the divers Ways whereby, in themselves, or by the application of Art to them, they may be made serviceable to Humane Life.

Now this was a Work for a Man of a thousand Hands, and as many Eyes, and depended upon a distinct, and comprehensive, History of Nature. It was a way laborious and tedious, yet useful and honourable, and in this, like that way of the Snail, which *shineth* though it is *slow*.

Such an useful and noble Philosophy did

our

our Author design, instead of the *Art of Disputation*, which then generally prevail'd, and which he compar'd to the condition of Children who are apt for *Talk*, but not for *Generation*. And certainly, that Character was most due unto himself which he gave to *Xenophanes*, of whom he said, that he was *a Man of a vast Conceit, and that minded nothing but Infinitum* (d).

(d) *Hist. of Life & Death. p. 15.*

Easie it is to add to things already *invented*; but to *invent*, and to do it under Discouragement, when the World is prejudiced against the Invention, and with loud Clamour hooteth at the Projector; this is not an Undertaking for Dulness, or Cowardize. To do this, argues an Inquisitive and *Sagacious Wit*; *A mind free from slavish prepossession*; *a piercing Judgment*, able to see through the mists of Authority; a great *Power* in the Understanding, giving to a Man sufficient *Courage* to bear up the Head against the common Current of Philosophical Doctrines, and *Force* to beat out its own way in untravelled Places.

With such Intellectual Ability, was the Lord *Verulam* endow'd: And he *stood on the old Paths*, and perceiv'd, the unsoundness of their Bottom; their intricate Windings; their tendency to an useless End, or
rather

rather to endless Disputation; and the daily Justlings and Rencounters of those who travail'd in them: And he looked attentively round about him, and he espied a new, and better, and larger, and safer way; and he journey'd far in it himself; and he left a Map of it for Posterity, who might further pursue it; and he has been happy in being follow'd, by Men of the ablest Understandings, with singular success; and the *Societies* for improving of Natural Knowledg, do not at this day, depart from his Directions, though they travel further than Death would suffer him to adventure.

I can, at present, call to remembrance but one Man, who hath undervalued his Lordship's Method; and it is the same Man who hath libell'd the Holy Scriptures themselves; the Infidel *Spinoza* (e). This Man objecteth against his Way, that it faileth in the very entrance of it, through a mistake about the *Original of Error*.

(e) *B. D.* Spinoza *in Ep.* 2. *ad H.* Oldenburg. *with op. Posth.* p. 398, 399.

His Lordship's Opinion is the same with that which *de Chart* insisteth on, in his latter Philosophy. Both shew that therefore Man deceives himself, because his *Will* (being larger in its desires, than the *Understanding*

ing is in its Comprehensions; and hastning its opinion of such Objects as it covets to know, before it hath sufficiently attended to them; and obtain'd a clear and distinct perception of them) does cause it to yield a blind and rash, and therefore groundless Assent to insufficient Evidence.

His Lordship hath expressed it *thus*, after his better way of saying things. "The "*Understanding* (f) is not only made up "of dry Light, but it receives an infusion "from the *Will* and Affections: And that "begets such Sciences as the Heart desireth. "For a Man soonest believes that which "he would have to be true. Wherefore "he rejects *difficult Truths*, through impa-"tience in inquiring; and *sober Truths*, be-"cause they restrain his hope [or desire;] "and the *deeper Natural Truths*, by reason of "Superstition; and the *Light of Experiments*, "by reason of Arrogance and Pride, lest the "Mind should seem to be conversant in mean "and transitory Things; and *Paradoxes*, out "of respect to the opinion of the Vulgar. In "sum, the *Will* seasons and infects the *Mind*, "by innumerable Ways, and by such as are, "sometimes, not at all perceived.

Now, how, think you, doth *Spinoza* shew this opinion, to be a gross and fundamental *Mistake*? Why; by denying that there

(f) *Nov. Organ.* l. 1. *Aph.* 49. p. 44, 45.

is

is any such thing in Man as a *Will:* (as if that general name was ever used to signifie a particular Act, and not rather to express the general notion of that Power:) By telling us that all Volitions are particular Acts, and as fatally determin'd by a Chain of Physical Causes, as any effects whatsoever of Natural Bodies. So that we are like to learn well, from his Philosophy, how to amend our Erroneous Assent, whilst it teacheth us that it is necessary, and not to be mended, unless Men could have other Bodies, and there were another Scheme of Nature.

It must be confess'd, that the Lord I write of, was not without Infirmities, Intellectual or Moral: And the latter of these have made the greater Noise from the greatness of his Fall. I do not, here, pretend to speak of an Angel, but of a Man: And no Man, *great in Wit,* and *high in Office,* can live free from suspicion of both kinds of Errors. For that *Heat* which is instrumental in making a *great Wit,* is apt to disorder the attention of the Mind, and the stability of the Temper. And *High Place,* because it giveth power to Opportunity, though no Athority to offend, is ever look'd on with a jealous Eye: And corrupt Men who mete by their own Measures, think no Man can be Great, and Innocent too. His

His Lordship own'd it under his Hand, (g) that, *He was frail, and did partake of the Abuses of the Times:* And, surely, he was a partaker of their Severities also; though they proved, by accident, happy Crosses and Misfortunes. Methinks they are resembled by those of Sir *George Sommers*, who being bound, by his Employment, to another Coast, was by Tempest, cast upon the *Barmudas*. And there, a Shipwrack'd Man made full discovery of a new temperate fruitful Region, which none had before inhabited; and which Mariners, who had only seen its Rocks, had esteemed an inaccessible and enchanted Place. The great cause of his Suffering, is to some, a secret. I leave them to find it out, by his words to King *James* (h), *I wish* (said he) *that as I am the first, so I may be the last of Sacrifices in your Times.* And when from private Appetite, it is resolv'd, that a Creature shall be sacrific'd; it is easie to pick up sticks enough, from any Thicket whither it hath straid, to make a Fire to offer it with.

But whatsoever his Errors were, or the causes of his Misfortunes, they are overballanc'd by his Vertues, and *will die with Time.* His Errors were but as some Excrescencies, which grow on those Trees that are

(g) *In his Letter to King James, March 25. 1620. In the Cab.*

(h) *See Mr. Bushels Extract.* p. 19.

re fit to build the Palaces of Kings: For though they are not proper and natural Parts, yet they do not very much deprive the Body of its use and value. And, further, (to express my self by a more decent Image, a Comparison of his own;) "His "Fall will be to Posterity, but as a little "Picture of *Night-work*, remaining a- "mongst the Fair and Excellent Tables of "his *Acts and Works* (i).

These I distinguish, into two kinds,

(i) *Epist. to Bishop Andrews*

His *Mechanical Inventions*, and his *Writings*.

I doubt not but his *Mechanical Inventions* were many. But I can call to mind but Three, at this time, and of them I can give but a very broken Account: And, for his Instruments and Ways in recovering deserted *Mines*, I can give no account at all; though certainly, without new Tools and peculiar Inventions, he would never have undertaken that new and hazardous Work. Of the three Inventions which come now to my Memory, the

First was *an Engine representing the motion of the Planets.* Of this I can say no more than what I find, in his own words, in one of his Miscellany Papers in Manuscript.

The

The words are these: "I did, once, cause to be represented to me, by *Wires*, the motion of some *Planets*, in fact as it is, without *Theories* of *Orbs*, &c. And it seemed a strange and extravagant Motion. One while, they moved in *Spires forwards*; another while they did unwind themselves in *Spires backwards*: One while they made larger Circles, and higher; another while smaller Circles, and lower: One while they mov'd to the North, in their Spires, another while to the South, &c.

His *Second Invention* was a *secret Curiosity of Nature, whereby to know the Season of every Hour of the Year, by a Philosophical Glass, placed (with a small proportion of Water) in a Chamber.* This Invention I describe in the words of him, from whom I had the notice of it, Mr. *Thomas Bushel* (k), one of his Lordships Menial Servants; a Man skilful in discovering and opening of *Mines*, and famous for his curious *Water-Works*, in *Oxfordshire*, by which he imitated *Rain, Hail*, the *Rain-bow, Thunder* and *Lightning*.

This secret cannot be that Instrument which we call *Vitrum Calendare*, or the *Weather-Glass*, the Lord *Bacon* in his Wri-

(k) See his Extract. p. 17.

Writings (*l*), speaking of that as a thing in ordinary use, and commending, not Water ‖ but rectifi'd Spirit of Wine, in the use of it. Nor (being an Instrument made with Water) is it likely to have shewed changes of the Air with so much exactness, as the later Baroscope made with Mercury. And yet, it should seem to be a secret of high value by the Reward, it is said to have procured. For the Earl of *Essex* (as he in his *Extract. pag.* 17. reporteth) when Mr. *Bacon* had made a Present of it to him, was pleas'd to be very bountiful in his Thanks, and bestow upon him *Twicknam-Park*, and its Garden of Paradise, as a place for his Studies. I confess, I have not faith enough to believe the whole of this Relation. And yet I believe the Earl of *Essex* was extremely Liberal, and free even to Profuseness; that *he was a great lover of Learned Men, being, in some sort, one of them himself* (*m*); and that with singular Patronage, he cherish'd the hopeful Parts of Mr. *Bacon*, who also studied *his* Fortunes and Service. Yet Mr. *Bacon* himself, where he professeth his unwillingness to be short, in the commemoration of the Favours of that Earl; is, in this great one, perfectly silent (*n*). But there is, in his *Apologie*, another Story, which may seem to

(*l*) *Hist. of life and death*, p. 22. ‖ *In Formâ Calidi*, §. 24. p. 176. *Org.*

(*m*) *Ms. Hist. of Q. Eliz.* p. 39.

(*n*) *Bacon's Apol. conc. the Earl of Essex*. p. 54, 55.

to have given to Mr. *Bushel*, the occasion of his Mistake. "After the Queen had de-
"ny'd to Mr. *Bacon*, the Solicitor's Place,
"for the which the Earl of *Essex* had been
"a long and earnest suitor on his behalf, it
"pleased that Earl to come to him, from
"*Richmond*, to *Twicknam-Park*; and thus
"to break with him: Mr. *Bacon*, the *Queen*
"hath deny'd me the *Place* for you.———
"you fare ill, because you have chosen *me*
"for your Mean and Dependance: You
"have spent your thoughts and time in my
"Matters; I die— if I do not do somewhat
"towards your Fortune. You shall not
"deny to accept a piece of Land which I
"will bestow upon you. And it was, it seems, so large a piece, that he under-sold it for no less than Eighteen Hundred Pounds.

His *Third Invention* was, a kind of *Mechanical Index of the Mind*. And of this, Mr. *Bushel* (*o*) hath given us the following Narrative and Description. "His Lord-
"ship presented to Prince *Henry*, Two Tri-
"angular Stones (as the First-fruits of his
"Philosophy) to imitate the Sympatheti-
"cal Motion of the *Load-stone* and *Iron*,
"although made up by the Compounds of
"Meteors (as Star-shot Jelly) and other
"like Magical Ingredients, with the reflect-
"ed

(*o*) *In his Extract.* p. 17, 18.

"ed Beams of the Sun, on purpose that
"the warmth distill'd into them through the
"moist heat of the Hand, might discover
"the affection of the Heart, by a visible
"sign of their Attraction and Appetite to
"each other, like the hand of a Watch,
"within ten Minutes after they are laid on
"a Marble Table, or the Theatre of a great
"Looking-Glass. I write not this as a
"feigned Story, but as a real Truth; for
"I was never quiet in my Mind, till I had
"procured these Jewels of my Lord's Phi-
"losophy from Mr. *Archy Primrose*, the
"Prince's Page.

Of this I find nothing, either in his Lordship's Experiments (p) touching *Emission*, or *Immateriate Virtues, from the Minds and Spirits of Men*; or, in those concerning the *secret Virtue of Sympathy and Antipathy* (q). Wherefore I forbear to speak further in an Argument about which I am so much in the dark.

(p) *Nat. Hist. Cent.* 10. *Exp.* 939. &c. p. 205.

(q) *Ibid. Exp.* 960. &c. p. 211.

I proceed to subjects upon which I can speak with much more assurance, his Inimitable *Writings*.

Now, of the Works of the Lord *Bacon*, many are extant, and some are lost, in whole, or in part.

His *Abecedarium Naturæ*, is in part lost, and there remaineth nothing of it besides the Fragment, lately retrieved, and now first publish'd. But this loss is the less to be lamented, because it is made up with advantage, in the second and better thoughts of the Author, in the two first Parts of his Instauration. The World hath sustain'd a much greater loss in his *Historia Gravis & Levis*, which (I fear) is wholly perished. It is true, he had gone no further than the general Delineation of this Work; but those Out-lines drawn by so great an Artist, would have much directed others, in describing those important *Phenomena* of Nature.

Also his Collection of Wise and Acute Sentences, entituled by him, *Ornamenta Rationalia*; is either wholly lost; or, in some obscure place, committed to Moths and Cobwebs. But this is, here in some sort supplied, partly out of his own Works, and partly out of those of one of the Ancients.

Lost, likewise, is a Book which he wrote in his Youth, he call'd it [*Temporis Partus Maximus*] (r) the Greatest Birth of Time: Or rather, *Temporis Partus Masculus*, the Masculine Birth of Time. For so *Gruter* found it call'd in some of the Papers of Sir *William Boswel* (s). This was a kind of Embrio of the Instauration: And

(r) *See the Epist. to Fulgen.*
(s) *See the Page after the Title of Ser p a Philosophica.*

and if it had been preserved, it might have delighted and profited Philosophical Readers, who could then have seen the Generation of that great Work, as it were from the first Egg of it.

Of those Works of the Lord *Bacon's* which are *Extant*, some he left imperfect, that he might pursue his Design in others; As the *New Atlantis*: Some he broke off on purpose, being contented to have set others on-wards in their way; as *The Dialogue of a Holy War*. In some he was prevented by Death; as in the History of *Henry* the Eighth. Of some he despaired; as of the *Philosophia Prima*, of which he left but some few Axioms. And lastly, some he perfected; as some parts of the *Great Instauration*. And amongst all his Works, that of his *Instauration*, deserveth the first place. He thought so himself, saying to Dr. *Andrews*, then Lord Bishop of *Winchester* (t), "This is the Work, which, in "my own judgment, (*Si nunquam fallit* "*Imago*) I do most esteem.

In this Work, he designed to take in pieces the former Model of Sciences; to lay aside the rotten Materials; to give it a new Form, and much Enlargement; and to found it, not upon Imagination, but Reason helped by Experience. This

(t) *In Ep. St. Dedic. before his Advertisement touching a holy War.*

Great Instauration, was to consist of *Six Parts*.

The *First Part* proposed was, the *Partitions of the Sciences*: And this the Author perfected in that Golden Treatise of the *Advancement of Learning*, addressed to King *James*, a Labour which he termed *(u)* the comfort of his other Labours. This he first wrote in two Books, in the *English* Tongue, in which his Pen excelled. And of this First Edition that is to be meant, which, with some Truth, and more Modesty, he wrote to the Earl of *Salisbury*; telling him *(w)*, "That, in his Book, he was "contented to awake better Spirits, being "himself like a Bell-ringer, who is first up "to call others to Church. Afterwards he enlargeth the Second of those Two Discourses, which contained especially the abovesaid Partition, and divided the Matter of it into Eight Books. And, knowing that this Work was desired beyond the Seas, and being also aware, that Books written in a modern Language, which receiveth much change in a few Years, were out of use; he caus'd that part of it which he had written in *English*, to be translated into the *Latine* Tongue, by Mr. *Herbert*, and some others, who were esteemed Masters in the *Roman* Eloquence. Notwithstanding

(u) *In his Letter to Sir T. Bodley, p. 34. Resusc.*

(w) *In a Letter in Resusc. p. 31.*

ing which, he so suted the Style to his Conceptions, by a strict Castigation of the whole Work, that it may deservedly seem his own. The Translation of this Work (that is, of much of the Two Books written by him in *English*) he first commended to Dr. *Playfer*, a Professour of Divinity in the University of *Cambridg*; using, amongst others, these words to him. " The (*x*) privateness of the Language considered, wherein the Book is written, excluding so many Readers; as, on the other side, the obscurity of the Argument, in many parts of it, excludeth many others; I must account it, a second Birth of that Work, if it might be translated into *Latine*, without manifest loss of the Sence, and Matter. For this purpose I could not represent to my self any Man, into whose hands I do more earnestly desire that Work should fall, than your Self: For, by that I have heard, and read, I know no Man a greater Master, in commanding Words to serve Matter."

The Doctor was willing to serve so Excellent a Person, and so worthy a Design; and, within a while, sent him a Specimen of a *Latine* Translation. But Men, generally, come short of themselves when they
strive

(x) *Collect.* of *Letters in Resusc.* p. 33, 34.

strive to out-doe themselves. They put a force upon their Natural Genius, and, by straining of it, crack and disable it. And so, it seems, it happened to that Worthy and Elegant Man. Upon this great Occasion, he would be over-accurate; and he sent a Specimen of such superfine Latinity, that the Lord *Bacon* did not encourage him to labour further in that Work, in the penning of which, he desired not so much neat and polite, as clear Masculine, and apt Expression.

The whole of this Book was rendred into *English* by Dr. *Gilbert Wats*, of *Oxford*; and the Translation has been well received by many. But some there were, who wished that a Translation had been set forth, in which the Genius and Spirit of the Lord *Bacon* had more appeared. And I have seen a Letter, written by certain Gentlemen to Dr. *Rawley*, wherein they *thus* importune him for a more accurate Version, by his own Hand. "It is our "humble sute to you, and we do earnestly "solicit you,— to give your self the "Trouble, to correct the too much defe-"ctive Translation of *de Augmentis* "*Scientiarum*, which Dr. *Watts* hath set "forth. It is a thousand pities, that so "worthy a Piece should lose its Grace
"and

"and Credit, by an ill Expositor; since "those Persons, who read that Translati- "on, taking it for Genuine, and upon that "presumption not regarding the *Latine* "Edition, are thereby robbed of that be- "nefit which (if you would please to "undertake the Business) they might re- "ceive. This tendeth to the dishonour of "that Noble Lord, and the hindrance of "the *Advancement of Learning.*

This Work hath been also translated into *French* upon the motion of the *Marquis Fiat*. But in it there are many things wholly omitted, many things perfectly mistaken, and some things (especially such as relate to Religion) wilfully perverted. Insomuch that, in in one place, he makes his Lordship to magnifie the Legend: A Book, sure of little Credit with him, when he thus began one of his Essays * ; "I had "rather believe all the Fables in the Le- "gend, and the Talmud, and the Alco- "ran, than that his Universal Frame is "without a Mind.

* *Essay of Atheism.*

The fairest, and most correct Edition of this Book in *Latine*, is that in Folio, printed at *London, Anno* 1623. And whosoever would understand the Lord *Bacon's* Cypher (y), let him consult that accurate Edition. For, in some other Editions

(y) *In* l. 6. c. 1.

which

which I have perused, the form of the Letters of the Alphabet, in which much of the Mysterie consisteth, is not observed: But the *Roman* and *Italic* shapes of them are confounded.

To this Book we may reduce the first four Chapters of that imperfect Treatise, published in *Latine* by *Isaac Gruter* (z), and called *The Description of the Intellectual Globe*; they being but a rude draught of the Partition of the Sciences, so accurately and methodically disposed, in this Book of the Advancement of Learning. To this Work, also, we may reduce, the Treatise called *Thema Cœli*, published likewise in *Latine*, by *Gruter*. And it particularly belongeth to the Fourth Chapter, and the Third Book of it; as being a Discourse tending to an improvement of the System of the Heavens, which is treated of in that place, the Houses of which (had God granted him life) he would have understood as well almost as he did his own. For the same Reason, we may reduce, to the same place of the *Advancement*, the Fifth, Sixth, and Seventh Chapters, of the *Descriptio Globi Intellectualis*, above remembred (a).

The Second Part of his Great Instauration (and so considerable a part of it, that the Name of the whole is given to it) is his

(z) *Inter Scripta Philos.* fol. 75.

(a) See Verulam's *Scripta Philos.* p. 90, &c.

his *Novum Organum Scientiarum*, written by himself in the *Latine* Tongue, and printed also most beautifully and correctly in Folio, at *London* (b). This Work he Dedicated to King *James*, with the following Excuse; That, if he had stolen any time, for the Composure of it, from his Majestie's other Affairs, he had made some sort of Restitution, by doing Honour to his Name and his Reign. The King wrote to him, then Chancellor, a Letter of thanks, with his own Hand (c); and this was the first part of it. "My Lord, I have recei-
"ved your Letter, and your Book, than
"the which you could not have sent,
"a more acceptable Present, to me. How
"thankful I am for it, cannot better be
"expressed by me, than by a firm Resolu-
"tion I have taken; First, to read it
"through with Care and Attention;
"though I should steal some Hours from
"my Sleep; having, otherwise, as little
"spare Time to read it, as you had to
"write it: And then to use the liberty of
"a true Friend, in not sparing to ask you
"the question in any Point, whereof I
"stand in doubt, (*Nam ejus est explicare,*
"*cujus est condere;*) as, on the other part,
"I will willingly give a due commendation
"to such Places, as in my Opinion, shall
"de-

(b) 1620: *and in 2d part Ref. part of this Orga. is publ. in an Engl. Version.*

(c) *Dated Octob. 16. 1620. See Collect. of Letters in Resusc. p. 83.*

"deserve it. In the mean time, I can with
"comfort, assure you, that you could not
"have made choice of a Subject, more be-
"fitting your Place, and your Universal,
"and Methodical Knowledg.——

Three Copies of this *Organum,* were sent by the Lord *Bacon* to Sir *Henry Wotton,* one who took a pride (as himself saith) in a certain Congeniality with his Lordship's Studies. And how very much he valued the *Present,* we may learn from his own words. "You Lordship (said he*) hath
"done a great and ever-living Benefit to
"all the Children of Nature, and to Na-
"ture her self in her uttermost extent of
"Latitude: Who, never before, had so
"noble, nor so true an Interpreter, or
"(as I am readier to style your Lordship)
"never so inward a Secretary of her Cabi-
"net. But of your Work (which came
"but this Week to my hands) I shall find
"occasion to speak more hereafter; ha-
"ving yet read only the First Book there-
"of, and a few Aphorisms of the Second.
"For it is not a Banquet that Men may su-
"perficially taste, and put up the rest in
"their Pockets; but, in truth, a solid
"Feast, which requireth due Mastication.
"Therefore, when I have once, my self,
"perused the whole, I determine to have
"it

* *Sir H. Wotton's Remains,* p. 298, 299.

* Ἀφορισμὸς, ὁ, ὁ determinatio, distinctio, separatio, [&] brevis sententia. in which last sense it [is] used [in] first book "it read, piece by piece, at certain Hours, "in my Domestic College, as an Ancient "Author: For I have learned thus much "by it already, that we are extremely mis- "taken in the Computation of Antiquity, "by searching it backwards; because, in- "deed, the first Times were the youngest; "especially in points of Natural Discovery "and Experience.——

This *Novum Organum* containeth in it, Instructions concerning a better and more perfect use of Reason in our Inquisitions after things. And therefore the Second Title which he gave it was, *Directions concerning Interpretations of Nature.* And, by this Art, he designed a Logick more useful than the Vulgar, and an *Organon* apter to help the Intellectual Powers, than that of *Aristotle.* For he proposed here, not so much the Invention of Arguments, as of Arts; and in Demonstration, he used Induction, more than Contentious Syllogism; and in his Induction, he did not straightway proceed from a few particular Sensible Notions, to the most general of all; but raised Axioms by degrees, designing the most general Notions for the last place; and insisting on such of them as are, not merely Notional, but, coming from Nature, do also lead to her.

This

This Book containeth Three Parts, *The Preface*; the *Diſtribution* of the Work of the Great Inſtauration; *Aphoriſms*, guiding to the Interpretation of Nature.

The Preface conſidereth the preſent unhappy ſtate of Learning, together with Counſels and Advices to advance and improve it. To this Preface therefore, are to be reduced the *Indicia*, and the *Proem* in *Gruter* (*d*), concerning the Interpretation of Nature; the Firſt Book *de Augmentis Scientiarum*, which treateth generally of their Dignity and Advancement; and his Lordſhip's *Cogitata & Viſa* (*e*), written by him, in *Latine*, without Intention of making them publick in that Form, and ſent to Dr. *Andrews* (*f*), as likewiſe to Sir *Thomas Bodely*, with a deſire to receive their Cenſures and Emendations. The *latter* returned him a free and friendly Judgment of this Work, in a large and learned Letter, publiſhed in the *Cabala*, in the *Engliſh* Tongue, and by *Gruter* in the *Latine* (*g*). The like, perhaps, was done by the *former*, though his Anſwer be not extant.

To *the Diſtribution*, belongeth that *Latine* Fragment in *Gruter* (*h*), called, The Delineation, and Argument, of the Second Part of the Inſtauration. So doth that (*i*) of the Philoſophy of *Parmenides* and

(*d*) *Script. p.* 285. & 479.

(*e*) *Pub. by* Gruter *among the* Scripta.

(*f*) *Anno* 1607. *ſee* Refuſc. *p.* 35.

(*g*) *Inter Scripta Philoſ.* p 62.

(*h*) *Inter Scripta.* p. 293.

(*i*) Pag. 208.

and *Telesius*, and (especially) *Democritus*. For (as he sheweth in the beginning of that Part) he designed first to consider the Learning of which the World was possessed; and then to perfect that; and that being done, to open new Ways to further Discoveries.

To the Aphorisms is reducible, his Letter to Sir *Henry Savil*, touching *Helps for the Intellectual Powers*, written by his Lordship in the *English* (*k*) Tongue. A part of Knowledg then scarce broken (*l*), Men believing that Nature was here rather to be follow'd than guided by Art; and as necessary (in his Lordship's Opinion) as the grinding and whetting of an Instrument, or the quenching it, and giving it a stronger Temper.

Also there belong to this place, the Fragment, call'd *Aphorismi & Consilia, de Auxiliis mentis*. And *Sententiæ Duodecim de Interpretatione Naturæ*; both published by *Gruter* in the *Latine* Tongue, in which his Lordship wrote them (*m*).

In the bringing this Labour to Maturity, he used great and deliberate Care; insomuch that Dr. (*n*) *Rawley* saith, he had seen Twelve Copies of it, revised Year by Year, one after another; and every Year alter'd and amended in the Frame thereof, till at last

(k) Re-fusc. p. 225, &c.
(l) See of late, Spinoza on that Subject.

(m) See Script. p. 448, 451.

(n) D.R. in Life of Lord Bacon.

d

last it came to the Model in which it was committed to the Press. It was like a mighty Pyramid, long in its Erection; and it will, probably, be like to it in its Continuance.

Now he received from many parts beyond the Seas, Testimonies touching this Work, such, as beyond which he could not (he saith, *) expect at the first, in so abstruse an Argument; yet nevertheless (he saith again) he had just cause to doubt that it flew too high over *Mens Heads*: He purpos'd therefore, (though he broke the order of Time) to draw it down to the sense by some Patterns, of *Natural Story and Inquisition*.

<small>* *In Epi. to Bishop Andrews.*</small>

And so he proceeded to

The Third Part of the Instauration, which he called the *Phænomena of the Universe*, or the History Natural and Experimental, subservient to the building of a true Philosophy.

This Work consisteth of several Sections:

The First is his *Parasceve*, or Preparatory to the History Natural and Experimental. It is a short Discourse written in *Latine*, by the Author, and annexed to the *Novum Organum Scientiarum*. There is delivered in it, in Ten Aphorisms, the general

ral manner of framing a Natural History. After which followeth a Catalogue of particular Histories, of Cœlestial and Aereal Bodies, and of those in the Terrestrial Globe, with the Species of them: Such as Metals, Gems, Stones, Earths, Salts, Plants, Fishes, Fowls, Insects; Man, in his Body, and in his Inventions mechanic and liberal.

A late Pen has travelled in the Translation of this little Description of Natural History; and it is extant in the Second Part of the *Resuscitation*.

To this *Parasceve*, it is proper to reduce the *Fragment of the Abecedarium Naturæ*; and a short Discourse written in *Latine* by his Lordship; and published by *Gruter* (*n*): It being (what also its Title shews) a *Preface to the Phænomena of the Universe*; or, *The Natural History*.

(n) See *Ver. Scr. Phil. p.* 323.

Neither do we, here, unfitly place the *Fable of the New Atlantis*: For it is the Model of a College to be Instituted by some King who philosophizeth, for the Interpreting of Nature, and the Improving of Arts. His Lordship did (it seems) think of finishing this Fable, by adding to it a Frame of Laws, or a kind of *Utopian* Commonwealth; but he was diverted by his desire of Collecting the Natural History

story which was first in his esteem. This Supplement has been lately made by another Hand (o): A great and hardy Adventure, to finish a Piece after the Lord *Verulam*'s Pencil. This Fable of the *New Atlantis* in the *Latine* Edition of it, and in the *Franckfort* Collection, goeth under the false and absurd Title of *Novus Atlas*: As if his Lordship had alluded to a Person, or a Mountain, and not to a great Island, which according to *Plato*, perished in the Ocean.

The Second Section is, the History of Winds, written in *Latine* by the Author, and by *R. G.* Gentleman, turned into *English*. It was Dedicated to King *Charles*, then Prince, as the First-fruits of his Lordship's Natural History; and as a grain of Mustard-seed, which was, by degrees, to grow into a Tree of Experimental Science. This was the Birth of the first of those Six Months, in which he determin'd (God assisting him) to write Six several Histories of Natural Things. To wit, of *Dense and Rare Bodies*, of *Heavy and Light Bodies*; of *Sympathy and Antipathy*; of *Salt, Sulphur, and Mercury*; of *Life and Death*; and (which he first perfected) that of *Winds*, which he calls the Wings by which Men flie on the Sea, and the

Besoms

(o) See R. H. contin. of N. Atlantis Octo. Lon. 1660.

Beesoms of the Air and Earth. And he, rightly, observeth concerning those *Postnati* (for, as he saith, they are not a part of the Six Days Works, or Primary Creatures) that the Generation of them has not been well understood, because Men have been Ignorant of the Nature and Power of the Air, on which the Winds attend, as *Æolus* on *Juno*.

The *English* Translation of this Book of Winds, is printed in the Second Part of the *Resuscitatio*, as it is called, though improperly enough; for it is rather a Collection of Books already Printed, than a Resuscitation of any considerable Ones, which before slept in private Manuscript.

The *Third Section is*, the History of *Density* and *Rarity*, and of the Expansion and Coition of Matter in Space. This Discourse was written by his Lordship in *Latine*; and was publish'd very imperfectly by *Gruter*, amongst other Treatises, to which he gave the Title of *Impetus Philosophici* (*o*); and very perfectly and correctly by Dr. *Rawley*, out of whose Hands none of his Lordship's Works came lame and ill shapen into the World.

In this Argument, his Lordship allowing that nothing is substracted, or added to the total Sum of Matter, does yet grant,

(o) *See Verulamii Scripta, p 336, 337, &c.*

that in the same Space there may be much more or less of Matter; and that (for Instance sake) there is ten times more of Matter in one Tun of Water, than in one of Air. By which his Lordship should seem to grant, what yet I do not find he does in any other place; either that there is a *Vacuum* in Nature, or *Penetration* of parts in Bodies.

The Third Section is, the History of *Gravity* and *Levity*, which (as before was said) was but design'd; and remaineth not (that I can hear of) so much as in the rude draught of its Designation. Only, there are published his Lordship's Topics, or Articles of Inquisition, touching *Gravity* and *Levity*, in his Book of Advancement (*q*); and a brief *Aditus* to this History, annexed to the *Historia Ventorum*. In that *Aditus*, or Entrance, he rejecteth the Appetite of heavy Bodies to the Center of the Earth, as a Scholastic Fancy: He taketh it for a certain Truth, That Body does not suffer but from Body, or that there is any local motion which is not solicited, either from the parts of the Body it self which is moved; or from Bodies adjacent, either contiguously, or in the next Vicinity, or at least within the Orb of their Activity: And lastly, he commendeth

(q) De *Augm. Scient.* l. 5. c. 3. p. 386.

deth the Magnetic Virtues introduced by *Gilbert*, whom yet in this he difalloweth, that he made himfelf as 'twere a Magnet, and drew every thing to his Hypothefis.

The Fourth Section is, the Hiftory of *Sympathy* and *Antipathy*. Of this we have only the *Aditus* annexed to that of *Hiftoria Gravis & Levis*; and a few Inftances in his *Sylva Sylvarum* (r). In this Hiftory he defigned to avoid Magical Fancies, which raife the Mind, in thefe things, to an undue height; and pretence of occultnefs of Quality, which layeth the Mind afleep, and preventeth further Inquiry into thefe ufeful fecrets of Nature.

(r) See *Exper.* 95, 96, 97. 462, 480, to 498.

The Fifth Section is, the Hiftory of *Salt*, *Sulphur*, and *Mercury*, the three Principles of the common *Chymifts*; of which three, he thought the firft to be no primordial Body, but a Compound of the two others, knit together by an acid Spirit. The *Aditus* (ſ) to this is annexed to that of *Hiftoria Sympathiæ & Antipathiæ Rerum*; but the Treatife it felf was (I think) never written.

(ſ) *All thofe Aditus are tranfl. into Engl. by the Tranf. of the Hiftory of Winds.*

The Sixth Section is, the Hiftory of *Life and Death*; written by his Lordfhip in *Latine*; and firft turn'd into *Englifh* by an injudicious Tranflator; and rendred much better a fecond time, by an abler Pen, made

d 4 abler

abler still by the Advice and Assistance of Dr. *Rawley.*

This Work, though ranked last, amongst the Six Monthly Designations; yet was set forth in the second Place: His Lordship (as he saith) inverting the Order, in respect of the prime use of this Argument, in which the least loss of time was, by him, esteemed very precious. The Subject of this Book (which Sir *Henry Wotton* (*t*) calleth, none of the least of his Lordship's Works) and the Argument of which, some had before undertaken (*u*); but to much less purpose is the first of those, which he put in his Catalogue of the *Magnalia Naturæ.* And doubless, his Lordship undertook both a great and a most desirable Work, of making *Art short,* and *Life easie and long.* "And it was his Lord-
" ship's wish, that the nobler sort of Phy-
" sicians might not employ their times
" wholly in the sordidness of Cures, nei-
" ther be honoured for necessity only; but
" become Coadjutors and Instruments of
" the Divine Omnipotence and Clemence,
" in prolonging and renewing the Life of
" Man: And in helping Christians who
" pant after the Land of Promise, so to
" journey through this World's Wilderness,
" as to have their Shoes and Garments,
" (these

(*t*) *Remains,* p. 455.
(*u*) Pansa *de pro. pag. vitâ* 8vo. Lips. 1615.

" (these of their frail Bodies) little worn
" and impair'd.

The *Seventh* and greatest Branch of the Third Part of the *Instauration, is his* Sylva Sylvarum, *or Natural History*; which containeth many *Materials* for the building of Philosophy, as the *Organum* doth *Directions* for the *Work*. It is an History not only of Nature freely moving in her Course, (as in the production of Meteors, Plants, Minerals); but also of Nature in constraint, and vexed and tortur'd by Humane Art and Experiment. And it is not an History of such things orderly ranged; but thrown into an Heap. For his Lordship, that he might not discourage other Collectors, did not cast this Book into exact Method; for which reason it hath the less Ornament, but not much the less Use.

In this Book are contain'd Experiments of Light, and Experiments of Use (as his Lordship was wont to distinguish); and amongst them some *Extraordinary*, and others *Common*. He understood that what was Common in one Country, might be a Rarity in another: For which Reason, Dr. *Caius*, when in *Italy*, thought it worth his pains to make a large and Elegant Description of *Our way of Brewing*. His Lordship also knew well, that an Experiment manifest

fest to the *Vulgar*, was a good ground for the Wise to build further upon. And himself rendred *Common ones, extraordinary* by *Admonitions*, for further Trials and Improvements. Hence his Lordship took occasion to say (w), that his writing of *Sylva Sylvarum*, was (to speak properly) not a Natural History, but a high kind of Natural Magic: Because it was not only a description of Nature, but a breaking of Nature into great and strange Works.

(w) *Nat. Hist. Cent.* 1. p. 25. *Exper.* 93.

This Book was written by his Lordship in the *English* Tongue, and translated by an obscure Interpreter, into *French*, and out of that Translation, into *Latine*, by *James Gruter*, in such ill manner, that they darkned his Lordship's Sence, and debased his Expression. *James Gruter* was sensible of his Miscarriage, being kindly advertised of it by Dr. *Rawley.* And he left behind him divers amendments, published by his Brother *Isaac Gruter*, in a second Edition (x). Yet still so many Errors have escaped, that the Work requireth a Third Hand.

(x) *Amstel.* 1661. *in* 16°.

Mounsieur *Ælius Deodatus* had once engaged an able Person in the translation of this Book; one who could have done his Lordship right, and oblig'd such Readers as understood not the *English* Original. He
be-

began, and went through the *Three first Centuries*, and then desisted; being desired by him who set him on work, to take his hand quite off from that Pen, with which he moved so slowly. His Translation of the *Third Century* is now in my Hands; but that of the two first, I believe is lost.

His Lordship thus began that Third Century in *English*. " All Sounds (whatsoe-
" ver) move round; that is to say, on all
" sides; upwards, downwards, forwards,
" and backwards. This appeareth in all
" Instances.

" *Sounds* do not require to be convey-
" ed to the sense in a right Line, as *Visibles*
" do, but may be arched. Though it be
" true, they move strongest in a right Line;
" which nevertheless is not caused by the
" *rightness* of the Line, but by the *short-*
" *ness* of the Distance; *Linea recta brevis-*
" *sima*. And therefore we see, if a *Wall*
" be between, and you speak on the one
" side, you hear it on the other; which is
" not because the Sound passeth through
" the *Wall*, but archeth over the *Wall*.

These words are thus turned, by *James Gruter*, in his last Edition; and tollerably well: Especially if we compare with some other places in his Translation.

Omnes

Omnes soni, qualescunq; sint, in circulum moventur; hoc est, in omnes partes, sursum, deorsum, antrorsum, retrorsum; quod omnes docent instantiæ.

Soni non requirunt ut rectâ lineâ ad sensum devehantur, quemadmodum visibilia, sed potest esse arcuata; quamvis verum sit, quòd fortissimè per rectam lineam moveant: Neq; tamen id lineæ debetur rectitudini, sed minori intervallo;. Linea enim recta est brevissima. Hinc, si quis ab alterâ interjecti Parietis parte vocem proferat, ab alterâ queat exaudiri; non quòd vox Parietem transeundo penetret, sed quòd arcuata ultra parietem ascendat.

But the Translator, employed by *Mounsieur Deodate*, turned them after this better manner.

Omnes in universum Soni in Orbem feruntur: In omnem videlicet partem; sursum, deorsum, antrorsum, & retrorsum. Hoc in omnibus exemplis cernitur.

Soni non in rectâ tantùm lineâ ad sensum deferri necesse habent, quemadmodum visilia; sed & inflexa & arcuata devehi possunt: Quanquam in rectâ lineâ fortissimè moveantur. Ubi tamen non hoc imputandum Rectitudini Lineæ, sed brevitati Intervalli. Recta enim linea eadem brevissima est. Itaq; experimur, muro interjecto vocem, ex adversâ parte

parte muri exaudiri, quæ ex alterâ ejus parte prolata fuerit. Auditur autem, non quòd per murum penetret, sed quòd eum transcendat motu flexuoso.

The Judicious Reader may discern by this little, how much this latter Translator excell'd the former, in comprehending and expressing his Lordship's Sence. And yet I cannot say, that throughout those Three Centuries in which he hath labour'd, he hath every where truly hit his Conceit. His Lordship had a very peculiar Vein with him; and I may resemble it to the singurity in the *Face* of *Cardan*, who tells us, in his own Life, that he set to Painters of divers Countries, yet could never have the Air of *it* taken by them.

Whilst I am speaking of this Work of his Lordship's, of *Natural History*, there comes to my mind a very Memorable Relation, reported by him who bare a part in it, the Reverend Dr. *Rawley*. One day, his Lordship was dictating to that Doctor, some of the Experiments in his *Sylva*. The same day, he had sent a Friend to Court, to receive for him a final Answer, touching the effect of a Grant which had been made him by King *James*. He had hitherto, only hope of it, and hope deferr'd; and he was desirous to know the event of
the

the Matter, and to be free'd, one way or other, from the suspence of his thoughts. His Friend returning, told him plainly, that he must thenceforth, despair of that Grant, how much soever his Fortunes needed it. *Be it so*, said his Lordship; and then he dismissed his Friend very chearfully, with thankful acknowledgments of his Service. His Friend being gone, he came straightway to Dr. *Rawley*, and said thus to him. Well Sir! *Yon Business won't go on; let us go on with this, for this is in our Power.* And then he dictated to him afresh, for some Hours, without the least hesitancie of Speech, or discernible interruption of Thought.

To this Work of *Natural History*, may be reduc'd his Lordship's Treatises, *De Sono & Auditu, De Metallis & Mineralibus, De Magnete, De Versionibus, Transmutationibus, Multiplicationibus, & Effectionibus Corporum, De Luce & Lumine* (y). All publish'd by Dr. *Rawley*, in the Collection call'd *Opuscula Varia Posthuma* Francisci Baconi.

We may likewise reduce to the same place, the Paper *De Fluxu & Refluxu Maris*, published by *Isaac Gruter*, amongst the *Scripta* (z); and that other *De Ratione*

(y) *The Paper* De Luce & Lumine *is also extant among the* Scripta Philosophica, *p.* 485. (z) Scripta Philosophica, *p.* 178. &c.

Inte-

Inveniendi causas Fluxus & Refluxus Maris; (a) as also the *Baconiana Physiologica* and *Medica,* in these *Remains.*

There may be further added, his *Cogitationes, De Naturâ Rerum*; *De Sectione Corporum*; *Continuo & Vacuo*; and the Fragment called *Filum Labyrinthi sive Legitima Inquisitio de Motu:* All publish'd by the same Mr. *Gruter,* in the same Book. Likewise the Treatises, *De Motûs sive Virtutis activæ variis Speciebus,* & *Historia Naturalis & Experimentalis de Formâ Calidi*; joyned to the *Historia Ventorum* (b), and inserted also into the *Organum* (c); and by *R. G.* made English.

For it was his Lordship's design (d), not merely to exhibit an History of Bodies, but moreover to procure a distinct and comparative one, of their Virtues, such as those of Density and Rarity; Consistency and Fluidity; Gravity and Levity; Heat and Cold.

Such a Collection of *Natural History,* was of necessity to be undertaken a-new. For the Collections, which were before in Mens Hands, were but a small and inconsiderable

(a) See this (turn'd into English by R. G.) in Resusc. Part 2. p. 90.
See it in Latine *at the end of the Tract.* De Motu, *annexed to the* Histor. Ventor. p. 91.

(b) *Hist. Vent.* p. 129, 191. *see* Resusc. 2d *Part.* p. 52.
(c) *Nov. Organ. De Motu.* p. 314. *de Forma Calidi.* p. 158.
(d) *Nov. Organ. in distrib. Op.* p. 13.

ble heap, when the Chaff and Fable were sifted from them; though the more considerable for that Separation. And further, as his Lordship noteth (e), too many of these Histories were at first framed rather for Delight, and Table-talk, than for Philosophy. Stories were feigned for the sake of their Morals; and they were frequently taken upon groundless Trust; and the later Writers borrowed out of the more Ancient, and were not Experimenters, but Transcribers: And such a one was *Pliny* himself, both in his larger and lesser Work; I mean that of *Solinus*, who is but *Pliny* contracted.

(e) *De Augment. Scien.* l. 2. c. 3. p. 135.

There are who have accused the Lord *Bacon* himself, for taking Experiments too readily upon Trust, and without deliberate and discreet Choice. To such I will return Answer in his own words. "The Rejection (f) which I continually use, of Experiments (though it appeareth not) is infinite; but yet, if an Experiment be probable in the Work, and of great use I receive it, but deliver it as doubtful.

(f) *Nat. Hist. Cent.* 1. p. 6. *Exper.* 25.

The *Fourth Part of the Instauration* designed, was *Scala Intellectûs*.

To this there is some sort of entrance in his Lordship's distribution of the *Novum Organum*,

Organum, and in a Page or two under that Title of *Scala*, published by *Gruter* (g): But the Work it self passed not beyond the Model of it in the Head of the Noble Author.

(g) See *Scripta*, p. 379.

That which he intended, was a particular Explication, and Application of the *Second Part of the Instauration*, (which giveth general Rules for the Interpretation of Nature) by gradual Instances and Examples.

He thought that his Rules, without some more sensible Explication, were like Discourses in Geometry, or Mechanics, without Figures, and Types of Engines. He therefore designed to select certain Subjects in Nature, or Art; and as it were, to draw to the Sense a certain Scheme of the beginning and progress of Philosophical Disquisition in them; shewing by degrees, where our consideration takes Root, and how it spreadeth and advanceth. And some such thing is done by those who, from the *Cicatricula*, or from the *Punctum Saliens*, observe and register all the *Phænomena* of the Animal unto its Death, and after it also in the Medical, or Culinarie, or other use of its Body; together with all the train of the Thoughts occasioned by by those *Phænomena*, or by others in compare with them.

And because he intended to exhibit such Observations, as they gradually arise; therefore he gave to that Designed Work, the Title of the *Scale*, or *Ladder of the Understanding*. He also expressed the same Conceit by another Metaphor (*h*), advising Students to imitate Men, who by going by degrees from several Eminencies of some very high Mountain, do at length arrive at the Top, or Pike of it.

(h) See Scripta, p. 384.

The *Fifth Part of the Instauration*, design'd, was, what he call'd *Prodromi sive Anticipationes Philosophiæ Secundæ*. To this we find a very brief Entrance, in the *Organum* (*i*), and the *Scripta*, publish'd by *Gruter* (*k*). And though his Lordship is not known to have composed any part of this Work by it self, yet something of it is to be Collected from the Axioms, and greater Observations intersperfed in his Natural Histories, which are not pure but mixed Writings. The Anticipations he intended to pay down as Use, till he might furnish the World with the Principal, in

(i) In Distrib. Op. p. 17.
(k) Vi- rul. scrip. p. 385. Prodromi, &c.

The *Sixth and last Part of his Instauration*, designed, which was, *Philosophia Secunda sive Scientia Activa*. This General Philosophy, founded upon Sensible Nature, or Arti-

Artificial Experiments, and built up by degrees in Obfervations and Axioms, he at length defpaired of, and commended to Pofterity. Time only can throughly finifh what his Lordfhip began, and fufficiently commend his Diligence and Sagacity, who collected fo many Materials, and difpos'd them into fuch Order; and made in fo fhort a Time, and (for the moft part) in the midft of Civil Bufinefs, fuch mighty Preparations towards the building of the *Houfe of Wifdom*.

After having mentioned the feveral Parts of this great Work, which concerneth, efpecially, *Body Natural*; we proceed to enumerate others of his Lordfhip's Writings, which concern *Civil*, or *Religious Matters*. And though moft of them are of a mixed nature, and Hiftory is feldom written without fome Political Reflections; yet to thofe who are not over Nice, the divifion of them into Hiftorical and Political, may be paffable.

His Hiftorical Works are thefe:

The Firft, Is the Hiftory of *Henry* the Seventh (*l.*), written Elegantly, by his Lordfhip in the *Englifh* Tongue, and Addreffed to his Highnefs the Prince of *Wales*; and turned afterwards into *Latine*. An Hiftory which required fuch a Reporter:

(l) *Publifhed firft 1622.*

thofe

those Times being Times both of great Revolution, and Settlement, through the Division and Union of the Roses.

This was the First Book which he Compos'd after his Retirement from an Active Life *(m)*. Upon which occasion he wrote thus to the Bishop of *Winchester (n)*. Being (as I am) no more able to do my Country Service, it remaineth unto me, to do it Honour: Which I have endeavoured to do in my Work, of the Reign of King *Henry* the Seventh.

The Second is, the Fragment of the *History of Henry the Eighth*, printed at the end of his Lordship's Miscellany Works, of which the best Edition is that in Quarto, in the Year 1629. This Work he undertook, upon the Motion of King *Charles* the First, but (a Greater King not lending him time) he only began it; for that which we have of it, was (it seems) but one Mornings Work.

The Third is, a Memorial, intituled the *Felicities of Queen Elizabeth (o)*. This was written by his Lordship, in *Latine (p)* only. A Person of more good Will, than Ability, translated it into *English (q)*, and call'd it, in the singular, *Her Felicity*. But we have also a Version, much more Accurate and Judicious, performed by Doctor

---

(m) *See the Cat. of his Works then written in his Life, by* D. R.

(n) *In Epist. bef. Dial of an holy War.*

(o) *See in the* Resusc. *the Letter to* Mr. Matthew. *p.* 37.

(p) *Publ. among his Opuscula.* p. 177.

(q) *-- inno* 1651. *in* 16°.

Doctor *Rawley* (r), who was pleased to take that Labour upon him, because he understood the value his Lordship put upon this Work; for it was such, that I find *this Charge* given concerning it, in his last *Will and Testament*. "In particular, I wish the "Elogie which I writ, in *Felicem Memo-* "*riam Elizabethæ*, may be published.

(r) *Publ. in* Resusc. *p.*181, &c.

For the Occasion of it, his Lordship telleth it thus, in a Letter to Sir *George Carey* (ſ), then in *France*, to whom he sent it.——"Because one must begin, I thought to "provoke your remembrance of me by "a Letter: And thinking to fit it with "somewhat besides Salutations, it came "to my mind, that this last Summer- "Vacation, by occasion of a factious Book "that endeavour'd to verifie *Misera Fœmi-* "*na,* (the Addition of the Pope's Bull) "upon Queen *Elizabeth*; I did write a few "Lines in her Memorial, which I thought "you would be pleased to reade, both for "the Argument; and because you were "wont to bear affection to my Pen. *Ve-* "*rum ut aliud ex alio :* If it came handsome- "ly to pass, I would be glad the President "de * *Thou* (who hath written an History, "as you know, of that Fame and Dili- "gence) saw it: Chiefly, because I know "not whether it may not serve him for "some

(ſ) Resusc. *p.*45.

* Thuanus.

"some use in his Story: Wherein I would
"be glad he did right to the Truth, and
"to the Memory *of that Lady*; as I per-
"ceive by that he hath already written,
"he is well inclined to do.

The *Fourth is*, the *Beginning of the History of Great Britain*. This was an Essay, sent to King *James*, whose Times it considered. A Work worthy his Pen, had he proceeded in it; seeing (as he (t) saith) he should have written of Times, not only since he could remember, but since he could observe; and by way of Introduction, of Times, (as he further noteth) of strange Variety; the Reign of a Child; the offer of an Usurpation by the *Lady Jane*, though it were but as a Diary Ague; the Reign of a Lady married to a Forreigner, and the Reign of a Lady solitary and unmarried.

(t) *See* Collect. *of Letters in* Refusc. p. 30. Letter *to* King James. *And* p. 28, 29, 30. *the* Letter *to the Lord* Chancellor Egerton, *concerning this Subject*.

His Lordship, who had given such proof of his Skill in writing an History of *England*, leaving the World, to the unspeakable loss of the learned part of it; his late Majesty, a great favourer of that Work, and wise in the choice of fit Workmen, encourag'd Sir *Henry Wotton* to endeavour it, by his Royal Invitation, and a Pension
of

of 500 *l. per annum.* This Proposal was made to that Excellent Man, in his declining Years; and he died after the finishing some short Characters of some few Kings; which Characters are publish'd in his *Remains* (*u*). But this new Undertaking diverted him from a Work, in which he had made some considerable Progress, the Life of *Luther*, and in it, the History of the Reformation, as it was begun and carried on in *Germany*: Of which Work, the Papers (they say) are lost, and in a Current of Time of no great depth, sunk beyond all possible Recovery.

(u) *Reliqu. Wotton.* p. 100.

The *Fifth is*, the *Imago Civilis Julii Cæsaris.*

The *Sixt, Imago Civilis Augusti Cæsaris.* Both of them (*w*) short personal Characters, and not Histories of their Empire: And written by his Lordship in that Tongue, which in their Times, was at its height, and became the Language of the World. A while since, they were translated into *English*, and inserted into the First Part of the *Resuscitation* (*x*).

(w) *Among the Opuscula.* p. 195.

(x) See *Resusc. Edw.* 3d. p. 214.

In the Seventh Place, I may reckon his Book *De Sapientiâ Veterum*, written by him in *Latine* (*y*), and set forth a second time with Enlargement; and translated into *English*

(y) See *his Letter to Mr. Matthews in Resusc.* p. 38.

English by Sir *Arthur Gorges* (z): A Book in which the Sages of former Times, are rendred more Wise than it may be they were, by so dextrous an Interpreter of their Fables. It is this Book which Mr. *Sandys* means, in those words which he hath put before his Notes, on the *Metamorphosis of Ovid* *. "Of Modern Wri-
"ters, I have received the greatest Light
"from *Geraldus*, *Pontanus*, *Ficinus*, *Vi-*
"*ves*, *Comes*, *Scaliger*, *Sabinus*, *Pierius*,
"and the Crown of the latter, the Vicount
"of Saint *Albans*.

(z) *This Translation is lately added to the Essays, in Octavo.*

* *Pag.* 18.

It is true, the design of this Book was, Instruction in Natural and Civil Matters, either couched by the Ancients under those Fictions, or rather made to seem to be so, by his Lordship's Wit, in the opening and applying of them. But because the first ground of it is Poetical Story, therefore let it have this place, till a fitter be found for it.

For his Lordship's *Political Writings*, they are such as relate, either to Ecclesiastical, or Civil Polity. His Writings which relate to *Ecclesiastical Polity*, (for he was not willing (a) that all his Labours should go into the City, and none into the Church) are the three following.

(a) *See his Epistle to Bishop Andrews.*

The

The *First* is a Discourse (*b*), bearing the Title of *Certain Considerations*, touching the better Pacification and Edification of the Church of *England*; and dedicated to King *James*. The *Second* (*c*) is, an *Advertisement*, touching the Controversies of the Church of *England*. The *Third* is, a Dialogue touching an *Holy War*: All written at first in *English*, by his Lordship. The *First* of these toucheth the Settlement of Doctrine: The *Second*, the Settlement of Discipline amongst the *Christians* in *England*: The *Third*, of Propagation of the Faith amongst *Unbelievers*. In all which it is plain, that his Lordship dealt in the Affairs of the Church, as he was wont to do in Civil Matters, *Suavibus Modis*, and in the Mean. Accordingly he was wont to compare himself to the Miller of *Granchester*, a Village by *Cambridg*. Of him his Lordship telleth, that he was wont to pray *for Peace among the Willows:* For whilst the Winds blew, the Wind-mills wrought, and his Water-mill was less Custom'd (*d*). His Lordship was for pacifying Disputes, knowing that *Controversies of Religion*, would hinder the *Advancement of Sciences*.

(*b*) *In* Refusc. p. 233. *it was published before without his Lordship's Name in Quarto,* 1640.
(*c*) *In* Refusc. p. 162.
(*d*) *See Letter to Mr Matthew, in* Refusc. p. 36.

His Writings which relate to *Civil Polity*, are very considerable; and yet they fall

much

much short of that which he had sometimes in design. For he aimed at the complete Model of a Commonwealth, though he hath left only some preparations towards it in his *Doctrine of Enlarging the bounds of Empire*; and in a few *Aphorisms* concerning *Universal Justice* (*e*). He also made a Proposal to King *James*, of a Digest of the Laws of *England*. But other Studies, together with want of Time and Assistance, prevented the ripening of these Thoughts.

(e) *In Augm. Scient.* l. 8 c. 3. p. 668. to p. 690, &c.

Now his Lordship's Writings in this Argument of Civil Polity, are either more *General*, or such as have more *Especial* respect to the several Dominions of the King of *England*. His Political Writings of a more *general* Nature, are his *Apothegms*, and *Essays*, besides the *Excerpta*, out of the *Advancement* above remembred. Both these contain much of that Matter which we usually call *Moral*, distinguishing it from that which is *Civil*: In the handling of which sort of Argument, his Lordship has been esteemed so far to excel, that he hath had a Comment written on him as on an Author in *Ethics* (*f*), and an Advancer of that most useful part of Learning. Notwith-

(f) See V. Placcii Comment. in l. 7. *Aug. Scient. de Philosophiâ Morali augendâ. in Octavo. Franc. an.* 1677.

withstanding which, I am bold to put these Books under this Head of *Matter Political:* Both because they contain a greater portion of that Matter; and because in true Philosophy, the Doctrine of *Politics* and *Ethics*, maketh up but one Body, and springeth from one Root, the End of God Almighty in the Government of the World.

The *Apothegms* (of which the first (g) is the best Edition) were (what he saith also (h) of his Essays) but as *the Recreations of his other Studies*. They were dictated one Morning, out of his Memory; and if they seem to any, a *Birth* too inconsiderable for the Brain of so great a Man; they may think with themselves how little a time *he went with it*, and from thence make some allowance. Besides, his Lordship hath receiv'd much Injury by late Editions (i), of which some have much enlarged, but not at all enriched the Collection; stuffing it with Tales and Sayings, too infacetious for a Ploughman's Chimney-Corner. And particularly, in the Collection not long since publish'd (k), and call'd *The Apothegms of King* James, *King* Charles, *the Marquess of* Worcester, *the Lord* Bacon, *and Sir* Thomas Moor; his Lordship is dealt with very rudely. For,

(g) *Apoth. printed in Oct. Lon.1625.*
(h) *See his Epistle to Bishop Andrews.*

(i) *Even by that added (but not by Dr. Rawley) to the Resuscitatio, Edw. 3d.*
(k) *In Octavo. Lon.1669.*

besides

besides the addition of Insipid Tales, there are some put in which are Beastly and Immoral (*l*): Such as were fitter to have been joyned to *Aretine*, or *Aloysia*, than to have polluted the chaste Labours of the Baron of *Verulam*.

(*l*) *Ex. gr. Apotheg.* 183, 184.

To those *Apothegms*, may be referred these now publish'd, *The Essays*, or *Counsels Civil and Moral*, though a By-work also, do yet make up a Book of greater weight by far, than the *Apothegms*: And *coming home to Men's Business and Bosomes*, his Lordship entertain'd this persuasion concerning them (*m*), that the *Latine Volume might last as long as Books should last*. His Lordship wrote them in the *English* Tongue, and enlarged them as Occasion serv'd, and at last added to them the *Colours of Good and Evil*, which are likewise found in his Book *De Augmentis* (*n*). The *Latine* Translation of them was a Work performed by divers Hands; by those of Doctor *Hacket* (late Bishop of *Lichfield*) Mr. *Benjamin Johnson* (the learned and judicious Poet) and some others, whose Names I once heard from Dr. *Rawley*; but I cannot now recal them. To this *Latine* Edition, he gave the Title of *Sermones Fideles*, after the manner of the *Jews*, who call'd the words *Adagies*, or Observations of

(*m*) See *Epist. Ded. to the D. of Bucks.*

(*n*) Lib. 6. c. 3. p. 453.

of the *Wise*, *Faithful Sayings*; that is, credible Propositious worthy of firm Assent, and ready Acceptance. And (as I think) he alluded more particularly, in this Title, to a passage in *Ecclesiastes* *, where the Preacher saith that he sought to find out *Verba Delectabilia*, (as *Tremellius* rendreth the *Hebrew*) pleasant *Words*, (that is, perhaps, his Book of *Canticles*); and *Verba Fidelia* (as the same *Tremellius*) *Faithful Sayings*; meaning, it may be, his Collection of *Proverbs*. In the next Verse, he calls them *Words of the Wise*, and so many Goads and Nails given *Ab eodem Pastore*, from the same Shepherd [of the Flock of *Israel*.]

* Ecclef. 12.10,11.

In a late *Latine* Edition of these Essays, there are subjoyned two Discourses, the one call'd *De Negotiis*, the other *Faber Fortunæ*. But neither of these are Works newly publish'd, but Treatises taken out of the Book *De Augmentis* (*o*).

(*o*) Lib. 8. c. 2. p. 585, &c.

To this Book of *Essays* may be annexed, that Fragment of an *Essay of Fame*, which is extant already in the *Resuscitatio* (*p*).

(*p*) Refusc.p.281.

His Lordship's *Political Writings* of a more *special* Nature, as relating to the Polity, and various Affairs of the several Dominions of the King of *England*, are very many, though most of them short.

As

As *First*, a Discourse of the Union of England and *Scotland* (q).

Secondly, Articles and Considerations, touching the Union aforesaid (r).

Thirdly, Considerations touching the Plantation in *Ireland* (s).

Fourthly, Considerations touching the Queen's Service in *Ireland* (t).

Fifthly, Considerations touching a War with *Spain* (u), then the Over-match in this part of the World; though now in meaner Condition.

Sixthly, His several *Speeches*; by which I mean not only those which go under that Name, but likewise his several *Charges*; they being much of the same Nature, though deliver'd *ex Officio*, which the other were not always. These Speeches and Charges, are generally Methodically, Manly, Elegant, Pertinent, and full of Wise Observations; as those are wont to be which are made by Men of *Parts and Business*. And I shall not pass too great a Complement upon his Lordship, if I shall say, That 'twas well for *Cicero*, and the honour of his Orations, that the Lord *Bacon* compos'd his in another Language.

Now his Speeches and Charges are very many, and I set them down in the following Catalogue.

(q) *In Resusc. p.* 197.
(r) *Page* 206.
(s) *Pag.* 255.
(t) *P.*16. *Of Coll. of Letters*.
(u) *Pub. in the Misf. works in Quarto, An.* 1629. *& reprinted in* 2d. *part of Resusc.*

His

the Lord Bacon's Works. 63

His Speeches in Parliament to the Lower House, are Eight.

The *First*, 39 *Elizabeth*, upon the Motion of Subsidy (*w*).   (w) Refuse. p. 1. of D. R's Edition.

The *Second*, 5 *Jacobi*, concerning the Article of General Naturalization of the Scotish Nation (*x*).   (x) P.10.

The *Third*, concerning the Union of Laws (*y*).   (y) P.24.

The *Fourth*, 5 *Jacobi*, being a Report in the House of *Commons*, of the Earls of *Salisbury*, and *Northampton*, concerning the Grievances of the Merchants, occasioned by the Practice of *Spain* (*z*).   (z) P.29.

The *Fifth*, 7 *Jacobi*, persuading the House of Commons, to desist from further Question of receiving the King's Messages by their Speaker, and from the Body of the Council, as well as from the King's Person (*a*).   (a) P.45.

The *Sixth*, 7 *Jacobi*, in the end of the Session of Parliament, persuading some Supply to be given to his Majesty, which seemed then to stand upon doubtful Terms; and passed upon this Speech (*b*).   (b) P.47.

The *Eighth*, 12 *Jacobi*, when the House was in great Heat, and much troubled about the *Undertakers*, who were thought to be some able and forward Gentlemen, who were said to have undertaken that the
King's

King's Business should pass in that House, as his Majesty could wish (*c*). (*c*) P. 48.

His Speeches in the *House of Lords*, are Two.

The *First*, To the *Lords*, at a Conference in the Parliament, 7 *Jacobi*, by him then Solicitor; moving them to joyn with the Commons, to obtain liberty to treat of a Composition with his Majesty, for *Wards* and *Tenures* (*d*). (*d*) P. 42.

The *Second*, (when he was Chancellor) to Mr. Serjeant *Richardson*, chosen then Speaker of the House of Commons; being a Reply to his Excuse and Oration (*e*). (*e*) P. 94.

His Speeches to King *James*, were also Two.

The *First*, A Speech by him, chosen by the Commons, to present a Petition touching *Purveyors*, deliver'd to his Majesty at *White-Hall*, in the second Year of his Reign (*f*). (*f*) P. 5.

The *Second*, a Speech used to the King, by him, then Solicitor, and chosen by the Commons for the presenting of the *Instrument of their Grievances*, in the Parliament 7 *Jacobi* (*g*). (*g*) P. 41.

His Speeches in the *Chancery*, are Two likewise.

The

The *First*, At the taking of his Place in Chancery, when made Lord-Keeper (*h*). (h)P.79.

The *Second*, To Sir *William Jones*, upon his calling to be Lord Chief Justice of *Ireland*, Anno 1617. (*i*). (i)P.89.

In the *Star-Chamber*, he used a Speech to the Judges and others, before the *Summer* Circuits, being then Lord-Keeper, and also *Lord-Protector*; for his Majesty was at that time in *Scotland*, Anno 1617. (*k*). (k)P.87.

In the *Common-Pleas*, he used a Speech to Justice *Hutton*, when he was called to be one of the Judges in the *Common-Pleas*. (*l*). (l)P.93.

In the *Exchequer-Chamber*, he used a Speech to Sir *John Denham*, when he was call'd to be one of the Barons of the Exchequer (*m*). (m)P.91.

There also he used an Argument (being Solicitor General) in the Case of the *Post-nati* of *Scotland* (*n*), before the Lord-Chancellor, and all the Judges of *England* (*o*). The Question in this Case was, Whether a Child born in *Scotland* since King *James*'s coming to the Crown of *England*, was Naturaliz'd in *England* or no? His Lordship argued for the Affirmative. (n) *Publ. first in 4°. Lon.*1641. (o) *See it in* Resusc. *part 2.* p. 37.

For his *Charges*, they were these following.

First,

First, His Charge at the Sessions, holden for the Verge in the Reign of King *James*, declaring the Latitude and Jurisdiction thereof (p).

(p) *Pub. in 4°. Lon. 1661. and reprinted in the 2d. part of Refusc.*

By the *Verge*, is meant a Plat of twelve Miles round, laid to the King's settled Mansion-House, subject to special exempted Jurisdiction, depending upon his Person and great Officers. This his Lordship called an Half-pace, or Carpet spread about the King's Chair of Estate; and he judged that it ought to be cleared and void, more than other places of the Kingdom, that Offences might not seem to be shrowded under the King's Wings.

Secondly, His Charge in the Star-Chamber against Duels (q); to which may be added the *Decree* of the Star-Chamber in the same Case (r).

(q) *See Refusc. 2d. part. p. 1.*
(r) *In part 2. of Refusc. p. 9.*

Thirdly, His Charge in the Star-Chamber against *William Talbot*, touching the Doctrine of *Suarez*, concerning the Deposing and Killing of Excommunicated Kings (s).

(s) Ref. 1 part. p. 53.

Fourthly, His Charge in the same Court against Mr. *J. S.* for Scandalizing and Traducing in the Public Sessions, Letters sent from the Lords of the Council, touching the *Benevolence* (t).

(t) P. 60.

Fifthly, His Charge in the same Court against *M. L. S. W.* and *H. J.* for Traducing

cing the King's Justice in the proceedings
against *Weston*, one of the Instruments in
the empoysoning of Sir *Thomas Overbu-*
ry (u). (u) P. 72.

Sixthly, His Charge in the *Kings-Bench*
against *Owen*, for affirming conditionally,
That if the King were Excommunicated, it
were lawful to kill him (w). (w) P. 68.

Seventhly, His Charge in the *Kings-Bench*
against the Lord *Sanquere* (x), a Scotish No- (x) *In*
bleman, who in private Revenge, had sub- *part 2. of*
orned *Robert Carlile* to murther *John Tur-* *Refusc.*
ner, a Master of Fence. p. 15.

Eighthly, His Charge before the Lord
High Steward, Lord *Elesmere*, and the
Peers, against the Countess and Earl of
Somerset (y).

His Lordship's *Seventh Writing*, touching (y) *Now*
Civil Policy in Special, is his *Reading* on the *first publ.*
Statute of *Uses* (z). *at the be-*
ginning of
these Re-
mains.

The *Eighth* is call'd, *Observations* upon a
Libel, publish'd *Anno* 1592, in Defamation (z) *Pub.*
of the Queen's Government (a). In these *in 4º. Lon.*
Observations, his Lordship hath briefly set 1642.
forth the present State of those Times; (a) Re-
but he hath done the same thing more at fusc. p.
large in his *Memorial* of Queen *Elizabeth*. 103.

The *Ninth* is, A true *Report* of the *Trea-*
son of Dr. *Roderigo Lopez* (a *Spaniard*, and
a Physician attending upon the Person of

f 2   the

the Queen); who was in Confederacy with certain Spanish Agents, and hired by the King of *Spain*, to poyson her Majesty (*b*).

(b) Pag. 151.

The *Tenth* is, His *Apologie* touching the Earl of *Essex*, in which he cleareth himself of Ingratitude by the plain reasons of the Case, and doth not (as many others have done) increase the suspicion by the very Excuse (*c*).

(c) *Publ. in* 4° Lon. 1642. *and in* 16° *An.* 1651. *and reprinted in the* 2d *part of* Refusc.

The *Eleventh* is, *Advice* to King *James* touching Mr. *Sutton*'s Estate, in the settling of which, in the Hospital of the *Chartreaux*, the Event sheweth that his Lordship was mistaken, when he called it *A Sacrifice without Salt* (*d*). He proposed four other Ends of that great heap of Alms to the King's Majesty. As first, The Erection of a College for Controversies, for the encountring and refuting of *Papists*. Secondly, The Erection of a *Receipt* (for the word *Seminary* he refus'd to make use of) for Converts from the persuasions of *Rome*, to the Reformed Religion. Thirdly, A settlement of Stipends for Itinerary Preachers, in Places which needed them; as in *Lancashire* where such care had been taken by Queen *Elizabeth*. And lastly, An increase of Salary to the Professors in either University of this Land. Wherefore

(d) Refusc p 265.

fore his Lordship manifesting himself, not against the Charity, but the manner of disposing it, it was not well done of those who have publickly defam'd him, by declaring their jealousies of Bribery by the Heir.

The *Twelfth* is, A Proposition to King *James*, touching the *Compiling and Amendment of the Laws of* England, written by him when he was Attourney General, and one of the Privy-Council (*e*). <small>(e) Pag. 271.</small>

The *Thirteenth* is, An *Offer* to King *James*, of a *Digest* to be made of the Laws of *England* (*f*). <small>(f) *In the M.scellan. Works.* p. 137. & 2d *part of* Refusc.</small>

The *Fourteenth* is, The *Elements* of the Common Laws of *England*, in a *double Tract:* The one of the *Rules* and *Maxims* of the Common Law, with their Latitude and Extent. The other, of the *Use* of the Common Law, for the preservation of our Persons, Goods, and good Names (*g*). These he Dedicated to her Majesty, whose the Laws were, whilst the Collection was his. <small>(g) *In* 4°. *Anno* 1639.</small>

The *Fifteenth* is, a Draught of an Act against an *usurious shift of Gain* (*h*), in delivering Commodities in stead of Money. <small>(h) *See* Refusc. *part* 2. p. 62.</small>

Touching these latter Pieces, which may be termed Writings in *Juridical Polity*, and which he wrote as a debtor to his Profession;

f 3

sion; it is beyond my Skill, as well as out of the way of my Studies, to pass a special Judgment on them. Onely I may note it in the general, that if he reached not so far in the Common Law, as Sir *Edward Cook*, and some other Ornaments of the long Robe: the prepossession of his Mind by Philosophical Notions, and his regard to Matters of *Estate*, rather than to those of *Law*, may be assigned as the true Causes of it: For doubtless Parts were not wanting. On this Subject it is, that he thus writeth to Sir *Thomas Bodley* (i). "I think "no Man may more truly say with the "Psalm, *multùm incola fuit Anima mea*, than "my self. For I do confess, since I was "of any Understanding, my Mind hath, "in effect, been absent from that I have "done: And, in absence are many Errors, "which I do willingly acknowledg, and "amongst the rest this great one that led "the rest; That knowing my self, by in-"ward Calling, to be fitter to hold a Book "than to play a Part, I have led my Life "in civil Causes, for which I was not very "fit by Nature, and more unfit by the pre-"occupation of my Mind.

(i) *Coll. of Letters in Resusc. p. 34.*

To a like purpose is *this*, in a Manuscript Letter to the Lord Chancellor *Egerton*, which I have sometimes perus'd.

——I

—"I am not (*k*) so deceived in my "self, but that I know very well, (and I "think, your Lordship is *major Corde*, and "in your Wisdom you note it more deep- "ly than I can in my self) that in Practising "the Law, I play not my best Game, which "maketh me accept it with a *nisi quid* "*potius*; as the best of my Fortune, and a "thing better agreeable to better Gifts than "mine, but not to mine.

(*k*) M S. *Letter of L. Bacons.*

And it appeareth, by what he hath said in a Letter to the Earl of *Essex* (*l*), that he once thought not to practise in his Pro- fession. "I am purposed (said he) not "to follow the practice of the Law. —And "my Reason is only, because it drinketh "too much Time, which I have dedicated "to better purposes.

(*l*) *Coll. in Resusc. p.* 111.

To this Head of *Polity*, relating to the Affairs of these Kingdoms, we may reduce most of his *Lordship's Letters*, published correctly in the *Resuscitatio*, and in these *Remains*, and from uncorrect Copies, in the *Cabala*. These they though often contain private Matters, yet commonly they have Matters of Estate intermingled with them. Thus, his Letter to the Lord-Treasurer *Burghley* (*m*), was writ in Excuse of his Speech in Parliament, against the Triple Subsidy. So, many of the Letters to the

(m) P. 1.

Earl

(n) Pag. 4, 5, 7.
(o) P. 76.
(p) P. 48, 51.
(q) P. 55.
(r) P. 58.
(ſ) P. 57.
(t) P. 59, 61, 70.
(u) P. 66.

Earl of *Eſſex* (*n*), and Sir *George Villiers* (*o*), relate plainly to the *Iriſh* Affairs. So, ſome Letters to King *James*, relate to the Caſes of *Peacham* (*p*), *Owen* (*q*), and others (*r*); to the Matter of his Revenue (*ſ*); to the New Company (*t*), who undertook to Dye and Dreſs all the Cloaths of the Realm; to the *Præmunire* in the Kings-Bench, againſt the Chancery (*u*). Moſt of the reſt are a Miſcellany, and not reducible to one certain Head.

Laſt of all, For his Lordſhip's Writings upon *Pious Subjects*, though for the Nature of the Argument, they deſerve the firſt place; yet they being but few, and there appearing nothing ſo extraordinary in the compoſure of them, as is found in his Lordſhips other *Labours*; they have not obtain'd an earlier mention.

They are only theſe:

His *Confeſſion of Faith*, written by himſelf in *Engliſh*, and turn'd into *Latine* by Dr. *Rawley* (*w*).

(w) Publ. in Engl. at the end of the Reſuſ. and in Latine in the Opuſcula, p. 207.

The *Queſtions* about an *Holy War*, and the *Prayers*, in theſe *Remains*. And a *Tranſlation* of certain of *David's Pſalms*, into Engliſh Verſe. With this laſt Pious Exerciſe he diverted himſelf in the time of his Sickneſs, in the Year Twenty Five. When he ſent it abroad into the World,

he

(x), he made a Dedication of it to his good Friend, Mr. *George Herbert:* For he judged the Argument to be futable to him in his double Quality, of a *Divine*, and a *Poet.* His Lordſhip had very great judgment in Poetry, as appeareth by his Diſcourſe (y) about it; and he had ſome ſort of Talent that way alſo. Hence, when the Queen had a purpoſe to Dine at his Lodging at *Twicknam* Park, he prepared a Sonnet (z), tending to the Reconcilement of her Majeſty to the Earl of *Eſſex* then in Diſfavour. But it was very ſeldom that he courted theſe Muſes, and therefore his Vein does not appear ſo Elegant and Happy, as Exerciſe might have made it. The truth is, 'tis one of the hardeſt things in the World, to excel in Poetry; and to Attempt, and not to Excel, is to loſe both Time and Reputation: For in this Art, Mediocrity will not paſs for Vertue. In this ſqueamiſh Age, (as *Mounſieur Rapine* ſaith, in his *Judicious Reflections*) Verſes are *Ridiculous*, if they be not *Admirable.* They are, it ſeems, like ſome Modern Diſhes, which if they have not an high taſte, occaſion Diſguſt.

(x) *'Twas publ. in* Lond. An. 1625. *in* 4° *and hath lately been put into the 2d part of* Refuſc.

(y) *In* l. 2. *de* Augm. Scient. c. 13.

(z) *See* Apol. *for the Earl of* Eſſex. p. 73.

Now of theſe ſeveral Works of his Lordſhip's already Publiſh'd (of which a great part

part (*a*) was written in that *non ignobile Quinquennium*, of his receſs from Buſineſs) there is not yet made any exact Collection, either in *Latine*, or *Engliſh*; though ſome attempts have been made in both thoſe Languages. The firſt *Latine Collection* was ſet forth accurately, for ſo much of it, by Dr. *Rawley*, under the Title of *Opera Moralia & Civilia* (*b*). But it contained only the *Hiſtory of* Henry *the Seventh*; *the Eſſaies*; *the Book of the Wiſdom of the Ancients*; *the Dialogue of an Holy War*; *the New* Atlan*tis*; *the Book* de Augmentis; *the Hiſtory of Winds*; *the Hiſtory of Life and Death*. The ſecond *Latine Collection* was lately publiſh'd (*c*) at *Francfort on the Meyn*. It pretendeth, in the Title, to contain all his Lordſhip's Extant Works, whether Philoſophical, Moral, Political, or Hiſtorical: Although, beſides the Books in the forementon'd Collection; it containeth only his *Lordſhip's Life* (without any mention of Dr. *Rawley*, who wrote it); the *Organon*; the *Scripta*; the *Sylva Sylvarum*; the *Felicities of Queen* Elizabeth; the *Images of* Julius, *and* Auguſtus Cæſar; *and the Epiſtle to* Fulgentius, without the *Opuſcula*, to which that Epiſtle is annexed. In this Collection, the *Nova Atlantis* is (as I noted a while ago) moſt abſurdly called *Novus Atlas*; and

---

(a) *See them in* S.W. Dugdale, *at the end of theſe Remains*.

(b) Londini, 1638. in Fol. *ſee* Dr. Rawley's *Letter to* M. Deodate, *and his Anſwer*.

(c) Fran. ad Moenum, 1665. in Fol.

and the other Books are most falsly Printed. And yet the Stationer (who, I suppose by his performance, was both Corrector and Publisher) does tell us of this Edition, that it was purged of all Faults. But his Collection cannot be so purged, unless the whole Volume be made one entire Blot. Posterity (I hope) will do his Lordship Honour, and Benefit to themselves, in a larger and more accurate Collection of his Works. These *Latine* ones, as also the *Miscellanies*, and the two parts of the *Resuscitatio*, (which are the only attempt in English) being far short of perfection.

Thus far I have travell'd in an Account, (such as it is) of those Genuine Writings of the *Lord Bacon*, which are already publish'd; and which, being (like *Medals of Gold*) both *rich* in their *Matter*, and *beautiful* in their *Form*, have met with a very great, and well nigh, equal number of Purchasers and Admirers.

This general Acceptance of his Works, has expos'd him to that ill and unjust usage which is common to Eminent Writers. For on such are fathered, sometimes Spurious Treatises; sometimes most Corrupt Copies of good Originals; sometimes their Essays and first Thoughts upon good Subjects, though

though laid aside by them Unprosecuted and Uncorrected; and sometimes the very Toys of their Youth, written by them in trivial or loose Arguments, before they had arriv'd either at ripeness of Judgment, or sobriety of Temper.

The veriest *Straws* (like that of *Father Garnet*) are shewn to the World as admiral *Reliques*, if the least stroaks of the *Image* of a celebrated Author, does but seem to be upon them.

The Press hath been injurious in this kind, to the Memory of Bishop *Andrews*, to whom it owed a deep and solemn Reverence. It hath sent forth a Pamphlet upon an Idle Subject, under the venerable Name of that great Man, who (like the Grass in hot Countries, of which they are wont to say that it groweth Hay) was born Grave and Sober: And still, further to aggravate the Injury, it hath given to that Idle Subject, the idler Title of the *Ex-ale-tation of Ale.*

In such an unbecoming manner it hath dealt, long ago *(d)*, with the very Learned and Ingenious Author of the *Vulgar Errors*. It hath obtruded upon him, whilst alive, a dull and worthless Book stollen, for the most part out of the *Physic's* of *Magirus*, by a very Ignorant Person: A Plagiary so Ignorant,

(d) *About the Year* 1658.

ignorant and so unskilful in his *Rider*, that not distinguishing betwixt *Lævis* and *Levis*, in the said *Magirus*, he hath told us of the *Liver*, that one part of it is *gibbous*, and the other *light*. And yet he had the confidence to call this Scribble, *The Cabinet of Nature unlocked*: An arrogant and fanciful Title, of which his true Humility would no more have suffer'd him to have been the Father, than his great Learning could have permitted him to have been the Author of the Book. For I can assure the Reader upon my knowledg, that as he is a Philosopher very inward with Nature, so he is one who never boasts of his Acquaintance with her.

Neither hath the Lord *Bacon* gone without his share in this Injustice from the Press. He hath been ill dealt with in the Letters printed in the *Cabala*, and *Scrinia*, under his Name: For Dr. *Rawley* professed, that though they were not wholly False, yet they were very corrupt and embased Copies. This I believe the rather, having lately compar'd some Original Letters with the Copies in that Collection, and found them imperfect. And to make a particular Instance; in comparing the Letter of Sir *Walter Raleigh* to Sir *Robert Car*, of whom a Fame had gone that he had begg'd his
Estate;

Estate; I found no fewer then forty Differences, of which some were of moment.

Our Author hath been still worse dealt with, in a Pamphlet in *Octavo*, concerning the Trial of the *Earl* and *Countess* of *Somerset*: And likewise in one in *Quarto*, which beareth the Title of *Bacon's Remains*, though there cannot be spied in it, so much as the *Ruines* of his beautiful Genius.

His Lordship, and other such memorable Writers, having formerly been subject to such Abuses; it is probable that many will, at first, suspect the faithfulness of this Collection; and look upon that as adulterate Ware, which is of such a sudden here brought forth to them, out of the Dark.

But let them first make trial, and then pass Sentence. And if they have sufficient knowledg of the peculiar *Air* of this Author, they will not only believe that these *Remains* are his, but also set a value upon them as none of his most useless and wast Papers. They say, the Feather of a *Phœnix* is of price: And here such will own, they have some little of the Body, as well as part of the Plumage.

It is difficult to imitate such great Authors, in so lively and exact a form, as without suspicion, to pass for them. They who

who are the most artificial Counterfeits in this way, do not resemble them as the Son does the Father, but at best, as the dead Picture does the living Person. And those who have true skill in the Works of the Lord *Verulam*, like great Masters in Painting, can tell by the *Design*, the *Strength*, the *way of Colouring*, whether he was the Author of this or the other Piece, though his Name be not to it.

For the Reader, who has been less versed in his Books, he may understand, that nothing is here offered to him as the *Labour* of that *Lord*, which was not written either by his own Hand, or in Copies transcrib'd by the most faithful Pen of his Domestic *Chaplain*, Dr. *William Rawley*: A Person whom his Lordship chiefly us'd in his Life-time, in Writing down, Transcribing, Digesting, and Publishing his Composures; and to whom, at his death, he expressed his Favour, by bequeathing to him in Money, One Hundred Pounds, and in Books, the great *Bibles* of the *King of Spain*.

I refer him, who doubteth of my Veracity in this Matter, to my worthy Friend Mr. *John Rawley*, (the Executor of the said Reverend Doctor) by whose care most of these Papers have been preserved

for

for the public Good; and who can bear me witness, (if occasion serveth) that I have not herein impos'd upon the World.

It is true, that Dr. *Rawley*, in his Preface to the *Opuscula* of his Lordship, hath forbidden us to expect any more of his *Remains* in *Latine*, or *English*: He addeth in express Terms, that nothing further remained in his Hands. He meant, when he said this, that such Writings of his Lordship, were to be esteemed as not in being, which were not worthy to appear. This meaning of his, he more plainly deliver'd in his Preface to the Collection, called *Resuscitatio*.

There he saith, "That he had left no-"thing to a future hand, which he found to "be of moment, or communicable to the pub-"lic, save only some few *Latine* Works "soon after to be publish'd. He deliver'd himself from the Obligation of that Promise in the Year fifty eight; publishing then, with all due care, those *Latine* Works (*e*). Soon after, he was accus'd by an obscure Prefacer, to a new Edition of the *Essays*, in *Octavo*, as one that had still concealed some of his Lordship's Philosophical Treasures. In vindication of himself from this Censure, I find him using these words in one of his papers, wherein he animadverteth on that pre-

(e) *Opus. Posth. Philos. Civil. Theologica F.B. B. de Ver.*

preface. "I have publish'd all I thought "fit, or a well advised Man would have "thought fit to be publish'd by me. He judged some papers, touching *Matters of Estate*, to tread too near to the heels of Truth, and to the times of the Persons concerned, from which now they are further remov'd, by the distance of Twenty Years. He thought his Lord's Letters concerning his Fall, might be injurious to his Honour, and cause the old Wounds of it to bleed anew; whereas if the remembrance of them had not been fresh in the Minds of many, and in the Books of some, the Collection of the *Cabala*, had revived part of it in a corrupt Copy; and the matter of those Letters is of such a nature, (as afterwards I shall shew) that it rather cleareth his Lordship's Fame, than throws more dirt upon it. For the *Philosophical Remains*, he judged them unfit to be committed to the Press, because they were but Fragments; and such too, as his Lordship's last Hand had not rendred Correct. The excess of Veneration which he had for his Lordship, inclin'd him to think nothing worthy to bear his Name, which was not a Masterpiece. And for this Reason, If Surreptitious Copies had not moved him to do his Lordship right by printing the

the true ones, we had wanted divers Papers which the World now enjoys, and receives with thankfulness. And where the substance is Gold, Men will readily accept it, though in the Ore and unrefined: Nor is it any disparagement to the *Inventory* of his Lordship's philosophical Goods, if there are numbred amongst them certain broken uncoined pieces of valuable Metal.

Some few imperfect Papers, about his Lordship's private Affairs, or of very little moment in Philosophy, are still kept where they ought to be, in private Hands. But those which have been judged worthy the Light, by those Learned and Prudent Men whom I have consulted, are now, with no small Labour, communicated to the World. For so blotted were some of the Papers, so torn, so disjoynted, so intermixed in Contents of a different Nature; that the *Sense*, as it now stands, may seem like *Mercury* reduced to its *proper Form*, after its divers Shapes and Transmutations.

Now these *Remains* which I have been moved to publish, I have digested according to the nature of their Contents, and reduc'd them to these several Heads of Arguments, *Civil* and *Moral*; *Physiological*; *Medical*; *Theological*; and *Bibliographical*.

Under

the Lord Bacon's Works.

Under the firſt Head of *Remains, Civil and Moral*, are contained theſe Papers.

The Firſt is, His *Charges* againſt the *Counteſs* and *Earl* of *Somerſet*, touching the death of Sir *Thomas Overbury*.

The proper place for theſe *Charges* was, in the firſt part of the *Reſuſcitatio* (*f*), be- (f) *Reſuſc. p. 72* fore his Charge againſt three Perſons for Scandal, and traducing of the King's Juſtice, in the proceedings againſt *Weſton*. But Dr. *Rawley* (as appeared by a Note of his, on the Margent of thoſe papers) did at that time forbear the inſerting of them, leſt they ſhould be offenſive to ſome then alive. Now, more than Sixty Years have paſſed, ſince the end of that Tragedy; and the News of it was told in the Ears of the World; and the Story was made publick and laſting by the Preſs, both before and after (*g*) the Doctor's death. And (g) *See it in Sir* what Curtain ſoever our Prudence would W. *Dug-* draw, we could not conceal ſo public a dale's *Ba-* Matter. Nor is it fitting we ſhould. For *ron. of Eng. Tome 2d.* thereby we ſhould endeavour to hide from *p. 425. &c.* Men, one uſeful Memorial of Divine Juſtice: A Memorial apt to deter Greatneſs from a Practice, which if it were common, there would be no ſafe eating or drinking, or breathing in Courts.

g 2   At

At the Trial, some Body, of bad Memory, and no better Pen, wrote down most imperfectly, a little of that which Mr. *Attorney* had spoken, largely and elegantly upon this solemn Occasion: And, in the Year fifty one, (a time of general Licence) this Scribble was publish'd (*h*). The Publisher had the confidence to affirm, that the Narrative was Collected out of the Papers of Sir *Francis Bacon* (*i*), which, by the Copies I set forth, 'tis manifest the Relator never had seen. But a good Name in the Title-page, was an useful Bush for the putting off the crude and unfined Matter in the Book it self.

Little hath the Relator told of much which was said by Mr. *Attorney*; and that which he hath told, he hath repeated in such ill manner, that it is no longer Sir *Francis Bacon*'s, but his own.

In *one Place* (*k*), he introduceth Mr. *Attorney*, speaking thus. "This is the "second time since the King's coming these "thirteen Years, that any *Peers* have been "Arraigned, and both these times your "*Grace* hath had the Place of *High Steward*. "The first was *Grey*, and *Cobham*; and "though they were Convicted, yet Exe-"cution follow'd not; no Noble Blood "hath been spilt since his Majestie's Reign.

(*h*) *In the Pamphlet entituled, a True and Historical Rel. of the Person of Sir Tho. Overbury in 12°.*
(*i*) *'Tis said in the Title Page.*

(*k*) *Pag. 127, 104.*

The

"The first was Revenge, of Treason against Male-contents; and this of the particular offence to a private Subject, against those that have been so high in the King's Grace and Favour; and therefore deserves to be written in a Sun-beam: but his being the best Master in in the World, hinders him not from being the best King; for *He can as well plain a Hill, as raise a Wall*; a good Lesson to put to my Lords the Peers: He is Lieutenant to him who is no respecter of persons.

Now how curtail'd, how incoherent, how mean and unelegant is this, in comparison of that which Mr. *Attorney* spake? For he spake that which followeth.

"In all this mean time, the King hath Reigned in his White Robe, not sprinkled with any one drop of Blood of any of his *Nobles* of this Kingdom: Nay, such have been the depths of his Mercy, as even those Noble-mens Bloods (against whom the proceeding was at *Winchester*) *Cobham* and *Grey*, were attainted and corrupted, but not spilt, or taken away; but that they remained rather *Spectacles* of Justice in their continual Imprisonment, than *Monuments* of Justice in the memory of their Suffering.

"It

"It is true, that the Objects of his Ju-
"ftice then, and now, were very diffe-
"ring: For then it was the Revenge of an
"Offence againſt his own Perſon and
"Crown, and upon Perſons that were
"Male-contents, and Contraries to the
"*State* and *Government*: But now it is the
"the Revenge of the Blood and Death of
"a particular *Subject*, and the Cry of a
"*Priſoner*: It is upon Perſons that were
"highly in his Favour, whereby his Ma-
"jeſty, to his great Honour hath ſhewed
"to the World, as if it were written with a
"Sun-beam, that he is truly the Lieute-
"nant of him, with whom there is no re-
"ſpect of Perſons; That his Affections
"Royal are above his Affections Private;
"That his Favours and Nearneſs about
"him are not like *Popiſh Sanctuaries*, to pri-
"vilege Malefactours; and that his being
"the beſt Maſter in the World, doth not
"let him from being the beſt King in the
"World. His People, on the other ſide,
"may ſay to themſelves, I will lie down
"in peace; for God, and the King, and
"the Law, protect me againſt the great
"and ſmall. It may be a Diſcipline alſo,
"to great Men, ſpecially ſuch as are ſwol-
"len in their Fortunes from ſmall begin-
                                    "nings:

"nings; that *The King is as well able to le-*
"*vel Mountains, as to fill Valleys,* if such be
"their desert.

In another place (*l*), he thrusteth into the Speech of Sir *Edward Cook*, a part of Sir *Francis Bacon*'s, and (like the worser sort of Thieves) he does not only rob, but mangle him. Sir *Francis Bacon* spake on this manner: "My Lords! He is not "the Hunter alone that lets slip the Dog "upon the Deer; but he that *lodges the* "*Deer,* or rouses him, or puts him out; "or *he that sets a Toyl* that he cannot "escape.

(*l*) Page 119. Of the Arraignment of the L. of Somerset.

Instead of which, the Relator hath substituted this absurd Sentence. "It is not he "only that slips the Dog, but he that *loves* "the Toyl, that kills the Deer.

This (I thought) was not unnecessary to be said in Vindication of Mr. *Attorney*'s Honour, which is vilely traduc'd in this Pamphlet, where the *Daw* would personate the *Orator*.

The Second Paper is, his Letter to the University of *Cambridg,* (to whom he was of Counsel) upon occasion of his being Sworn of the Privy-Council to the King. This I judged fit to bear that other company which is already printed (*m*), and answereth to their Congratulation at his first

(*m*) Resusc. Letters, p. 83.

first coming to the Place of *Lord-Keeper*.

The *Third* is, his Letter to King *James*, touching the Place of Lord High Chancellour of *England*, upon the approaching death of the Chancellour *Egerton*.

The *Fourth* is, a Letter to the same Prince, for the relief of his Estate. This, with that *other of Submission* in the *Cabala*, seem to some to blemish his Lordship's Honour; to others, to clear it: For *in this*, he appealeth to the King himself, whether he had not ever found him direct and honest in his Service, so as not once to be rebuked by him, during Nineteen Years Employment. He sheweth that his Fall was not the King's Act; and that the Prince was ready to reach out his Hand to stay him from falling. In the other he maketh this profession of his being free from malicious Injustice. "For the Bribery and Gifts "wherewith I am charged, when the Books "of Hearts shall be opened, I hope I shall "not be found to have the troubled Foun-"tain of a corrupt Heart, in a depraved "habit of taking Rewards to pervert Ju-"stice, howsoever I may be frail, and par-"take of the abuses of the Times."

The *Fifth* Paper is, a Collection of his remaining *Apothegms*, inferiour in number to those already published, but not in weight.

weight. Some of these he took from Eminent Persons, and some from meaner ones, having set it down from his Observation (*n*), that *The Bolt of the Rustic, often hits the Mark*; and that the Sow, in rooting, may describe the letter A, though she cannot write an entire Tragedy.

The *Sixth* is, a Supply of his Collection of Judicious and Elegant Sentences, called by him *Ornamenta Rationalia*. He also gave to those Wise and Polite Sayings, the Title of *Sententiæ Stellares*; either because they were Sentences which deserved to be pointed to by an Asterisc in the Margent; or because they much illustrated and beautify'd a Discourse, in which they were disposed in due place and order; as the Stars in the Firmament, are so many glorious Ornaments of it, and set off with their Lustre, the wider and less adorned Spaces.

This Collection is either wholly lost, or thrown into some obscure Corner; but I fear the first. I have now three Catalogues in my Hands, of the unpublish'd Papers of Sir *Francis Bacon*; all written by Dr. *Rawley* himself. In every one of these appears the Title of *Ornamenta Rationalia*, but in the Bundles which came with those Catalogues, there's not one of those *Sentences* to be found. I held my self oblig'd,

(n) *In Impet. Philosoph. p. 476. Rusticorum Proverbia nonnulla apposite ad veritatem dicuntur Sus rostro, &c.*

lig'd in some sort, and as I was able, to supply this defect; it being once in my power to have preserved this Paper. For a Copy of it was long since, offer'd me by that Doctor's only Son, and my dear Friend (now with God) Mr. *William Rawley*, of whom, if I say no more, it is the *greatness of my Grief* for that irreparable loss, which causeth my *Silence*. I was the more negligent in taking a Copy, presuming I might, upon any occasion, command the Original; and because that was then in such good Hands. Now, there remains nothing with me, but a general Remembrance of the quality of that Collection. It consisted of divers short Sayings, aptly and smartly expressed, and containing in them much of good Sense in a little room.

These he either made, or took from others, being moved so to do by the same Reason which caus'd him to gather together his *Apothegms*, which (he saith) *he collected for his Recreation*, his Lordship's Diversions being of more value than some Men's Labours. Nor do such *Sentences* and *Apothegms*, differ much in their Nature. For *Apothegms* are only somewhat longer, and fuller of Allusion, and tell the Author, and the occasion of the *Wise Saying*; and are but the same Kernel, with the Shell and

and Leaf about it. That which he faith of the one, is true of the other. "They "are both *Mucrones Verborum* (*o*), pointed "Speeches, or Goads. *Cicero* (faith he) "calleth them *Salinas*, Salt-pits, that you "may extract Salt out of, and sprinkle it "where you will. They serve to be in-"terlaced in continued Speech: They serve "to be recited, upon occasion, in them-"selves.

(*o*) *In Preface to his Apothegms.*

Such *Ornaments* have been noted in all Ages and Places, and in many Collected.

Amongst the *Hebrews*, they had (of old) the Proverbs of *Agur*, and *Salomon*.

In Times more Modern, there have been set forth the *Pirke Avoth*; and the Sentences, Proverbs, Apothegms, and Similitudes of the *Hebrew* Writers, Collected in the *Florilegium Hebraicum* of *Buxtorf*.

Amongst the *Egyptians*, we find such Ænigmatic Proverbial Forms as these; *He hath a Wing of a Bat*. That is, the Man is impotent, yet daring; and so like a *Bat*, which adventures to flie, though it has no Feathers. *The Crab keeps the door of the Oyster*. That is, his Friend destroys him. For the *Crab* (they say) puts in his Claw when the *Oyster* gapes, and eats it up.

Amongst the *Arabians*, we find the Proverbs

verbs of *Lockman*, or *Æsop*; and those Collected by *Erpenius*.

Amongst the *Greeks*, we find the Sentences of their *Seven Wise Men*, of *Theognes*, and *Phocylides*, and of divers others preserved by *Stobæus*. *Pythagorus* had his ὑποθῆκαι (*p*), of which we should have known much more, if Time had not denied us the Book of *Aristotle* περὶ τῶν Πυθαγορέων. Thence, 'tis thought, *Laërtius*, and *Porphyrie*, cite certain Pythogoric Symbols (*q*), in which among others, the *Pleiades* are called *the Harp of the Muses*; and the *Northern Bears*, the *Hands of Rhea*. Which latter Symbol, is for such a Toy, pretty enough, if expounded of Matter fixed, and detained from the course of its Fluidity, by cold, or rest. But I pretend not so much intimacy with the *Magical Pythagoras*, as to be his Interpreter. To *Henry Stephens*, we owe a Collection of *Greek* Sentences, from the Comic Poets. The Monk *Thalasius*, wrote an Hundred Sentences concerning Charity and Continence, after the way of the Cloyster, that is, in a pious, but less acute manner (*r*).

Amongst the *Romans*, *Julius Cæsar*, and *Macrobius* wrote Collections of *Apothegms*; and the Sentences of *Laberius*, and also of *Publius*, (who was, indeed, by Birth a *Syrian*,

(*p*) See Salmas. *in Simplic. in Epict. ad calc.* p 12.

(*q*) Vide Jonsium *de Script. Hist. Phil.* p. 54. Also p. 76. & Jamblich. *de vita Pythag.* p. 131.

(*r*) See them in the Μικροπρεσβ p. 100.

Syrian, but by Education and Privilege a *Roman*) are to this Day preserved.

Some, a-while ago, have gathered and amassed the Sentences of *Cicero*, and of both the *Seneca*'s, though (I think) without much judgment, and as we gather Fishes in a Net, enclosing the good and bad together. Last Year, the *Sieur de Laval*, did publish his Collection of the Sentences of St. *Austin* (*f*). And it is not long since, *Mounsieur Hache* set forth a whole Folio of Sentences, Collected out of Twelve of the Tomes of the *Bibliotheca Patrum* (*t*).

Among the *Italians*, *Spaniards*, *French*, *Dutch*, *Turks*, (which two last I put together, for the alike bluntness and courseness of their Sayings) there are divers Collections of *Apothegms* and Proverbs.

Among our *Selves*, we have the like, and particularly the *Wise Sayings* by Mr. *Cambden*, and the *Jacula Prudentum*, in Mr. *Herbert*; which latter some have been bold to accuse as having too much Feather, and too little Point. But the sense of that Metaphor, may be more truly apply'd to the Collection call'd *Flores Edvardi Coci* (*u*). Those Sayings, as they are represented without the Context of that Eminent Lawyer, are like the Flowers in an Herbal, of which no Man would put the Generality into his Garden. The

(*f*) *Sent. tirées des Oeuvres de* S. *Aug. A. Paris, 1677. in Octavo.*

(*t*) *Sent. ex 12. Bib. Patr. tom is selecta per Fr. Hache, An. 1666.*

(*u*) *By Tho. Ash. Lon. 1617. in 16°.*

The use of such little things, no Man knew better than Sir *Francis Bacon*, who could turn every saying to Advantage; and if it wanted Lustre in it self, he could by Art create it, and by setting it well.

His own Collection was (as I remember) gathered partly out of his own Store, and partly from the Ancients, and accordingly 'tis supplied out of his own Works, and the *Mimi* of *Publius*.

Under the *Second Head* of *Remains Physiological*, or *Natural*, is contain'd in the *First place*,

A *Fragment* of his Lordship's *Abecedarium Naturæ*. This is commonly said to be lost, and it is well nigh so, the latter part of it only remaining. But where the whole is good, each part is of value. And Antiquaries who travel in the Dominions of the *Grand Signior*, do not despise the ancient Statues which they find there, though *Makometan* Superstition hath broken off their Heads.

This Work is said to be a *Metaphysical Piece*; but it is not so, in the strictest sense. Its principal design is the Partition of things into their several Classes; a design which his Lordship brought to more perfection in his *Organon*, and Book *De Augmentis Scientiarum*. And though in it were
handled

handled *Condittons of Being*, yet not abstractly from all Body, but with reference to it. And therefore his Lordship did not call it *Abecedarium Hyperphysicum*, but the *Alphabet of Nature*. And his Lordship giveth express Caution, in his Book of *Advancement* (*w*), that where he speaks of Conditions of Entities, which are called Transcendental; (such as, *Much, Little, The Same, Divers, Possible, Impossible*) he be not interpreted in a *Logical*, but *Physical* Sense. His Lordship was much averse to high and useless Speculations, and he was wont to express that Averseness in the following Comparison. The *Lark* (said he) is an high flier, and in its flight does nothing but Sing: But the *Hawk* flies high, and thence descends and catches its Prey.

(*w*) *De Augm. Scient.* l. 3. c. 2. p. 228.

The *Second Paper* about Natural things, is his Lordship's Inquisition touching the *Compounding of Metals*.

Then follow, in the *Third Place*, his *Articles of Questions*, touching *Minerals*. Of these, the first inquireth about the same Subject with the foregoing Paper; but finding them distinguish'd by his Lordship, I have not joyn'd them together.

These Questions were turn'd into *Latine*, and in that Tongue, publish'd by Dr. *Rawley*,

amongst

amongst his Lordship's *Opuscula*; but the *English* Originals are now, the first time set forth. And having by me three Copies, I publish them by that one on which his Lordship had endorsed with his own Hand, *This is the clean Copy.*

Now these Inquiries being in themselves Imperfect, and without much Solution of his Lordship's adjoyn'd; I have here added to them the several Answers of Dr. *Meverel*, to whom they were proposed by his Lordship. It has not been in my power, as yet, to inform my self duly about this *Doctor*; but doubtless, he was a *Chymist*, as those Times went, of the first Order. It was his Lordship's manner, on divers mornings, to set down Inquiries for the following Days, in some loose Papers. And in one of them, I find this, among other *Memoranda.* "To send to Dr. *Meverel.* "Take Iron and dissolve it in *Aqua Fortis*, "and put a Loadstone near it, and see "whether it will extract the Iron: Put also "a Loadstone into the Water, and see "whether it will gather a Crust about it.

After the Questions of his Lordship about Minerals, and the Answers of Dr. *Meverel*, there follows, in the *Fourth Place*, an *Inquisition* concerning the Versions, Transmutations, Multiplications, and

Effec-

Effections of Bodies, not hitherto publish'd in the *English* Tongue, in which his Lordship wrote it (*x*).

Fifthly, There is annexed a certain Speech touching the recovery of Drowned Mineral Works, prepared, as Mr. *Bushel* saith, for that *Parliament* under which he fell. His Lordship, no doubt, had such a Project; and he might prepare a Speech also, for the Facilitating of it. But that this is a true Copy of that Speech, I dare not avouch. His Lordship's Speeches were wont to be digested into more Method; his Periods were more round, his Words more choice, his Allusions more frequent, and manag'd with more decorum. And as no Man had greater command of Words, for the illustration of Matter, than his Lordship; so here he had Matter which refus'd not to be cloth'd in the best Words.

(*x*) *See D. R's. Translation among the Opuscula.*

The *Sixth Paper* about Natural Things, containeth certain Experiments about *weight in Air and Water*.

The *Seventh* containeth a few Proposals to the Country-Man, called *Experiments for Profit*. The *Eighth*, Experiments about the *Commixture of Liquors*. The *Ninth*, a Catalogue of *Bodies Attractive and not Attractive*, with Experimental Observations about them.

h

Under the *Third* Head of *Medical Remains*, is contain'd in the *First* place, a Paper which he called *Grains of Youth*. In it he prescribeth divers things, as means to keep up the Body in its Vigour. Amongst these is the Receipt of the *Methusalem Water, against the Driness of Age*, which his Lordship valued and used.

Next follows a *Catalogue of Astringents, Openers, and Cordials*, Instrumental to Health. Then comes in the *Third place*, an *Extract*, by his Lordship, for his own use, out of the *History of Life and Death*, together with some new Advices in order to Health.

Last of all, there are added *Four Medical Receipts*.

The *First* is, his *Lordship's Broth and Fomentation against the Stone*, which I judg'd acceptable to the Public, seeing his *Receipt against the Gout* had been so, though it worketh not an Infallible Cure. And here it may seem strange, that his Lordship does not mention Spirit of *Nitre*, which he so often used, and which a very ingenious Experimenter (*y*) hath noted, to be the best of *Acids* against the Stone.

The *Second* is, the Receipt of an Oyntment, called by his Lordship, *Unguentum Fragrans sive Romanum*. By this he meaneth an Unguent which consisteth of *Astringents,*

(*y*) *Dr. Grew, in his Exper. of the Luctation arising from Affus. of Menstruums upon all sorts of Bodies.* P. 102.

gents, preventing excess of Transpiration; and *Cordials* comforting the Parts. And he called it (I suppose) the *Roman Unguent*, because that People did eminently make use of Baths and Anointings. "He "himself held, that the anointing with Oyl, "was one of the most potent Operations "to long Life (z); and that it conduced "to Health, both in *Winter*, by the exclu- "sion of the cold Air; and in *Summer*, by "detaining the Spirits within, and prohi- "biting the resolution of them; and keep- "ing of the force of the Air, which is then "most predatory. Yet it was his Lordship's opinion, that it was best to anoint without Bathing, though he thought Bathing without Anointing bad.

(z) *Hist. of Life & Death, of the Oper. upon Exclusion of Air.* §. 21. p. 37.

The *Third* and *Fourth*, are Receipts to comfort the Stomach. One of them he calleth a Secret; and I suppose it might be communicated to him by Sir *Henry Wotton*. For Sir *Henry* speaks of his preparation of a certain Wood (*a*), as of a rare Receipt to Coroborate the *Viscera*, and to keep the Stomack in *Tono*.

(a) *In Reliqu. Wotton.* p. 473.

Under the *Fourth Head*, of *Theological Remains*, are contain'd only a few *Questions* about the lawfulness of a *Holy War*; and two Prayers, one for a *Philosophical Student*, the other for a *Writer*. The sub-

h 2 stance

stance of these two Prayers is extant in *Latine*, in the *Organon* (*b*), and *Scripta* (*c*).

(b) Nov. Organum, p. 19. ad Calc. partis primæ.
(c) Scripta Philos. p. 451. and after the Title-Page.

Under the *Fifth Head* of *Bibliographical Remains*, are contained some of his Lordship's own Papers concerning his Works, and likewise some Letters and Discourses of others upon the same Subject, together with a few interspersed Remarks concerning his Life.

His Lordship's Papers are these *Six*.

The *First* is, a Letter to *Elizabeth*, the Sister of King *Charles* the Martyr, and Wife to *Frederic*, Prince *Palatine* of the *Rhine*; a Princess who found so many Thorns in the Crown of *Bohemia*. She pleased to write to his Lordship, and he return'd Answer, and sent along with it as a Present, his *Discourse of a War with Spain*; though neither came to her Hands, till after his Lordship's Death.

The *Second* is, a Letter to the *University* of *Cambridg*, when he sent them his Book of the *Advancement of Learning*.

The *Third* is, a Letter to the same University, upon his sending to them his *Novum Organum*. This he wrote in a loose sheet of paper; the *former*, in one of the spare leaves at the beginning of the Book.

The *Fourth* is, a Letter to *Trinity College*, in *Cambridg* (of which Society he had been a Member)

Member) upon his sending thither the aforesaid Book *De Augmentis Scientiarum*.

The *Fifth* is, a Letter to the Bishop of *Lincoln*; in which I note the goodness of his Lordship's Nature, whilst he still maintaineth his Friendship with him, though he had succeeded him in his place of Lord-Keeper. For Envy hates every one that sits in that Chair from whence it self is fallen.

The *Sixth* is, a Letter to Father *Fulgentio*, a Divine (if I mistake not) of the *Republic of Venice*, and the same who wrote the Life of his Colleague, the excellent Father *Paul*.

The *Seventh* is, a Letter to the *Marquess Fiat*, then Embassadour from *France*, soon after the Marriage betwixt his late *Majesty* and *Henrietta Maria*, in the knitting of which he had been employ'd. This *Marquess* was the Person, who, impatient of seeing so Learned a Man, was admitted to his Lordship when he was very ill, and confin'd to his Bed; and who saluted him with this high Compliment: "Your Lord-"ship hath been to me hitherto like the An-"gels, of which I have often heard and "read, but never saw them before. To which piece of Courtship, he return'd such answer, as became a Man in those Circumstances.

stances. "Sir, the Charity of others, "does liken me to an Angel, but my own "Infirmities tell me I am a Man.

The *Eighth* is, a Transcript out of his Lordship's *Will*, concerning his Writings. There, in particular manner, he commendeth to the Press, the *Felicities* of Queen *Elizabeth*. This I noted before; and observe it here again as an Argument of the Impartiality of his Lordship's Judgment and Affection. He was zealous in bearing testimony to the wise Administration of the Public Affairs in those Times, in which himself advanced little either in Profit, or Honour. For he was hindred from growing at Court by a great Man, who knew the slenderness of his Purse, and also fear'd that if he grew, he might prove Taller than himself (d). The little Art used against him, was the representing of him as a *Speculator*; though it is plain, no Man dealt better, and with kinder ways, in public Business than himself: And it generally ripened under his Hands.

(d) See his Lordship's Letter to Sir R. C. in Coll. of Letters in 1st. part of Resusc. p. 87. and that in p. 110, 111.

For the Papers written by others, touching his Lordship and his Labours, they are these.

The *First* is, a Letter from the University of *Oxford*, to his Lordship, upon his sending to them his Book of *Advancement of of Learning,* in its second, and much enlarged Edition. It should seem by a Passage towards the end of this Letter, that the Letter which his Lordship sent to them, together with his Book, was written (like the first to the *University* of *Cambridg*) in one of the spare leaves of it, and contain'd some wholesome Admonitions in order to the pursuit of its Contents.

The *Second* is, a Letter from Dr. *Maynwaring,* to Dr. *Rawley,* concering his *Lordship's Confession of Faith.* This is that Dr. *Maynwaring,* whose Sermon upon *Eccles.*8.2. *&c.* gave such high Offence, about One and Fifty Years ago.

For some Doctrines, which he noteth in his Lordship's Confession, the Reader ought to call to mind, the times in which his Lordship wrote them, and the distaste of that Court against the proceedings of *Barnevelt,* whose State-faction blemish'd his Creed.

The rest are, Letters of Dr. *Rawley, Monnsieur Deodate, Isaac Gruter,* touching the Edition of his Lordship's Works: *An Account of his Lordship's Life* and *Writings,* by Sir *William Dugdale,* together with some new Insertions: *Characters* of his Lordship, and his *Philosophy,* by Dr. *Heylin,* Dr. *Sprat,* and Mr. *Abraham Cowley.*

All

All thefe Papers I have put under the Title of *Baconiana*, in imitation of thofe, who of late, have publifh'd fome Remains of Learned Men, and called them, *Thuana, Scaligerana, Perroniana*.

Thefe then are the particular Writings, in which I have labour'd, and in fetting forth of which, I have undertaken the lower Office of a Prefacer. And I think it more defireable to write a mean Preface to a good Book, than to be Author of a mean Book, though graced with a Preface from fome excellent Pen: As it is more Honour, with a plain *White Staff*, to go before the King, than being an unpolifh'd Magiftrate of a mean and antiquated Corporation, to be ufher'd forth with a Mace of Silver.

T. T.

Novemb. 30.
1678.

A TABLE OF THE Contents.

Baconiana Politico-moralia.

Under this Head are Contained,

1. SIR Francis Bacon's *Charge against* Frances *Countess of* Somerset, *about poysoning of Sir* Tho. Overbury. p. 3.
2. *His Charge against* Robert, *Earl of* Somerset, *touching the same matter.* p. 14.
3. *His Letter to the University of* Cambridg, *when he was sworn Privy-Counsellor.* In Latine, p. 37. *In* English, p. 39.
4. *His Letter to King* James, *touching the Chancellor's Place.* p. 41.

5. His

A Table of

5. *His Letter to King* James, *for the Relief of his Estate.* p. 45.
6. *His Remaining* Apothegms. p. 53.
7. *A Supply of his* Ornamenta Rationalia, *or* Judicious Sentences.
   1. *Out of the* Mimi *of* Publius, *in* Latine *and* English. p. 60.
   2. *Out of his own Writings.* p. 65.

Baconiana Physiologica, Containing

I. *A Fragment of his* Abecedarium Naturæ, *in* Latine, p. 77. *and* English, p. 84.
II. *His* Inquisition, *touching the Compounding of* Metals. p. 92.
III. *His* Articles *of* Questions, *touching* Minerals.
   1. *Concerning the* Incorporation *and* Union *of* Metals. p. 104.
   2. *Dr.* Meveril's *Answers to them.* p. 110.
   3. *Concerning the* Separation *of* Metals *and* Minerals. p. 114.
   4. *Dr.* Meverel's *Answers to them.* p. 116.
   5. *Concerning the* Variation *of* Metals *and* Minerals. p. 118.
   6. *Dr.* Meverel's *Answers.* p. 123.
   7. *Concerning the* Restitution *of* Metals. p. 127.
   8. *Dr.*

the Contents.

8. *Dr.* Meverel's *Answer.*   p. 128.

IV. *The Lord* Bacon's Inquisition, *concerning the Versions, Transmutations, Multiplications and Effections of Bodies.* p. 129.
V. *His Speech about the Recovery of Drown'd Mineral Works.*   p. 131.
VI. *His Experiments about Weight in Air and Water.*   p. 134.
VII. *His Experiments for Profit.*   p. 138.
VIII. *His Experiments about the Commixture of Liquors, by Simple Composition only.*   p. 140.
IX. *A Catalogue of Bodies Attractive and not Attractive, with Observations upon them, in* Latine, p. 145. *in* English, p. 149.

Baconiana Medica.

Under this Head are Contained,

1. *His Paper about Prolongation of Life,* called by him Grains of Youth.   p. 155.
2. *A Catalogue of Astringents, Openers, and Cordials, instrumental to long Life.* p. 161.
3. *An Extract, by his Lordship, out of his Book of the* Prolongation of Life, *for his own use.*   p. 167.
4. *His*

A Table of

4. His *Medical Receipts, against the Stone*, &c. p. 171.

Baconiana Theologica.

Under this Head are Contained,

1. His *Questions of the Lawfulness of a War, for the Propagation of Religion.* p. 179.
2. *Two Prayers of his, one called the Students, the other the Writers Prayer.* p. 181, 182.

Baconiana Bibliographica.

Under this Head are Contained,

I. *Papers (written by Himself) relating to his Books. As*

  1. His *Letter to the Queen of* Bohemia, *to whom he sent his Book of a War with* Spain. p. 187.
  2. *A Letter of the Lord* Bacon's *to the Uni-*

the Contents.

University of Cambridg, *upon his sending to them his Book* De Augm. Scient. *in* Latine, p. 189, *in* English, p. 190.

3. *His Letter to the same University, upon his sending to them his* Novum Organum, *in* Latin, p. 191. *in* Engl. p. 192.

4. *His Letter to* Trinity College *in* Cambridg, *upon his sending to them his Book of the* Advancement of Learning, *in* Latine, p. 193. *in* English, p. 194.

5. *His Letter to the Bishop of* Lincoln, *about his Speeches,* &c. p. 195.

6. *His Letter to Father* Fulgentio, *about all his Writings in* English, p. 196.

7. *To Marquess* Fiat *(about his Essays) in* French, p. 201. *in* English, p. 202.

8. *Part of his last Testament concerning his Writings.* p. 203.

II. *Papers (written by others) relating to his Books and Life. As*

1. *A Letter to him from the University of* Oxford *(in* Latine, p. 204. *in* English, p. 206. *) upon his having sent to them his Book* De Augmentis Scientiarum.

2. *A Letter from Dr.* Maynwaring *to Dr.* Rawley, *about the Lord* Bacon's *Confession of Faith.* p. 209.

3. *A Letter from Dr.* Rawley *to Mounsieur* Ælius Deodate *in* Latine, p. 214. *in* English

A Table of, &c.

English, p. 215. *concerning his publishing the Lord* Bacon's *Works.*

4. *Mounsieur* Deodate's *Answer, in* Latine, p. 217. *and* English, p. 219.
5. *Mr.* Isaac Gruter's *Three Letters to Dr.* Rawley *(in* Latine, p. 221, 231, 238. *in* English, p. 225, 234, 240.) *concerning the Lord* Bacon's *Works.*
6. *An Account of the Life, and Writings of the Lord* Bacon, *by Sir* W. Dugdale, *together with Insertions by the Publisher.* p. 242.
7. *A Character of the Lord* Bacon, *by* Dr. Heylin. p. 263.
8. *A Character by* Dr. Sprat. p. 264.
9. *A Character of his Philosophy, by Mr.* Cowley. p. 267.

ERRATA.

Liber cui Titulus (Baconiana, &c.)
IMPRIMATUR.

Ex *Ædibus* Lambethanis, Nov. 20. 1678.

Geo. Thorp, Rev$^{mo.}$ in C. P. & D. Dom. *Gulielmo* Archiep. Cant. a Sacris Domesticis.

ERRATA.

In the Introduction.

Page 6. Line 24. Read *Sprang*: P. 11. l. 12. r. *Site.* l. 28. for that, r. *the.* P. 13. Margent, l. 2. for with, r. *inter.* P. 15. l. 26. for to, r. *and.* P. 16 l. 9. for *to*, r. *for.* P. 24. l. 18. r. *enlarged.* l. 25. for were, r. *wear.* P. 27. l. 23. for his, r. *this.* P. 40. l. 9. for *precious*, r. *considerable.* P. 43. l. 29. r. *compare them.* P. 57. l. 13. for *of*, r. *the.* P. 59. l. 16. for *Edward* 3d. r. *Edit.* 3d. P. 60. l. 8. put a period after *publish'd.* P. 62. l. 19. r. *Methodical.* P. 71. l. 24. r. *though they.*

In the Book.

P. 20. l. 11. blot out *but.* P. 33. l. 4. for *in*, r. *is.* P. 37. l. 23. r. *relictum.* P. 61. l. 21. blot out *even.* P. 79. l. 24. blot out *Add.* P. 83. l. 12. r. *vellicationes.* P. 85. l. 21. for *Impossibility*, r. *in Possibility.* P. 89. l. 20. for *interspect*, r. *intersperse.* P. 95. l. 19. r. *it will.* P. 119. l. 2. r. *Arborescents.* P. 125. l. 18. r. *fittest.* P. 132. l. 26, 27. for *the whole Intellects*, r. *your noble Intellects.* P. 135. l. 29. r. *differ.* P. 139. l. 11. r. *rawns.* P. 146. l. 7. for *hewed*, r. *leaved.* P. 148. l. 10. r. *ipsam.* P. 149. l. 10. for *Sheaves*, r. *Shivers.* P. 162. l. 9. r. *mullein.* P. 165. l. 13. r. *Cupparus.* P. 167. l. 2. r. *Puls.* P. 168. l. 28. for *with juyce*, r. *which I use.* P. 189. l. 16. r. *legitimè.* P. 192. l. 15. r. *it is.* P. 199. l. 19, 20. r. *prodromi.* P. 201. l. 4. for *file*, r. *filz.* l. 9. for *non*, r. *mon.* l. 23. for *ex*, r. *et.* P. 208. l. 9. blot out *&c.* P. 215. l. 3. r. *generosissime Domine.* l. 4. r. *addictissimus.* P. 218. l. 2. r. *contriverim.* P. 222. l. 23. for *tum*, r. *Tu.* P. 232. l. 23. r. *vertit.* P. 237. l. 4. r. *would.* P. 239. l. 4. r. *inerat.* l. 12. r. *consecrari.* l. 14. r. *segnescens.* P. 249. l. 29, 30. for *carried*, r. *varied.* P. 250. l. 5. r. *you to call.* P. 253. l. 19. r. *Courts.* P. 254. Margent l. 1. for *R. this*, r. *L. this.* P. 257. Margent l. 1. for *'Twas*, r. *they were.* P. 259. l. 8, 9. after *Nature*, put a Semicolon ; after *parted*, a Colon.

Baconiana Politico-Moralia.
REMAINS
OF THE
Lord Bacon,
Civil and Moral.

LONDON,
Printed for *Richard Chiswel*, at the
Rose and Crown in St. *Paul's*
Church-Yard, 1679.

The Lord *Bacon*'s
REMAINS,
Civil and Moral.

The Charge ‖ by way of Evidence, by Sir Francis Bacon, his Majesties Attourney General, before the **Lord High Steward,** * *and the* **Peers,** *against* Frances *Countess of* Somerset, *concerning the poysoning of Sir* Thomas Overbury.

‖ Given *May* 24. 1616.

*The Lord Chancelor Egerton, Lord Elesmere, and the Earl of Bridgwater.

IT may please your Grace, my *Lord High Steward of England,* and you my Lords the *Peers.*

I am very glad to hear this unfortunate Lady doth take this Course, to confess fully, and freely, and thereby to give Glory to God, and to Justice. It is (as I may term it) the Nobleness of an Offender to confess; and therefore those meaner

B 2   Per-

Persons, upon whom Justice passed before, confessed not, she doth. I know your Lordships cannot behold her without compassion. Many things may move you, her Youth, her Person, her Sex, her noble Family, yea, her Provocations, (if I should enter into the Cause it self) and Furies about her; but chiefly her Penitency and Confession. But Justice is the work of this Day; the Mercy-Seat was in the inner part of the Temple; the Throne is publick. But since this Lady hath by her Confession prevented my Evidence, and your Verdict; and that this Day's labour is eased; there resteth in the Legal Proceeding, but for me to pray that her Confession may be recorded, and Judgment thereupon.

But because *your Lordships* the Peers are met, and that this day and to morrow are the Days that crown all the former Justice; and that in these great Cases it hath been ever the manner to respect Honour and Satisfaction, as well as the ordinary Parts and Forms of Justice; the Occasion it self admonisheth me, to give *your Lordships* and the Hearers this Contentment, as to make Declaration of the Proceedings of this excellent Work of the King's Justice, from the beginning to the end.

It may please your Grace, my *Lord High Steward*

Steward of England, this is now the second time, within the space of thirteen years Reign of our Happy *Sovereign*, that this high Tribunal Seat (ordained for the Trial of *Peers*) hath been opened and erected, and that with a rare event, supplied and exercised by one and the same Person, which is a great Honour unto you, my *Lord Steward*.

In all this mean time the King hath reigned in his white Robe, not sprinkled with any one Drop of the Blood of any of his Nobles of this Kingdom. Nay, such have been the Depths of his Mercy, as even those Noble-Mens Bloods, (against whom the Proceeding was at *Winchester*) *Cobham* and *Grey*, were attainted and corrupted, but not spilt or taken away; but that they remained rather *Spectacles of Justice* in their continual imprisonment, than *Monuments of Justice* in the Memory of their Suffering.

It is true, that the Objects of his Justice then and now were very differing; for then it was the Revenge of an Offence against his own Person and Crown, and upon Persons that were Male-Contents, and Contraries to the State and Government; but now it is the Revenge of the Blood and Death of a particular Subject, and the Cry of a Prisoner; it is upon Persons that were highly in his Favour;

vour; whereby his Majesty, to his great Honour, hath shewed to the World, as if it were written in a Sun-beam, that he is truly the Lieutenant of him *with whom there is no respect of Persons*; that his Affections Royal are above his Affections private; that his Favours, and Nearness about him, are not like *Popish Sanctuaries*, to privilege Malefactors; and that his being the best Master in the World, doth not let him from being the best King in the World. His People, on the other side, may say to themselves, I will lie down in Peace, for God, the King, and the Law, protect me against great and small. It may be a Discipline also to great Men, especially such as are swoln in their Fortunes from small beginnings, that the King is as well able to level Mountains, as to fill Vallies, if such be their desert.

But to come to the present Case, The great Frame of Justice (*my Lords*) in this present Action, hath a *Vault*, and hath a *Stage*: A *Vault*, wherein these Works of Darkness were contrived; and a *Stage*, with Steps, by which it was brought to Light.

For the former of these, I will not lead your *Lordships* into it, because I will engrieve nothing against a Penitent, neither will I open any thing against him that is absent.

The

Civil and Moral.

The one I will give to the Laws of Humanity, and the other to the Laws of Justice; for I shall always serve my Master with a good and sincere Conscience, and I know *that* he accepteth best. Therefore I will reserve that till to morrow, and hold my self to that which I called the *Stage* or *Theater*, whereunto indeed it may be fitly compared: for that things were first contained within the Invisible Judgments of God, as within a Curtain, and after came forth, and were acted most worthily by the King, and right well by his Ministers.

Sir *Thomas Overbury* was murthered by Poison, *Septemb.* 15. 1613. This foul and cruel Murder did for a time cry secretly in the Ears of God; but God gave no answer to it, otherwise than by that Voice, (which sometime he useth) which is *Vox Populi*, the Speech of the People: For there went then a Murmur that *Overbury* was poisoned; and yet the same submiss and low Voice of God (the Speech of the Vulgar People) was not without a Counter-tenor or Counter-blast of the Devil, who is the common Author both of Murder and Slander; for it was given out, that *Overbury* was dead of a foul Disease; and his Body (which they had made *Corpus Judaicum* with their Poisons, so as it had no whole part) must be said

said to be leprosed with Vice, and so his Name poisoned as well as his Body. For as to Dissoluteness, I have not heard the Gentleman noted with it; his Faults were of Insolency, Turbulency, and the like of that kind.

Mean time there was some Industry used (of which I will not now speak) to lull asleep those that were the Revengers of the Blood, the Father and the Brother of the Murdered. And in these terms things stood by the space of two years, during which time God did so blind the two great Procurers, and dazle them with their Greatness, and blind and nail fast the Actors and Instruments with security upon their Protection, as neither the one looked about them, nor the other stirred or fled, or were conveyed away, but remained here still, as under a privy Arrest of God's Judgments; insomuch as *Franklin*, that should have been sent over to the *Palsgrave* with good store of Money, was by God's Providence, and the Accident of a Marriage of his, diverted and stayed.

But about the beginning of the Progress the last Summer, God's Judgments began to come out of their depths. And as the revealing of Murder is commonly such as a Man said, *à Domino hoc factum est*; it is is God's work, and it is marvellous in our eyes: so in this particular it was most admirable; for it came forth first by a Complement, a matter of Courtesy. My Lord of *Shrewsbury*, that is now with God, recommended to a Councellor of State, (of special Trust by his place) the late Lieutenant * *Helwisse*, only for Acquaintance, as an honest and worthy Gentleman, and desired him to know him, and to be acquainted with him. That Councellor answered him civilly, That my Lord did him a favour, and that he should embrace it willingly; but he must let his Lordship know, that there did lie a heavy imputation upon that Gentleman, *Helwisse*, for that Sir *Tho. Overbury*, his Prisoner, was thought to have come to a violent and an untimely Death. When this Speech was reported back by my Lord of *Shrewsbury* to *Helwisse*, *percussit ilicò animum*, he was strucken with it, and being a politick Man, and of likelihood doubting, that the matter would break forth at one time or other, and that others might have the start of him, and thinking to make his own Case by his own Tale, resolved with himself upon this occasion, to discover unto my Lord of *Shrewsbury*, and that Councellor, that there was an Attempt (whereunto he was privy) to have poisoned *Overbury*, by the hands of his

*Called in Sir *H. Wotton*'s Reliq. p. 413. *Elvis* In Sir *A. Welden*'s Court of K. *James*, p. 107. *Elwaies*. In *Aulic. Coquin.* p. 141. *Ellowaies*. In Sir *W. Dugdales* Baron. of *Eng*. Tom 2. p. 425. *Elways*. In *Baker*, *Yelvis*. p. 434.

his Underkeeper, *Weston*; but that he checked it, and put it by, and diswaded it. But then he left it thus, that it was but as an Attempt, or an untimely Birth, never executed; and as if his own Fault had been no more, but that he was honest in forbidding, but fearful of revealing, and impeaching or accusing great Persons. And so with this fine point thought to save himself.

But that Councellor of Estate wisely considering, that by the Lieutenant's own Tale it could not be simply a Permission, or Weakness; for that *Weston* was never displaced by the Lieutenant, notwithstanding that Attempt; and coupling the Sequel by the beginning, thought it matter fit to be brought before his Majesty, by whose appointment *Helwisse* set down the like Declaration in writing.

Upon this Ground the King playeth *Salomon*'s part, *gloria Dei celare rem, & gloria Regis investigare rem*, and sets down certain Papers of his own hand, which I might term to be *Claves Justitiæ*, Keys of Justice, and may serve both for a Precedent for *Princes* to imitate, and for a Direction for *Judges* to follow. And his Majesty carried the Ballance with a constant and steady hand, evenly and without prejudice, whether it were a true Accusation of the one part, or a Practice and factious Scandal of the other.

Which

Which Writing, becauſe I am not able to expreſs according to the worth thereof, I will deſire your Lordſhips anon to hear read.

This excellent Foundation of Juſtice being laid by his Majeſties own hand, it was referred unto ſome Councellors to examine further, who gained ſome Degrees of Light from *Weſton*, but yet left it imperfect.

After it was referred to Sir *Ed. Cook*, Chief Juſtice of the Kings Bench, as a Perſon beſt practiſed in Legal Examinations, who took a great deal of indefatigable pains in it without intermiſſion, having (as I have heard him ſay) taken at leaſt three hundred Examinations in this Buſineſs.

But theſe things were not done in a Corner, I need not ſpeak of them. It is true, that my Lord Chief Juſtice, in the dawning and opening of the Light, finding the matter touched upon theſe great Perſons, very diſcreetly became Suitor to the King, to have greater Perſons than his own Rank joined with him; whereupon your Lordſhips, my Lord High Steward of *England*, my Lord Steward of the King's Houſe, and my Lord *Zouch*, were joined with him.

Neither wanted there (this while) Practice to ſuppreſs Teſtimony, to deface Writings, to weaken the Kings Reſolution, to
ſlander

slander the Justice, and the like. Nay when it came to the first solemn Act of Justice, which was the Arraignment of *Weston*, he had his lesson to stand mute, which had arrested the whole Wheel of Justice: but this dumb Devil, by the means of some discreet Divines, and the potent Charm of Justice together, was cast out; neither did this poisonous Adder stop his Ear to these Charms, but relented, and yeilded to his Trial.

Then followed the other Proceedings of Justice against the other Offenders, *Turnor, Helwisse, Franklin*.

But all these being but the Organs and Instruments of this Fact, (the Actors, and not the Authors) Justice could not have been crowned without this last Act against these great Persons; else *Weston*'s Censure or Prediction might have been verified, when he said, *He hoped the small Flies should not be caught, and the greater escape.* Wherein the King, being in great straits between the defacing of his Houour and of his Creature, hath (according as he useth to do) chosen the better part, reserving always Mercy to himself.

The time also of Justice hath had its true Motions. The time until this Ladies deliverance was due unto Honour, Christianity, and Humanity, in respect of her great Belly.

The time since was due to another kind of Deliverance too, which was, that some Causes of Estate which were in the Womb might likewise be brought forth, not for matter of Justice, but for Reason of State. Likewise this last Procrastination of Days had the like weighty Grounds and Causes.

But (my Lords) where I speak of a Stage, I doubt I hold you upon the Stage too long. But before I pray Judgment, I pray your Lordships to hear the Kings Papers read, that you may see how well the King was inspired, and how nobly he carried it, that Innocency might not have so much as Aspersion.

> *Frances*, Countess of *Somerset*, hath been indicted and arraigned, as accessary before the Fact, for the Murder and Impoisonment of Sir *Tho. Overbury*, and hath pleaded guilty, and confesseth the Indictment: I pray Judgment against the Prisoner.

The Charge of Sir Francis Bacon, *his Majesties Attourney General, by way of Evidence, before the Lord High Steward, and the Peers, against* Robert Earle of Somerset, *concerning the poisoning of* Overbury.

IT may please your Grace, my Lord High Steward of *England,* and you my Lords the Peers; You have here before you *Robert* Earl of *Somerset,* to be tried for his Life, concerning the procuring and consenting to the Impoisonment of Sir *Thomas Overbury,* then the King's Prisoner in the Tower of *London,* as an Accessary before the Fact.

I know your Lordships cannot behold this Nobleman, but you must remember his great favour with the King, and the great Place that he hath had and born, and must be sensible that he is yet of your Number and Body, a Peer as you are ; so as you cannot cut him off from your Body but with grief; and therefore that you will expect from us, that give in the

Kings

King's Evidence, found and sufficient matter of Proof, to satisfy your Honours and Consciences.

And for the manner of the Evidence also, the King our Master (who among his other Vertues, excelleth in that Vertue of the Imperial Throne, which is Justice) hath given us Commandment that we should not expatiate, nor make Invectives, but materially pursue the Evidence, as it conduceth to the Point in question ; a matter that (tho we are glad of so good a Warrant) yet we should have done of our selves ; for far be it from us, by any strains of Wit or Art to seek to play Prizes, or to blazon our Names in Blood, or to carry the Day otherwise than upon just Grounds. We shall carry the Lanthorn of Justice (which is the Evidence) before your Eyes upright, and be able to save it from being put out with any Winds of Evasions, or vain Defences, that is our part ; not doubting at all, but that this Evidence in it self will carry that force, as it shall little need Vantages or Aggravations.

My Lords, The Course which I shall hold in delivering that which I shall say (for I love Order) is this,

First,

First, I will speak somewhat of the nature and greatness of the Offence which is now to be tried, and that the King, however he might use this Gentleman heretofore, as the *Signet upon his Finger* (to use the Scripture Phrase) yet in this Case could not but put him off, and deliver him into the hands of Justice.

Secondly, I will use some few words touching the Nature of the Proofs, which in such a Case are competent.

Thirdly, I will state the Proofs.

And *lastly*, I will produce the Proofs, either out of the Examinations and Matters in Writing, or Witnesses *viva voce*.

For the Offence it self; it is of Crimes (next unto High-Treason) the greatest; it is the foulest of Fellonies. And take this Offence with the Circumstances, it hath three Degrees or Stages; that it is Murder; that it is Murder by Impoisonment; that it is Murder committed upon the Kings Prisoner in the Tower: I might say, that it is Murder under the Colour of Friendship; but that is a Circumstance moral, I leave that to the Evidence it self.

For Murder, my Lords, the first Record of Justice which was in the World was a Judgment upon Murder, in the person of *Adam's*

Adam's first born, *Cain*: And though it were not punished by Death, but with Banishment and mark of Ignominy, in respect of the primogeniture, or of the population of the World, or other points of God's secret Will, yet it was adjudged, and was (as I said) the first Record of Justice. So it appeareth likewise in Scripture, that the murder of *Abner* by *Joab*, though it were by *David* respited in respect of great Services past, or Reason of State, yet it was not forgotten. But of this I will say no more. It was ever admitted, and so ranked in God's own Tables, that Murder is of offences between Man and Man (next to Treason and Disobedience of Authority, which some Divines have referred to the First Table, because of the Lieutenancy of God in Princes and Fathers) the greatest.

For Impoisonment, I am sorry it should be heard of in this Kingdom: It is not *nostri generis nec sanguinis*; It is an Italian Crime fit for the Court of *Rome*, where that Person that intoxicateth the *Kings* of the Earth with his Cup of Poison in Heretical Doctrine, is many times really and materially intoxicated and impoisoned himself.

But it hath *three Circumstances*, which make it grievous beyond other Murders:
Whereof

Whereof the *first* is, That it takes a Man in full Peace; in God's and the King's Peace; He thinks no harm, but is comforting Nature with Refection and Food: So that (as the Scripture saith) *His Table is made a Snare.*

The *second* is, That it is easily committed, and easily concealed; and on the other side, hardly prevented, and hardly discovered: For Murder by violence Princes have Guards, and private Men have Houses, Attendants, and Arms: Neither can such Murders be committed but *cum sonitu,* and with some overt and apparent Act, that may discover and trace the Offender. But for Poison, the said Cup it self of Princes will scarce serve, in regard of many Poisons, that neither discolour nor distast; and so passeth without noise or observation.

And the *last* is, Because it containeth not only the destruction of the maliced Man, but of any other; *Quis modo tutus erit?* For many times the Poison is prepared for one, and is taken by another: So that Men die other Mens Deaths; *Concidit infelix alieno vulnere:* and it is as the Psalm calleth it, *Sagitta nocte volans;* The Arrow that flies by night, it hath no aim or certainty.

Now

Now for the *third Degree* of this particular Offence, which is, that it was committed upon the King's Prisoner, who was out of his own Defence, and meerly in the King's protection, and for whom the King and State was a kind of Respondent, it is a thing that aggravates the Fault much. For certainly (my Lord of *Somerset*) let me tell you this, That Sir *Tho. Overbury* is the first Man that was murdered in the Tower of *London*, since the murder of the two young Princes.

For the Nature of the Proofs, *your Lordships* must consider, that Impoisonment, of Offences is the most secret: So secret, as if in all Cases of Impoisonment you should require Testimony, you were as good proclaim Impunity. I will put Book-Examples.

Who could have impeached *Livia*, by Testimony, of the impoisoning of the Figs upon the Tree, which her Husband was wont, for his pleasure, to gather with his own hands.

Who could have impeached *Parisatis* for the poisoning of one side of the Knife that she carved with, and keeping the other side clean; so that her self did eat of the same piece of Meat that the Lady did that she did impoison? The Cases are infinite, (and indeed not fit to be spoken of) of the secrecy of Impoisonments; But wise Triers must take upon them, in these secret Cases; *Solomon's* Spirit, that where there could be no Witnesses, collected the Act by the Affection.

But yet we are not to come to one Case: For that which *your Lordships* are to try, is not the Act of Impoisonment (for that is done to your hand) all the World by Law is concluded, but to say that *Overbury* was impoisoned by *Weston*. But the Question before you is of the procurement only, and of the abetting (as the Law termeth it) as accessary before the Fact: Which abetting is no more, but to do or use any Act or Means, which may aid or conduce unto the Impoisonment.

So that it is not the buying or making of the Poison, or the preparing, or confecting, or commixing of it, or the giving or sending, or laying the Poison, that are the only Acts that do amount unto Abetment. But if there be any other Act or Means done or used, to give the opportunity of Impoisonment, or to facilitate the execution of it, or to stop or divert any impediments that might hinder it, and this be with an intention, to accomplish and atchieve the Impoisonment; all these are Abetments,

and

and Accessaries before the Fact. I will put you a familiar Example. Allow there be a Conspiracy to murder a Man as he journies by the ways and it be one Man's part to draw him forth to that Journey by invitation, or by colour of some business; and another takes upon him to disswade some Friend of his, whom he had a purpose to take in his Company, that he be not too strong to make his defence: And another hath the part to go along with him, and to hold him in talk till the first blow be given. All these (*my Lords*) without scruple are Abetters to this Murder, though none of them give the Blow, nor assist to give the Blow.

My Lords, he is not the Hunter alone that lets slip the Dog upon the Deer, but he that lodges the Deer, or raises him, or puts him out, or he that sets a Toyle that he cannot escape, or the like.

But this (*my Lords*) little needeth in this present Case, where there is such a Chain of Acts of Impoisonment as hath been seldom seen, and could hardly have been expected, but that Greatness of Fortune maketh commonly Grossness in offending.

To descend to the Proofs themselves, I shall keep this course.

First,

First, I will make a Narrative or Declaration of the Fact it self.

Secondly, I will break and distribute the Proofs, as they concern the Prisoner.

And *thirdly*, according to that distribution, I will produce them, and read them, or use them.

So that there is nothing that I shall say, but your Lordship (my Lord of *Somerset*) shall have three thoughts or cogitations to answer it: *First*, when I open it, you may take your aim: *Secondly*, when I distribute it, you may prepare your Answers without confusion: And *lastly*, when I produce the Witnesses, or Examinations themselves, you may again ruminate and readvise how to make your defence. And this I do the rather, because your Memory or Understanding may not be oppressed or overladen with length of Evidence, or with confusion of order. Nay more, when your Lordship shall make your Answers in your time, I will put you in mind (when cause shall be) of your omissions.

First therefore, for the simple Narrative of the Fact. Sir *Tho. Overbury*, for a time was known to have had great Interest, and great Friendship with my Lord of *Somerset*, both in his meaner Fortunes, and after:

Infomuch as he was a kind of Oracle of Direction unto him; and if you will believe his own vaunts (being of an infolent *Thrafonical* difpofition) he took upon him, that the Fortune, Reputation, and Underftanding of this Gentleman (who is well known to have had a better Teacher) proceeded from his Company and Counfel.

And this Friendfhip refted not only in Converfation and Bufinefs of Court, but likewife in Communication of Secrets of Eftate. For my Lord of *Somerfet*, at that time, exercifing (by his Majefties fpecial favour and truft) the Office of the Secretary provifionally, did not forbear to acquaint *Overbury* with the King's Packets of Difpatches from all parts, *Spain*, *France*, the *Low Countries*, &c. And this not by glimpfes, or now and then rounding in the Ear for a favour, but in a fetled manner: Packets were fent, fometimes opened by my Lord, fometimes unbroken unto *Overbury*, who perufed them, copied, regiftred them, made Tables of them as he thought good: So that I will undertake, the time was, when *Overbury* knew more of the Secrets of State, than the Council Table did. Nay, they were grown to fuch an inwardnefs, as they made a Play of all the World

befides

besides themselves: So as they had *Ciphers and Jargons* for the King, the Queen, and all the great Men; things seldom used, but either by Princes, and their Embassadours and Ministers, or by such as work and practise against, or at least upon Princes.

But understand me (my Lord) I shall not charge you this day with any Disloyalty; only I say this for a foundation, That there was a great communication of Secrets between you and *Overbury*, and that it had relation to Matters of Estate, and the greatest Causes of this Kingdom.

But (my Lords) as it is a principle in Nature, that the best things are in their corruption the worst: And the sweetest Wine makes the sharpest Vinegar: So fell it out with them, that this excess (as I may term it) of Friendship, ended in mortal Hatred on my Lord of *Somerset*'s part.

For it fell out, some twelve months before *Overbury*'s imprisonment in the Tower, that my Lord of *Somerset* was entred into an unlawful love towards his unfortunate Lady, then Countess of *Essex*; which went so far, as it was then secretly projected (chiefly between my Lord Privy Seal and my Lord of *Somerset*) to effect a Nullity

in

in the Marriage with my Lord of *Essex*, and so to proceed to a Marriage with *Somerset*.

This Marriage and Purpose did *Overbury* mainly oppugn, under pretence to do the true part of a Friend (for that he counted her an unworthy Woman) but the truth was, that *Overbury*, who (to speak plainly) had little that was solid for Religion or Moral Vertue, but was a Man possessed with Ambition and vain Glory, was loth to have any Partners in the favour of my Lord of *Somerset*, and specially not the *House of the Howards*, against whom he had always professed hatred and opposition. So all was but miserable Bargains of Ambition.

And (*my Lords*) that this is no sinister construction, will well appear unto you, when you shall hear that *Overbury* makes his brags to my Lord of *Somerset*, that he had won him the love of the Lady by his Letters and Industry: So far was he from Cases of Conscience in this Matter. And certainly (*my Lords*) howsoever the tragical misery of that poor Gentleman *Overbury* ought somewhat to obliterate his Faults; yet because we are not now upon point of Civility, but to discover the Face of Truth to the Face of Justice: And that it is material to the true understanding of the

the ſtate of this Cauſe, *Overbury* was nought and corrupt, the Ballades muſt be amended for that point,

But to proceed, When *Overbury* ſaw that he was like to be diſpoſſeſſed of my Lord here, whom he had poſſeſſed ſo long, and by whoſe Greatneſs he had promiſed himſelf to do wonders; and being a Man of an unbounded and impetuous ſpirit, he began not only to diſſwade, but to deter him from that Love and Marriage; and finding him fixed, thought to try ſtronger Remedies, ſuppoſing that he had my Lord's Head under his Girdle, in reſpect of communication of Secrets of Eſtate, or (as he calls them himſelf in his Letters, Secrets of all Natures) and therefore dealt violently with him, to make him deſiſt, with menaces of Diſcovery of Secrets, and the like.

Hereupon grew two ſtreams of hatred upon *Overbury*; *The one* from the Lady, in reſpect that he croſſed her Love, and abuſed her Name, which are Furies to Women; *The other* of a deeper and more Mineral Nature from my Lord of *Somerſet* himſelf; who was afraid of *Overbury*'s Nature, and that if he did break from him and fly out, he would mine into him, and trouble his whole Fortunes.

I.

I might add a *third* stream from the Earl of *Northampton*'s Ambition, who desires to be first in favour with my Lord of *Somerset*, and knowing *Overbury*'s malice to himself, and his House, thought that Man must be removed and cut off. So it was amongst them resolved and decreed, that *Overbury* must die.

Hereupon they had variety of Devices. To send him beyond Sea, upon occasion of Employment, that was too weak; and they were so far from giving way to it, as they crost it. There rested but two ways, Quarrel or Assault, and Poison. For that of Assault, after some proposition and attempt, they passed from it; It was a thing too open, and subject to more variety of chances. That of Poison likewise was a hazardous thing, and subject to many preventions and cautions, especially to such a jealous and working Brain as *Overbury* had, except he were first fast in their hands.

Therefore the way was first to get him into a Trap, and lay him up, and then they could not miss the Mark. Therefore in execution of this Plot, it was devised, that *Overbury* should be designed to some honourable Employment in Foreign Parts, and should under-hand by the Lord of *Somerset* be encouraged to refuse it; and so upon that contempt he should be laid Prisoner in the Tower, and then they would look he should be close enough, and Death should be his Bail. Yet were they not at their end. For they considered, that if there was not a fit Lieutenant of the Tower for their purpose, and likewise a fit under-keeper of *Overbury*: *First*, They should meet with many Impediments in the giving and exhibiting the Poison: *Secondly*, They should be exposed to note and observation, that might discover them: And *thirdly*, *Overbury* in the mean time might write clamorous and furious Letters to other his Friends, and so all might be disappointed. And therefore the next Link of the Chain, was to displace the then *Lieutenant Waade*, and to place *Helwisse* a principal Abetter in the Impoisonment: Again, to displace *Cary*, that was the under-Keeper in *Waade's time*, and to place *Weston*, who was the principal Actor in the Impoisonment: And this was done in such a while (that it may appear to be done, as it were with one breath) as there were but fifteen days between the commitment of *Overbury*, the displacing of *Waade*, the placing of *Helwisse*, the displacing of *Cary* the under-Keeper, the placing of *Weston*, and the first Poison given two days after.

Then

Then when they had this poor Gentleman in the Tower close Prisoner, where he could not escape nor stir, where he could not feed but by their Hands, where he could not speak nor write but through their Trunks; then was the time to execute the last Act of this Tragedy.

Then must *Franklin* be purveyour of the Poisons, and procure five, six, seven several Potions, to be sure to hit his Complexion. Then must Mris *Turner* be the *Say-Mistris* of the Poisons to try upon poor Beasts, what's present, and what works at distance of time! Then must *Weston* be the Tormenter, and chase him with Poison after Poison, Poison in Salts, Poison in Meats, Poison in Sweetmeats, Poison in Medicines and Vomits, until at last his Body was almost come, by use of Poisons, to the state that *Mithridate*'s Body was by the use of Treacle and Preservatives, that the force of the Poisons were blunted upon him: *Weston* confessing, when he was chid for not dispatching him, that he had given him enough to poison twenty Men. *Lastly*, Because all this asked time, courses were taken by *Somerset*, both to divert all means of *Overbury*'s Delivery, and to entertain *Overbury* by continual Letters, partly of Hopes and Projects for his Delivery, and partly of other Fables and Negotiations; somewhat like some kind of Persons (which I will not name) which keep Men in talk of Fortune-telling, when they have a fellonious meaning.

And this is the true Narrative of this Act of Impoisonment, which I have summarily recited.

Now for the Distribution of the Proofs, there are four Heads of Proofs to prove you guilty (my Lord of *Somerset*) of this Impoisonment; whereof two are precedent to the Imprisonment, the third is present, and the fourth is following or subsequent: For it is in Proofs, as it is in Lights; there is a direct Light, and there is a reflexion of Light, or Back-Light.

The *first* Head or Proof thereof is, That there was a root of Bitterness, a mortal Malice or Hatred, mixed with deep and bottomless Fears, that you had towards Sir *Thomas Overbury*.

The *second* is, That you were the principal Actor, and had your hand in all those Acts, which did conduce to the Impoisonment, and which gave opportunity and means to effect it; and without which the Impoisonment could never have been, and which could serve or tend to no other end, but to the Impoisonment.

The *third* is, That your hand was in the very Impoisonment it self, which is more than needs to be proved; that you did direct Poison, that you did deliver Poison, that you did continually hearken to the success of the Impoisonment, and that you spurred it on, and called for dispatch, when you thought it lingred.

And *lastly*, That you did all the things after the Impoisonment, which may detect a guilty Conscience for the smothering of it, and avoiding punishment for it, which can be but of three kinds. That you suppressed, as much as in you was, Testimony: That you did deface, and destroy, and clip, and misdate all Writings that might give light to the Impoisonment; and that you did fly to the Altar of Guiltiness, which is a Pardon, and a Pardon of Murder, and a Pardon for your Self, and not for your Lady.

In this (*my Lord*) I convert my speech to you, because I would have you attend the Points of your Charge, and so of your Defence the better. And two of these Heads I have taken to my self, and left the other two to the King's two Serjeants.

For the *first* main part, which is the mortal

mortal Hatred coupled with Fear, that was in my Lord of *Somerset* towards *Overbury*, although he did palliate it with a great deal of hypocrisie and dissimulation even to the end; I shall prove it (*my Lord Steward,* and you *my Lords and Peers*) manifestly, by matter both of Oath and Writing. The root of this Hatred was that that hath cost many a Man's Life; that is, Fear of discovering Secrets. Secrets (I say) of a high and dangerous nature; wherein the course that I will hold shall be this.

First; I will shew that such a Breach and Malice was between *my Lord* and *Overbury*, and that it burst forth into violent Menaces and Threats on both sides.

Secondly; That these Secrets were not light, but of a high nature, for I will give you the Elevation of the Pole. They were such as my Lord of *Somerset* for his part had made a Vow, That *Overbury* should neither live in Court nor Country. That he had likewise opened himself, and his own fears so far, that if *Overbury* ever came forth of the Tower, either *Overbury* or himself must die for it. And of *Overbury's* part, he had threatned my Lord, That whether he did live or die, my *Lord's* shame should never die, but he would leave him the most odious Man of the World. And farther that

that my Lord was like enough to repent it, in the place where *Overbury* wrote, which was the Tower of *London*. He was a true Prophet in that: So here in the height of the Secrets.

Thirdly; I will shew you, that all the King's Business was by my Lord put into *Overbury*'s Hands: So as there is work enough for Secrets, whatsoever they were. And like Princes Confederates, they had their *Ciphers* and *Jargons*.

And *lastly*; I will shew you that it is but a Toy to say that the Malice was only in respect he spake dishonourably of the Lady; or for doubt of breaking the Marriage: For that *Overbury* was a Coadjutor to that Love, and the Lord of *Somerset* was as deep in speaking ill of the Lady, as *Overbury*. And again, it was too late for that Matter, for the Bargain of the Match was then made and past. And if it had been no more but to remove *Overbury* from disturbing of the Match, it had been an easy matter to have banded over *Overbury* beyond Seas, for which they had a fair way; but that would not serve their turn.

And lastly, *Periculum periculo vincitur*, to go so far as an Impoisonment, must have a deeper malice than flashes: For the Cause must bear a proportion to the Effect.

For the next general Head of Proofs, which confifts in Acts preparatory to the middle Acts, they are in eight feveral points of the Compafs, as I may term it.

Firft; That there were devices and projects to difpatch *Overbury*, or to overthrow him, plotted between the Countefs of *Somerfet*, the Earl of *Somerfet*, and the Earl of *Northampton*, before they fell upon the Impoifonment: For always before Men fix upon a courfe of Mifchief, there be fome rejections; but die he muft one way or other.

Secondly; That my Lord of *Somerfet* was principal Practicer (I muft fpeak it) in a moft perfidious manner, to fet a Train or Trap for *Overbury* to get him into the Tower; without which they never durft have attempted the Impoifonment.

Thirdly; That the placing of the Lieutenant *Helwiffe* one of the Impoifoners, and the difplacing of *Waade*, was by the means of my Lord of *Somerfet*.

Fourthly; That the placing of *Wefton* the under-Keeper, who was the principal Impoifoner, and the difplacing of *Cary*, and the doing of all this within fifteen days after *Overbury*'s Commitment, was by the means and countenance of my Lord of *Somerfet*. And thefe two were the active
Inftru-

Instruments of the Impoisonment: And this was a Business that the Ladies power could not reach unto.

Fifthly; That because there must be a time for the Tragedy to be acted, and chiefly because they would not have the Poisons work upon the sudden: And for that the strength of *Overbury*'s Nature, or the very custom of receiving Poison into his Body, did overcome the Poisons that they wrought not so fast, therefore *Overbury* must be held in the Tower. And as my Lord of *Somerset* got him into the Trap, so he kept him in, and abused him with continual hopes of Liberty; and diverted all the true and effectual means of his Liberty, and made light of his Sickness and Extremities.

Sixthly; That not only the Plot of getting *Overbury* into the Tower, and the devices to hold him and keep him there, but the strange manner of his close keeping (being in but for a Contempt) was by the device and means of my Lord of *Somerset*, who denied his Father to see him, denied his Servants that offered to be shut up close Prisoners with him, and in effect handled it so, that he was close Prisoner to all his Friends, and open and exposed to all his Enemies.

Seventhly,

Seventhly, That the Advertisement which my Lady received from time to time, from the *Lievtenant* or *Weston,* touching *Overbury*'s state of Body or Health, were ever sent up to the Court, though it were in Progress, and that from my Lady: such a thirst and listening this Lord had to hear that he was dispatched.

Lastly, There was a continual Negotiation to set *Overbury*'s Head on work, that he should make some recognition to clear the honour of the Lady; and that he should become a good Instrument towards her and her Friends: All which was but entertainment: For *your Lordships* shall plainly see divers of my Lord of *Northampton*'s Letters (whose hand was deep in this Business) written (I must say it) in dark Words and Clauses; That there was one thing pretended, and another intended; That there was a real Charge, and there was somewhat not real; a main drift and a dissimulation. Nay further, there be some passages which the *Peers* in their wisdom will discern to point directly at the Impoisonment.

After this Inducement followed the Evidence it self.

The Lord Bacon's Letter to the University of Cambridg.

Rescriptum *Procuratoris Regis Primarii,* ad *Academiam Cantabrigiensem,* quando in Sanctius *Regis* Consilium cooptatus fuit.

GRatæ *mihi fuere Literæ vestræ, atque Gratulationem vestram ipse mihi gratulor. Rem ipsam ita mihi Honori, & voluptati fore duco, si in hâc mente maneam, ut* Publicis Utilitatibus, *studio indefesso, & perpetuis curis, & puro affectu, inserviam. Inter partes autem Reipublicæ, nulla Animo meo charior est, quàm* Academiæ *&* Literæ. *Idque & vita mea anteacta declarat,& scripta. Itaque quicquid mihi accesserit, id etiam vobis accessisse existimare potestis. Neque vero Patrocinium meum vobis sublatum aut diminutum esse credere debetis. Nam & ea pars Patroni, quæ ad consilium in causis exhibendum spectat, integra manet; Atque etiam (si quid gravius acciderit) ipsum perorandi Munus (licentiâ* Regis *obtentâ) relictam est; Quodque Juris* Patrocinio *deerit, id auctiore potestate*

state compensabitur. Mihi in votis est, ut quemadmodum à privatorum & clientelarum negotiis, ad Gubernacula Reipublicæ translatus jam sum; Ita & postrema Ætatis meæ pars (*si vita suppetit*) etiam à publicis curis ad otium & Literas deduci possit. Quinetiam sæpius subit illa Cogitatio, ut etiam in tot & tantis Negotiis, tamen singulis annis aliquos dies apud vos deponam; Ut ex majore vestrarum rerum notitiâ vestris utilitatibus melius consulere possim.

5. Julij 1616. *Amicus vester maximè*

Fidelis & Benevolus.

Fr. Bacon.

The same in English by the Publisher.

The Answer of the Lord Bacon, *then* Attorney General, *to the* University *of* Cambridg, *when he was sworn of the* Privy Council *to the* King.

YOur Letters were very acceptable to me; and I give *my self* joy, upon *your* Congratulation. The thing it self will (I suppose) conduce to my Honour and Satisfaction, if I remain in the mind I now am in; by unwearied study, and perpetual watchfulness, and pure affection, to promote the *Publick Good*. Now among the Parts of the *Common-wealth*, there are none dearer to me than the *Universities*, and *Learning*. And This, my *manner of Life* hitherto, and my *Writings*, do both declare. If therefore any good Fortune befalls me, you may look upon it as an accession to your selves. Neither are you to believe, that *my Patronage* is either quite removed from you, or so much as diminished. For, that part of an *Advocate* which concerneth the *giving of Counsel* in Causes, remaineth entire. Also (if any thing more weighty & urgent falleth out) the very Office of *Pleading* (the

King's leave being obtained) is still allow'd me. And whatsoever shall be found wanting in my Juridical Patronage, will be compensated by my more ample Authority. My wishes are, that as I am translated from the Business of private Men, and particular Clients, to the Government of the Common-wealth; so the latter part of my Age (if my Life be continued to me) may, from the Publick Cares, be translated to leisure and study.

Also this thought comes often into my mind, amidst so many Businesses, and of such moment, every year to lay aside some days to think on *You*: That so, having the greater insight into your Matters, I may the better consult your Advantage.

July the 5*th* 1616.

Your most faithful

and kind Friend,

Fr. Bacon.

Sir *Francis Bacon*'s *Letter* to *King James* touching the *Chancellor's* Place.

It may please Your most Excellent Majesty.

YOur worthy *Chancellour* * (I fear) goeth his last day. God hath hitherto used to weed out such Servants as grew not fit for Your *Majesty*. But now He hath gather'd to Himself one of the choicer Plants in Your *Majesties Garden*. But Your *Majesties* Service must not be mortal.

* *Chanc.* Egerton.

Upon this heavy Accident, I pray your *Majesty*, in all humbleness and sincerity, to give me leave to use a few words. I must never forget when I moved your *Majesty* for the *Attorney's Place*, that it was your own sole Act, and not my *Lord of Somerset*'s; who, when he knew your *Majesty* had resolv'd it, thrust himself into the Business to gain thanks. And therefore I have no reason to *pray to Saints*.

I shall now again make Oblation to your *Majesty*; first of my Heart; then of my Service; thirdly, of my Place of *Attorney*; and fourthly, of my Place in the *Star-Chamber*.

I hope I may be acquitted of Presumption,

tion, if I think of it; both because my Father had the Place, which is some civil inducement to my desire, (and I pray God your Majesty may have twenty no worse years than Queen *Elizabeth* had in her Model after my Father's placing) and chiefly because the Chancellor's place, after it went to the Law, was ever conferred upon some of the Learned Counsel, and never upon a Judg. For *Audley* was raised from King's Serjeant; my *Father* from Attorney of the Wards; *Bromlie* from Sollicitor; *Puckering* from Queen's Serjeant; *Egerton* from Master of the Rolls, having newly left the Attorney's place.———

For my self, I can only present your Majesty with *Gloria in Obsequio*; yet I dare promise, that if I sit in that Place, your Business shall not make such short turns upon you as it doth; But when a Direction is once given, it shall be pursued and performed: And your Majesty shall only be troubled with the true Care of a King; which is to think *what* you would have done in chief; and not *how* for the Passages.

I do presume also, in respect of my Father's Memory, and that I have been always gracious in the *Lower-House*, I have some interest in the Gentlemen of *England*; and

and shall be able to do some good Effect in rectifying that Body of Parliament, which is *Cardo Rerum*. For, let me tell your Majesty, That *that part* of the Chancellor's place, which is to judg in equity between Party and Party, that same *Regnum Judiciale* (which since my Father's time is but too much enlarged) concerneth your Majesty least, more than the acquitting of your Conscience for Justice. But it is the *other Parts* of a *Moderator* amongst your *Council*; of an *Overseer* over your *Judges*; of a *Planter* of fit *Justices* and *Governors* in the Country, that importeth your Affairs, and these Times, most.

I will add likewise, that I hope, by my Care, the *Inventive Part* of your *Council* will be strengthned; who, now commonly, do exercise rather their *Judgments* than their *Inventions*; and the *Inventive Part* cometh from Projectors, and Private Men; which cannot be so well: In which kind my *Lord of Salisbury* had a good Method.—

To conclude; If I were the Man I would be, I should hope, that as your Majesty of late hath won Hearts by Depressing, you should in this lose no Hearts by Advancing. For I see your People can better skill of *Concretum* than *Abstractum*; and that the

the Waves of their Affection flow rather after Persons than Things. So that Acts of this nature (if this were one) do more good than twenty Bills of Grace.

If God call my *Lord Chancellor*, the Warrants and Commissions which are requisite for the taking of *the Seal*, and for working with it, and for reviving of Warrants under his Hand, which die with him, and the like, shall be in readiness. And in this Time presseth more, because it is the end of a Term, and almost the beginning of the Circuits; so that the *Seal* cannot stand still. But this may be done as heretofore, by *Commission*, till your *Majesty* hath resolved on an *Officer*. *God* ever preserve your *Majesty*.

Your Majesties most

humble Subject, and

bounden Servant,

F. Bacon.

A Letter written * by the Lord Bacon to King James, for Relief of his Estate.

About a year and half after his Retirement.

May it please your most Excellent Majesty.

IN the midst of my misery, which is rather asswaged by Remembrance than by Hope; my chiefest worldly comfort is, to think, That since the time I had the first Vote of the Commons House of Parliament for Commissioner of the Union, until the time that I was this last Parliament, chosen by both Houses for their Messenger to your Majesty in the Petition of Religion, (which two were my first and last Services) I was ever more so happy as to have my poor Services graciously accepted by your Majesty, and likewise not to have had any of them miscarry in my Hands. Neither of which points I can any ways take to my self, but ascribe the former to your Majestie's Goodness, and the latter to your prudent Directions; which I was ever careful to have and keep. For as I have often said to your Majesty, I was towards you but as a Bucket, and a Cistern, to draw forth and conserve, your self was the Fountain.

Unto

Unto this comfort of nineteen years prosperity, there succeeded a comfort even in my greatest adversity, somewhat of the same nature; which is, That in those offences wherewith I was charged, there was not any one that had special relation to your Majesty, or any your particular Commandments. For as, towards Almighty God, there are Offences against the first and second Table, and yet all against God. So with the Servants of Kings, there are Offences more immediate against the Sovereign: Although all Offences against Law are also against the King. Unto which Comfort there is added this Circumstance, That as my Faults were not against your Majesty, otherwise than as all Faults are; so my Fall was not your Majesties Act, otherwise than as all Acts of Justice are yours. This I write not to insinuate with your Majesty, but as a most humble Appeal to your Majesties gracious remembrance, how honest and direct you have ever found me in your Service; whereby I have an assured belief, that there is in your Majesties own Princely Thoughts, a great deal of serenity and clearness to me your Majesties now prostrate and cast-down Servant.

Neither (my most gracious Sovereign) do

do I by this mention of my Services, lay claim to your Princely Grace and Bounty, though the priviledg of Calamity doth bear that form of Petition. I know well, had they been much more, they had been but my bounden Duty. Nay, I must also confess, that they were from time to time, far above my merit, over and super-rewarded by your Majesties Benefits which you heaped upon me. Your Majesty was and is that Master to me, that raised and advanced me nine times; thrice in Dignity, and six times in Office. The places indeed were the painfullest of all your Services; But then they had both Honour and Profits: And the then Profits might have maintained my now Honour, if I had been wise. Neither was your Majesties immediate liberality wanting towards me in some Gifts, if I may hold them. All this I do most thankfully acknowledg, and do herewith conclude, That for any thing arising from my self to move your Eye of pity towards me, there is much more in my present Misery, than in my past Services; save that the same your Majesties Goodness, that may give relief to the one, may give value to the other.

And indeed, if it may please your Majesty, this Theme of my Misery is so plentiful, as

it

it need not be coupled with any thing elfe. I have been fome Body by your Majefties fingular and undeferved favour, even the prime Officer of your Kingdom. Your Majefties Arm hath been over mine in Council, when you prefided at the Table; fo near I was: I have born your Majefties Image in Metal, much more in Heart: I was never in nineteen years Service chidden by your Majefty, but contrariwife often over-joyed, when your Majefty would fometimes fay, I was a good Husband for you, though none for my felf: fometimes, That I had a way to deal in Bufinefs *fuavibus modis*, which was the way which was moft according to your own Heart: And other moft gracious fpeeches of Affection and Truft, which I feed on to this day. But why fhould I fpeak of thefe things which are now vanifhed, but only the better to exprefs the Downfal?

For now it is thus with me: I am a year and an half old in Mifery; though I muft ever acknowledg, not without fome mixture of your Majefties Grace and Mercy; For I do not think it poffible, that any you once loved fhould be totally miferable. Mine own Means, through mine own Improvidence are poor and weak, little better than my Father left me. The poor Things

Things which I have had from your Majesty, are either in Question, or at Courtesy. My Dignities remain Marks of your Favour, but Burdens of my present Fortune. The poor Remnants which I had of my former Fortunes in Plate or Jewels, I have spread upon poor Men unto whom I owed, scarce leaving my self a convenient Subsistence. So as to conclude, I must pour out my Misery before your Majesty, so far as to say, *Si deseris tu, perimus.*

But as I can offer to your Majesties compassion little arising from my self to move you, except it be my extream Misery, which I have truly laid open; so looking up to your Majesty's own self, I should think I committed *Cain*'s fault if I should despair. Your Majesty is a King, whose Heart is as unscrutable for secret motions of Goodness, as for depth of Wisdom. You are, Creator-like, *Factive*, and not *Destructive*. You are the Prince, in whom hath been ever noted an aversation against any thing that favoured of an hard Heart; as, on the other side, your Princely Eye was wont to meet with any motion that was made on the relieving part. Therefore as one that hath had the happiness to know your Majesty near hand, I have (most Gracious Sovereign) Faith enough for a Miracle, much

much more for a Grace, that your Majesty will not suffer your poor Creature to be utterly defaced, nor blot that Name quite out of your Book, upon which your Sacred Hand hath been so oft for new Ornaments and Additions.

Unto this degree of compassion, I hope God above, (of whose Mercy towards me, both in my Prosperity and Adversity I have had great Testimonies and Pledges, though mine own manifold and wretched unthankfulnesses might have averted them) will dispose your Princely Heart, already prepared to all Piety. And why should I not think, but that *thrice Noble Prince*, who would have pulled me out of the Fire of a Sentence, will help to pull me (if I may use that homely phrase) out of the Mire of an abject and sordid condition in my last days: And that *excellent Favorite* of yours, (the goodness of whose Nature contendeth with the greatness of his Fortune; and who counteth it a Prize, a second Prize, to be a good Friend, after that Prize which he carrieth to be a good Servant) will kiss your Hands with joy for any Work of Piety you shall do for me. And as all commiserable Persons (especially such as find their Hearts void of all malice) are apt to think that all Men pity them; I assure my felf that the Lords of your Council, who out of their Wifdom and Noblenefs, cannot but be fenfible of humane Events, will in this way which I go for the Relief of my Eftate, further and advance your Majefty's Goodnefs towards me: For there is, as I conceive, a kind of Fraternity between Great Men that are, and thofe that have been, being but the feveral Tenfes of one Verb. Nay, I do further prefume, that both Houfes of Parliament will love their Juftice the better, if it end not in my ruin. For I have been often told, by many of my Lords, as it were in excufing the feverity of the Sentence, that they knew they left me in good Hands. And your Majefty knoweth well, I have been all my life long acceptable to thofe Aflemblies, not by flattery, but by moderation, and by honeft expreffing of a defire to have all things go fairly and well.

But if it may pleafe your Majefty, (for Saints I fhall give them Reverence, but no Adoration; my Addrefs is to your Majefty the Fountain of Goodnefs) your Majefty fhall, by the Grace of God, not feel that in Gift, which I fhall extreamly feel in Help: For my Defires are moderate, and my Courfes meafured to a Life orderly and referved, hoping ftill to do your Majefty honour

honour in my way. Only I moſt humbly beſeech your Majeſty, to give me leave to conclude with thoſe words which Neceſſity ſpeaketh: Help me, (dear Sovereign Lord and Maſter) and pity me ſo far, as I that have born a Bag, be not now in my Age forced in effect to bear a Wallet; nor I that deſire to live to ſtudy, may not be driven to ſtudy to live. I moſt humbly crave pardon of a long Letter, after a long ſilence. God of Heaven ever bleſs, preſerve, and proſper your Majeſty.

Your Majeſties poor

ancient Servant

and Beadſman,

Fr. St. *Alb.*

Certain Apothegms of the Lord Bacon's, hitherto unpublished.

1. *Plutarch* said well, It is otherwise in a Common-wealth of *Men* than of *Bees*. The Hive of a City or Kingdom is in best condition, when there is least of noise or Buzze in it.

2. The same *Plutarch* said, of Men of weak Abilities set in Great Place, that they were *like little Statues* set on *great Bases*, made to appear the less by their Advancement.

3. He said again; Good *Fame* is like *Fire*. When you have kindled it, you may easily preserve it; but if once you extinguish it, you will not easily kindle it again; at least, not make it burn as bright as it did.

4. The Answer of *Apollonius* to *Vespasian*, is full of excellent * Instruction: *Vespasian* asked him, *What was* Nero's *overthrow?* He answered, Nero *could touch and tune the Harp well; but in Government, sometimes he used to wind the Pins too high, sometimes to let them down too low.* And certain it is, that nothing destroyeth Authority

*This Apothegm is also found in his Essay of Empire, p. 107

thority so much as the unequal and untimely enterchange of Power *pressed* too far, and *relaxed* too much.

5. Queen *Elizabeth* seeing Sir *Edward*—— in her Garden, look'd out at her Window, and asked him in *Italian, What does a Man think of when he thinks of nothing?* Sir *Edward* (who had not had the effect of some of the Queen's Grants so soon as he had hop'd and desir'd) paused a little, and then made answer, *Madam, He thinks of a Woman's Promise.* The *Queen* shrunk in her Head, but was heard to say, *Well, Sir* Edward, *I must not confute you. Anger makes dull Men witty, but it keeps them poor.*

6. When any Great Officer, Ecclesiastical or Civil, was to be made, the *Queen* would enquire after the Piety, Integrity, Learning of the Man. And when she was satisfied in these Qualifications, she would consider of his Personage. And upon such an Occasion she pleas'd once to say to me, *Bacon,* How can the *Magistrate* maintain his Authority when the *Man* is despis'd?

7. In *Eighty Eight,* when the *Queen* went from *Temple-Bar* along *Fleetstreet,* the Lawyers were rank'd on one side, and the Companies of the City on the other; said Master *Bacon* to a Lawyer that stood next him,

do

do but observe the Courtiers. If they bow first to the Citizens, they are in Debt; if first to us, they are in Law.

8. King *James* was wont to be very earnest with the Country Gentlemen to go from *London* to their Country Houses. And sometimes he would say *thus* to them; Gentlemen, at *London* you are *like Ships in a Sea*, which show like nothing; but in your Country Villages, you are like *Ships in a River*, which look like great things.

9. Soon after the death of a great Officer, who was judged no advancer of the King's Matters, the King said to his Sollicitor *Bacon*, who was his Kinsman; Now tell me truly, what say you of your Cousin that is gone? Mr. *Bacon* answered, Sir, since your Majesty doth charge me, I'le e'ne deal plainly with you, and give you such a character of him, as if I were to write his Story. I do think he was no fit Counsellor to make your Affairs better; but yet he was fit to have kept them from growing worse. The King said, *On my So'l, Man, in the first thou speakest like a True Man, and in the latter like a Kinsman.*

10. King *James*, as he was a Prince of great Judgment, so he was a Prince of a marvellous pleasant humour; and there now come

into my mind two instances of it.

As he was going through *Lusen* by *Greenwich*, he ask'd what Town it was? they said, *Lusen*. He ask'd a good while after, What Town is this we are now in? They said, still 'twas *Lusen*. On my So'l, said the King, *I will be King of* Lusen.

11. In some other of his Progresses, he ask'd how far 'twas to a Town whose name I have forgotten; they said, *Six miles*. Half an hour after he ask'd again; one said, *Six miles and an half*: The King alighted out of his Coach, and crept under the Shoulder of his Led Horse. And when some ask'd his Majesty what he meant; *I must stalk*, said he, *for yonder Town is shie and flies me*.

12. Count *Gondomar* sent a Complement to my Lord St. *Albans*, wishing him *a good Easter*. My Lord thank'd the Messenger, and said, He could not at present requite the *Count* better, than in returning him the like; *That he wished his Lordship a good Passover*.

13. My Lord Chancellor *Elsmere*, when he had read a Petition which he dislik'd, would say; *What! you would have my hand to this now?* And the Party answering, yes; He would say further; *Well, so you shall. Nay, you shall have both my hands to't*. And so

so would, *with both his hands*, tear it in pieces.

14. I knew a * *Wise Man*, that had it for a by-word, when he saw Men hasten to a Conclusion; *Stay a little that we may make an end the sooner.*

<small>* See this also in his Essay of Dispatch, p. 143.</small>

15. Sir *Francis Bacon* was wont to say of an angry Man who suppressed his Passion, That *he thought worse than he spake:* and of an angry Man that would chide, That *he spoke worse than he thought.*

16. He was wont also to say, That Power in an ill Man, was like the *Power of a black Witch; He could do hurt, but no good with it.* And he would add, That *the Magicians could turn Water into Blood, but could not turn the Blood again to Water.*

17. When Mr. Attourney *Cook*, in the Exchequer, gave high words to Sr. *Francis Bacon*, and stood much upon his higher Place; Sir *Francis* said to him, *Mr. Attourney! The less you speak of your own greatness, the more I shall think of it; and the more, the less.*

18. Sir *Francis Bacon* coming into the Earl of *Arundel*'s Garden, where there were a great number of Ancient Statues of naked Men and Women, made a stand, and as astonish'd, cryed out, *The Resurrection.*

19. Sir *Francis Bacon* (who was always for

for moderate Counsels) when one was speaking of such a Reformation of the Church of *England*, as would in effect make it no Church; said thus to him, Sir, The Subject we talk of is the Eye of *England*: And *if there be a speck or two in the Eye, we endeavour to take them off; but he were a strange Oculist who would pull out the Eye.*

20. The same Sir *Francis Bacon* was wont to say, That those who left useful Studies for useless Scholastic Speculations, were like the *Olympic Gamsters, who abstain'd from necessary Labours, that they might be fit for such as were not so.*

21. He likewise often used this Comparison. * *The Empirical Philosophers are like to Pismires;* they only lay up and use their Store. *The Rationalists are like to Spiders;* they spin all out of their own Bowels. But give me a Philosopher, who *like the Bee,* hath a middle faculty, *gathering from abroad, but digesting that which is gathered by his own virtue.*

* See the Substance of this in Nov. Org. Ed. Lugd. Bat. *p.* 105. & inter Cogitata & visa. *p.* 53.

22. The Lord St. Alban, who was not overhasty to raise *Theories,* but proceeded slowly by Experiments, was wont to say to some Philosophers who would not go his Pace; *Gentlemen!* Nature *is a Labyrinth, in which the very hast you move with will make you lose your way.*

23. The

23. The same Lord when he spoke of the *Dutchmen*, used to say, That we could not abandon them for *our safety*, nor keep them for *our profit*. And sometimes he would express the same sense on this manner; *We hold the Belgic Lion by the Ears.*

24. The same Lord, when a Gentleman seem'd not much to approve of his Liberality to his Retinue, said to him; Sir, *I am all of a Piece; If the Head be lifted up, the inferiour parts of the Body must too.*

25. The Lord *Bacon* was wont to commend the Advice of the plain old Man at *Buxton* that sold Beesoms; A proud lazy young Fellow came to him for a Beesom upon Trust; to whom the *Old Man* said; Friend! hast thou no Mony? borrow of thy Back, and borrow of thy Belly; they'l ne're ask thee again, I shall be dunning thee every day.

26. *Solon* * said well to *Cræsus*, (when in ostentation he shewed him his Gold) Sir, *if any other come that has better Iron than you, he will be master of all this Gold.*

* See this in his Essay of the true Greatness of Kingdoms. p. 171.

27. *Jack Weeks* said of a great Man (just then dead) who pretended to some Religion, but was none of the best livers; *Well, I hope he is in Heaven. Every Man thinks as he wishes; but if he be in Heaven, 'twere pity it were known.*

Ornamenta

Ornamenta Rationalia.

A supply (by the Publisher) of certain weighty and elegant *Sentences*, some made, others collected, *by the Lord Bacon*; and by him put under the above-said Title; and at present not to be found.

A Collection of Sentences out of the Mimi of Publius; *Englished by the Publisher.*

1. A *Leator, quantò in Arte est melior, tantò est nequior.*

A Gamster, the greater Master he is in his Art, the worse Man he is.

2. *Arcum, intensio frangit; Animum, remissio.*

Much bending breaks the Bow; much unbending, the Mind.

3. *Bis vincit, qui se vincit in Victoriâ.*

He conquers twice, who upon Victory overcomes himself.

4. *Cùm*

4. *Cùm vitia profint, peccat, Qui rectè facit.*

If Vices were upon the whole matter profitable, the virtuous Man would be the sinner.

5. *Benè dormit, qui non fentit, quòd malè dormiat.*

He sleeps well, who feels not that he sleeps ill.

6. *Deliberare utilia, mora eft tutiffima.*

To deliberate about useful things, is the safest delay.

7. *Dolor decrefcit, ubi quò crefcat non habet.*

The flood of Grief decreaseth, when it can swell no higher.

8. *Etiam Innocentes cogit mentiri dolor.*

Pain makes even the Innocent Man a Lyar.

9. *Etiam celeritas in defiderio, mora eft.*

Even in desire, swiftness it self is delay.

10. *Etiam capillus unus habet umbram fuam.*

The smallest Hair casts a shadow.

11. *Fidem qui perdit, quò fe fervat in reliquum?*

He that has lost his Faith, what has he left to live on?

12. *Formofa Facies muta commendatio eft.*

A beautiful Face is a silent commendation.

13. *Fortuna*

13. *Fortuna nimium quem fovet, Stultum facit.*

Fortune makes him a Fool, whom she makes her Darling.

14. *Fortuna obesse nulli contenta est semel.*

Fortune is not content to do a Man but one ill turn.

15. *Facit gratum Fortuna, quam nemo videt.*

The Fortune which no Body sees, makes a Man happy and unenvied.

16. *Heu! quàm miserum est ab illo lædi, de quo non possis queri.*

O! what a miserable thing 'tis to be hurt by such a one of whom 'tis in vain to complain.

17. *Homo toties moritur quoties amittit suos.*

A Man dies as often as he loses his Friends.

18. *Hæredis fletus, sub personâ risus est.*

The Tears of an Heir are laughter under a Vizard.

19. *Jucundum nihil est, nisi quod reficit varietas.*

Nothing is pleasant, to which variety do's not give a relish.

20. *Invidiam ferre, aut fortis, aut fœlix potest.*

He may bear envy, who is either couragious or happy.

21. *In malis sperare bonum, nisi innocens, nemo potest.*

None but a virtuous Man can hope well in ill circumstances.

22. *In vindicando, criminosa est celeritas.*

In taking revenge, the very haste we make is criminal.

23. *In calamitoso risus etiam injuria est.*

When Men are in calamity, if we do but laugh we offend.

24. *Improbè Neptunum accusat, qui iterum Naufragium facit.*

He accuseth *Neptune* unjustly, who makes Shipwrack a second time.

25. *Multis minatur, qui uni facit injuriam.*

He that injures one, threatens an hundred.

26. *Mora omnis ingrata est, sed facit sapientiam.*

All delay is ungrateful, but we are not wise without it.

27. *Mori est fœlicis antequam Mortem invocet.*

Happy he who dies e're he calls for Death to take him away.

28. *Malus ubi bonum se simulat, tunc est pessimus.*

An ill Man is always ill; but he is then worst

worst of all when he pretends to be a Saint.

29. *Magno cum periculo custoditur, quod multis placet.*

Lock and Key will scarce keep that secure, which pleases every body.

30. *Malè vivunt qui se semper victuros putant.*

They think ill who think of living always.

31. *Malè secum agit Æger, Medicum qui hæredem facit.*

That sick Man do's ill for himself, who makes his Physician his Heir.

32. *Multos timere debet, quem multi timent.*

He of whom many are afraid, ought himself to fear many.

33. *Nulla tam bona est Fortuna, de quâ nil possis queri.*

There's no Fortune so good but it bates an Ace.

34. *Pars beneficii est, quod petitur, si bene neges.*

'Tis part of the Gift, if you deny *gentilely* what is asked of you.

35. *Timidus vocat se cautum, parcum sordidus.*

The *Coward* calls himself a *wary* Man; and the *Miser* says he is *frugal*.

36. O

36. *O Vita! misero longa, fœlici brevis.*
O Life! an Age to him that is in misery, and to him that is happy, a moment.

A Collection of Sentences out of some of the Writings of the Lord Bacon.

1. IT is a strange desire which Men have, to seek Power and lose Liberty.

2. Children increase the cares of Life; but they mitigate the remembrance of Death.

3. Round dealing is the honour of Man's Nature; and a mixture of falshood is like *allay* in Gold and Silver, which may make the Metal work the better, but it embaseth it.

4. Death openeth the Gate to good Fame, and extinguisheth Envy.

5. Schism, in the Spiritual Body of the Church, is a greater scandal than a corruption in Manners: As, in the natural Body, a Wound or Solution of Continuity, is worse than a corrupt Humour.

6. Revenge is a kind of *wild Justice*, which the more a Man's Nature *runs*

to, the more ought Law to *weed* it out.

7. He that studieth Revenge, keepeth his own Wounds green.

8. Revengeful Persons live and die like Witches. Their life is mischievous, and their end is unfortunate.

9. It was an high Speech of *Seneca*, (after the manner of the *Stoic's*) *That the good Things which belong to Prosperity, are to be wish'd; but the good things which belong to Adversity, are to be admir'd.*

10. He that cannot see well, let him go softly.

11. If a Man be thought *secret*, it inviteth *discovery:* as the more *close* Air sucketh in the more *open*.

12. Keep your *Authority* wholly from your Children, not so your *Purse*.

13. Men of Noble Birth are noted to be envious towards new Men when they rise. For the distance is alter'd; and it is like a deceit of the Eye, that when others come on, they think themselves go back.

14. That Envy is most malignant which is like *Cain's*, who envyed his Brother, because his Sacrifice was better accepted, when there was no body but *God* to look on.

15. The lovers of Great Place are impatient of Privateness, even in Age which requires

requires the Shadow: like old *Townsmen* that will be still *sitting at their Street-Door*, though there they offer Age to scorn.

16. In Evil, the best condition is, not to *will*; the next, not to *can*.

17. In great Place, ask counsel of both Times: of the *Ancient Time*, what is *best*; and of the *latter Time*, what is *fittest*.

18. As in Nature things move more *violently* to their *Place*, and *calmly* in their *Place*: So Virtue in Ambition is *violent*; in Authority, setled and calm.

19. *Boldness* in civil Business, is like *Pronuntiation* in the Orator of *Demosthenes*; the first, second, and third thing.

20. *Boldness is blind:* wherefore 'tis ill in *Counsel*, but good in *Execution*. For in Counsel it is good to *see dangers*, in Execution *not to see them*, except they be very great.

21. Without *good Nature*, Man is but a better kind of *Vermin*.

22. God never wrought Miracle to convince *Atheism*, because his ordinary Works convince it.

23. The great *Atheists* indeed are *Hypocrites*, who are always handling Holy Things, but without feeling; so as they must needs be cauteriz'd in the end.

24. The Master of *Superstition* is the People.

People. And in all Superstition, wise Men follow Fools.

25. In removing *Superstitions*, care would be had that (as it fareth in ill Purgings) *the good be not taken away with the bad*, which commonly is done, when the *People* is the *Physician*.

26. He that goeth into a Country before he hath some entrance into the Language, goeth to *School*, and not to *travel*.

27. It is a miserable state of mind (and yet it is commonly the case of Kings) *to have few things to desire, and many things to fear*.

28. Depression of the Nobility may make a King more *absolute*, but less *safe*.

29. All Precepts concerning Kings, are, in effect, comprehended in these Remembrances; *Remember thou art a Man*; *Remember thou art God's Vicegerent*. The one bridleth their *Power*, and the other their *Will*.

30. Things will have their *first* or *second* agitation. If they be not tossed upon the *Arguments of Counsel*, they will be tossed upon the *Waves of Fortune*.

31. The true composition of a Counsellor, is rather to be skill'd in his Masters *Business* than his Nature; for then he is like to *advise him*, and not to *feed* his humour.

32. Private

32. Private Opinion is more *free*, but Opinion before others is more *reverend*.

33. *Fortune* is like a *Market*, where many times if you stay a little the *price will fall*.

34. Fortune sometimes turneth the *handle of the Bottle*, which is easie to be taken hold of; and after the *belly*, which is hard to grasp.

35. Generally it is good to commit the beginning of all great Actions, to *Argus* with an *hundred Eyes*; and the ends of them to *Briareus* with an *hundred hands*; *first to watch, and then to speed*.

36. There's great difference betwixt a *cunning Man* and a *wise Man*. There be that can pack the Cards, who yet can't play well; they are good in *Canvasses* and *Factions*, and yet otherwise mean Men.

37. Extreme self-lovers will set a Man's House on fire, tho it were but to *roast their Eggs*.

38. New Things, like Strangers, are more admir'd, and *less favour'd*.

39. It were good that Men in their Innovations, would follow the Example of Time it self, which indeed innovateth *greatly*, but *quietly*; and by degrees scarce to be perceived.

40. They that reverence too much *old Time*,

Time, are but a scorn to *the New*.

41. The *Spaniards* and *Spartans* have been noted to be of small dispatch. *Mi venga la muerte de Spagna*; let my death come from *Spain*, for then it will be sure to be long a coming.

42. You had better take, for Business, a Man somewhat *absurd*, than *overformal*.

43. Those who want Friends to whom to open their Griefs, are Cannibals of their own Hearts.

44. Number it self importeth not much in Armies, where the People are of weak courage. For (as *Virgil* says) *it never troubles a Wolf how many the Sheep be*.

45. Let States, that aim at Greatness, take heed how their Nobility and Gentry multiply too fast. In *Coppice Woods*, if you leave your *Staddles* too *thick*, you shall never have clean *Underwood*, but *Shrubs and Bushes*.

46. A Civil War is like the *heat of a Feaver*; but a Forreign War is like the *heat of Exercise*, and serveth to keep the Body in health.

47. *Suspicions* among thoughts, are like *Bats* among Birds, They ever *fly by twilight*.

48. Base Natures, if they find themselves once suspected, will never be true.

49. Men

49. Men ought to find the difference between *saltness* and *bitterness*. Certainly he that hath a Satyrical Vein, as he maketh others afraid of his Wit, so he had need be afraid of others Memory.

50. *Discretion* in Speech is more than Eloquence.

51. Men seem neither well to understand their *Riches*, nor their *Strength:* of the former they believe *greater things* than they should, and of the latter *much less*. And from hence certain fatal Pillars have bounded the progress of Learning.

52. *Riches* are the *Baggage* of Vertue; they can't be spar'd, nor left behind, but they hinder the *march*.

53. Great *Riches* have *sold* more Men than ever they have *bought out*.

54. *Riches have Wings* ; and sometimes they fly away of themselves, and sometimes they must be set flying to bring in more.

55. He that defers his Charity 'till he is dead, is (if a Man weighs it rightly) rather liberal of another Man's, than of his own.

56. *Ambition* is like *Choler*; if it can move, it makes Men *active*; if it be stop'd, it becomes adust, and makes Men *melancholy*.

57. To take a Souldier without Ambition, is to pull off his Spurs.

58. Some ambitious Men seem as Skreens to Princes in matters of *Danger* and *Envy*. For no Man will take such parts, except he be like the *Seeld Dove*, that mounts and mounts because he cannot see about him.

59. Princes and States should chuse such Ministers as are more sensible of *Duty* than *Rising*; and should discern a *busy Nature* from a *willing Mind*.

60. A Man's Nature *runs* either to *Herbs* or *Weeds*; Therefore let him seasonably water the one, and destroy the other.

61. If a Man look sharply and attentively, he shall see *Fortune*; for though she be *blind*, she is not *invisible*.

62. *Usury* bringeth the Treasure of a Realm or State into few hands: For the Usurer being at certainties, and others at uncertainties; at the end of the Game, *most of the Mony will be in the Box*.

63. Beauty is best in a Body that hath rather *dignity of Presence*, than *beauty of Aspect*. The beautiful prove accomplish'd, but not of great Spirit; and study, for the most part, rather *Behaviour* than *Vertue*.

64. The best part of Beauty, is that which a Picture cannot express.

65. He who builds *a fair House* upon an *ill* Seat, commits himself to *Prison*.

66. If you will work on any Man, you must

must either know his *Nature* and Fashions, and so *lead him*; or his *Ends*, and so *perswade* him; or his weaknesses and disadvantages, and so awe him; or those that have interest in him, and so govern him.

67. Costly Followers (among whom we may reckon those who are importunate in Suits) are not to be liked; lest while a Man maketh his Train longer, he maketh his Wings shorter.

68. Fame is like a River that beareth up things light and swollen, and drowns things weighty and solid.

69. *Seneca* saith well, That *Anger is like Rain, which breaks it self upon that it falls.*

70. Excusations, Cessions, Modesty it self well govern'd, are but Arts of Ostentation.

71. High Treason is not written in Ice; that when the *Body* relenteth, the *Impression* should go away.

72. The best Governments are always subject to be like the fairest *Crystals*; wherein every *Isicle* or *Grain* is seen; which, in a fouler Stone is never perceiv'd.

73. Hollow Church Papists are like the *Roots* of *Nettles*, which themselves sting not; but yet they bear all the stinging Leaves.

Baroniana

Baconiana Physiologica.

Or, Certain

REMAINS

OF

Sir Francis Bacon,

Baron of *Verulam*, and Viscount of St. *Alban*.

IN

ARGUMENTS

Appertaining to

Natural Philosophy.

LONDON,

Printed for *R. C.* at the Rose and Crown in St. *Paul's* Church-yard. 1679.

THE
Lord Bacon's
Physiological Remains.

Fragmentum Libri *Verulamiani* cui Titulus *Abecedarium Naturæ.*

CUm tam multa producantur à Terrâ & Aquis, tam multa pertranseant Aerem, & ab eo excipiantur, tam multa mutentur, & solvantur ab Igne, minus perspicuæ forent Inquisitiones cæteræ, nisi Naturâ Massarum istarum quæ toties occurrunt bene cognitâ, & explicatâ. His adjungimus. Inquisitiones de Cœlestibus & Meteoricis, cum & ipsæ sint Massæ Majores, & ex Catholicis.

M.ss.

Maſſ. Maj.
Inquiſitio ſexageſima ſeptima.
Triplex Tau, ſive de Terrâ.

Maſſ. Maj.
Inquiſitio ſexageſima octava.
Triplex Upſilon, ſive de Aquâ.

Maſſ. Maj.
Inquiſitio ſexageſima nona.
Triplex Pſy, ſive de Aere.

Maſſ. Maj.
Inquiſitio ſeptuageſima.
Triplex Chy, ſive de Igne.

Maſſ. Maj.
Inquiſitio ſeptuageſima prima.
Triplex Pſi, ſive de Cœleſtibus.

Maſſ. Maj.
Inquiſitio ſeptuageſima ſecunda.
Triplex Omega, ſive de Meteoricis.

Conditiones

Conditiones Entium.

Supersunt ad inquirendum in Abecedario Conditiones Entium, quæ videntur esse tanquam Transcendentia, & parùm stringunt de Corpore Naturæ, tamen eo, quo utimur, inquirendi modo, haud parum afferent Illustrationis ad reliqua. Primò igitur, cum optimè observatum fuerit à Democrito *Naturam rerum esse copiâ Materiæ, & Individuorum varietate amplam, atq; (ut ille vult) infinitam; Coitionibus verò, & speciebus in tantum finitam, ut etiam angusta, & tanquam paupercula, videri possit. Quandoquidem tam paucæ inveniantur species, quæ sint aut esse possint, ut exercitum millenarium vix conficiant: Cumque Negativa Affirmativis subjuncta, ad informationem Intellectus plurimum valeant; constituenda est Inquisitio de Ente, & non Ente. Ea ordine est septuagesima tertia, & quadruplex* Alpha *numeratur.*

Cond. Ent.
Quadruplex Alpha; *sive de Ente & non Ente.*

Ad Possibile & Impossibile, nil aliud est, quàm Potentiale ad Ens, aut non Potentiale ad ad Ens. *De eo Inquisitio septuagesima quarta conficitur; quæ quadruplex* Beta *numeratur.*

Cond. Ent.
Quadruplex Beta; *sive de Possibili & Impossibili.*

Etiam Multum, Paucum, Rarum, Con*suetum sunt potentialia ad* Ens *in* Quanto. *De iis Inquisitio septuagesima quinta esto, quæ quadruplex* Gamma *numeretur.*

Cond. Ent.
Quadruplex Gamma; *sive de Multo & Pauco.*

Durabile & Transitorium, Æternum & Momentaneum, sunt potentialia ad Ens *in Duratione. De illis septuagesima sexta Inquisitio esto, quæ quadruplex* Delta *numeratur.*

Cond. Ent.
Quadruplex Delta; *sive de Durabili & Transitorio.*

---

*N*aturale *& M*onstrosum, *sunt potentialia ad* Ens, *per cursum Naturæ, & per deviationes*

ationes ejus. De *iis Inquisitio septuagesima septima esto, quæ quadruplex* Epsilon *numeratur.*

Cond. Ent.

Quadruplex Epsilon; *sive de Naturali & Monstroso.*

Naturale & Artificiale sunt potentialia ad Ens, sine Homine, & per Hominem. De *iis Inquisitio septuagesima octava conficitor, quæ quadruplex* Zeta *numeretur.*

Cond. Ent.

Quadruplex Zeta; *sive de Naturali & Artificiali.*

Exempla in explicatione ordinis Abecedarij, non adjunximus, quia ipsæ Inquisitiones continent totas Acies Exemplorum.

Tituli secundùm quos Ordo Abecedarij est dispositus, nullo modo eam Authoritatem habento, ut pro veris, & fixis rerum divisionibus recipiantur. Hoc enim esset profiteri scire nos quæ inquirimus. Nam nemo res verè dispertit, qui non naturam ipsarum penitùs cognovit. Satis sit, si ad ordinem inquirendi (id quod nunc agitur) commodè se habeant.

G   Norma

Norma Abecedarij.

Abecedarium hoc modo conficimus & regimus. Historia & Experimenta, omnino primas partes tenent. Ea si enumerationem & seriem rerum particularium exhibeant, in Tabulas conficiuntur, aliter sparsim excipiuntur.

Cùm vero Historia & Experimenta sæpissimè nos deserant, præsertim Lucifera illa, & Instantiæ Crucis, per quas, de veris rerum causis, Intellectui constare possit ; Mandata damus de Experimentis novis. Hæc sint tanquam Historia Designata. Quid enim aliud nobis primò viam ingredientibus relinquitur ?

Modum Experimenti subtilioris explicamus, ne error subsit, atq; ut alios, ad meliores modos excogitandos, excitemus.

Etiam Monita, & Cautiones, de Rerum fallacijs & inveniendi erroribus, quæ nobis occurrunt, aspergimus. Observationes nostras, super Historiam, & Experimenta, subteximus, ut Interpretatio Naturæ magis sit in Procinctu.

Etiam Canones, sed tamen Mobiles, & Axiomata inchoata, qualia nobis inquirentibus, non pronunciantibus, se offerunt constituimus. Utiles enim sunt, si non prorsus veræ.

Deniq; tentamenta quædam Interpretationis quandoq; molimur, licèt prorsus humi repentia, & vero Interpretationis nomine, nullo modo

(*ut*

(ut arbitramur) decoranda. *Quid enim nobis supercilio opus est, aut impostura, cum toties profiteamur, nec nobis Historiam & Experimenta, qualibus opus est, suppetere, nec absq; his, Interpretationem Naturæ perfici posse, ideoq; nobis satis esse, si initiis rerum non desimus.*

Perspicuitatis autem, & Ordinis gratiâ, Aditus quosdam ad Inquisitiones, instar præfationum, substernimus. Item Connexiones & Vincula, ne Inquisitiones sint magis abruptæ, interponimus.

Ad usum vero vellicationis quasdam, de Practicâ, suggerimus.

Etiam Optativa eorum, quæ adhuc non habentur, unâ cum proximis suis, ad erigendam humanam industriam, proponimus.

Neq; sumus nescii, Inquisitiones inter se, aliquando complicari, ita ut nonnulla ex Inquisitis, in Titulos diversos incidant. Sed modum eum adhibebimus, ut & repetitionum fastidia, & rejectionum molestias, quantum fieri possit, vitemus; postponentes tamen hoc ipsum (quando necesse fuerit) perspicuitati docendi, in Argumento tam obscuro.

Hæc est Abecedarii Norma & Regula. Deus Universi Conditor, Conservator, & Instaurator, Opus hoc & in Ascensione ad Gloriam suam, & in Descensione ad bonum humanum, pro suâ erga homines benevolentia & Misericordia protegat & regat, per Filium suum unicum Nobiscum Deum.

The same in *English* by the Publisher.

A Fragment *of a Book written by the Lord* Verulam, *and Entituled,* The Alphabet of Nature.

* See the distributi- on, in l. 2. c. 3. *de Augm. Scient.* p. 234, 135, 136. Ed. Lugd. Bat. *l* 3. c. 4 p. 231. *An. l* c. 4. Globi In- tellect. p. 88, 89.

SEeing so many things are produc'd by the *Earth*, and Waters; so many things pass through the *Air*, and are received by it; so many things are chang'd and dissolv'd by *Fire*; other Inquisitions would be less perspicuous, unless the Nature of those *Masses* which so often occur, were well known and explain'd. To these we add Inquisitions concerning *Celestial Bodies*, and *Meteors*, seeing they are some of greater *Masses*,& of the number of Catholic Bodies. *

Greater Masses.

The 67*th* Inquisition. The three-fold *Tau*, or concerning the *Earth*.

The 68*th* Inquisition. The three-fold *Upsilon*, or concerning the *Water*.

The 69*th* Inquisition. The three-fold *Phi*, or concerning the *Air*.

The 70*th* Inquisition. The three-fold *Chi*, or concerning the *Fire*.

The

The 71*st* Inquisition. The Three-fold *Psi*, or concerning *Celestial Bodies*.
The 72*d* Inquisition. The three-fold *Omega*, or concerning *Meteors*.

Conditions of Entities.

THere yet remain, as Subjects of our Inquiry, in our *Alphabet*, the *Conditions of Beings*, which seem, as it were, *Transcendentals*, and such as *touch* very little of the *Body* of Nature. Yet by that manner of Inquisition which we use, They will considerably illustrate the other Objects.

First; Therefore seeing (as *Democritus* excellently observed) *the Nature of Things is in the plenty of Matter, and variety of Individuals, large, and* (as he affirmeth) *Infinite; but in its Coitions and Species so Finite, that it may seem narrow and poor;* seeing so few *Species* are found, either in actual Being, or Impossibility, that they scarce make up a *muster of a Thousand*; And seeing Negatives, subjoin'd to Affirmatives, conduce much to the Information of the Understanding: It is fit that an Inquisition be made concerning *Being*, and *not Being*.

That is the 73*d* in order, and reckon'd the *Four-fold Alpha*.

Conditions of Beings.

The *four-fold Alpha*; or, concerning *Being*, and *not Being*.

Now *Possible* and *Impossible*, are nothing else but Conditions *potential to Being*, or *not potential to Being*. Of this the 74*th* Inquisition consists, and is accounted the *four-fold Beta*.

Conditions of Beings.

The *four-fold Beta*; or concerning *Possible* and *Impossible*.

Also, *Much, Little; Rare, Ordinary;* are Conditions potential to Being *in Quantity*. Of them let the 75*th* Inquisition consist, and be accounted the *four-fold Gamma*.

Conditions of Beings.

The *four-fold Gamma*; or, concerning *much* and *little*.

Durable

Durable and *Transitory*, *Eternal* and *Momentary*, are *potential* to Being in *Duration*. Of these let the 76th Inquisition consist, and be call'd the *four-fold Delta*.

Conditions of Beings.

The *four-fold Delta*; or, concerning *Durable* and *Transitory*.

Natural and *Monstrous*, are *potential* to Being, either by the *course* of Nature, or by its *deviations* from it. Of these let the 77th Inquisition consist, which is accounted the *four-fold Epsilon*.

Conditions of Beings.

The *four-fold Epsilon*; or, concerning what is *Natural* or *Monstrous*.

Natural and *Artificial*, are potential to Being, either with or without the Operation of Man. Of these let the 78th Inquisition consist, and be accounted the *four-fold Zeta*.

Conditions of Beings.

The *four-fold Zeta*; or, of that which is *Natural* and *Artificial*.

We have not subjoined Examples in the Explication of the Order of this our *Alphabet* : for the Inquisitions themselves contain the whole Array of Examples.

It is by no means intended, that the *Titles*, according to which the Order of this *Alphabet* is dispos'd, should have so much authority given to them, as to be taken for true and *fixed partitions of Things*. That were to profess we already knew the things after which we inquire; for no Man do's *truly* dispose of things into their several *Classes*, who do's not beforehand very well understand the Nature of them. It is sufficient, if these Titles be conveniently adapted to the Order of Inquiry; the thing which is at present design'd.

The Rule (or Form) *of the Alphabet.*

After this manner we *compose* and *dispose* our *Alphabet*.

We begin solely with *History* and *Experiments.*

riments. These, if they exhibit an enumeration and series of particular Things, are dispos'd into *Tables*; otherwise they are taken seperately, and by themselves.

But seeing we are often at a loss for *History* and *Experiments*, especially such as are *Luciferous* [or Instructive] and [as we call * them] *Instances of the Cross*; by which the Understanding might be helped in the knowledg of the true Causes of Things: We propose the task of making *new Experiments*. These may serve as an *History in Design.* For what else is to be done by us who are but breaking the Ice?

* See Nov. Organ. *l* 2 Aph. 36. *p.* 254.? ⁋ Lugd. Bat.

For the mode of any more abstruse, Experiment, we explain it, lest any mistake arise about it; and to the intent also that we may excite others to excogitate better Methods.

Also we interspect certain *Admonitions* and *Cautions* concerning such Fallacies of Things, and Errors in Invention, as we meet with in our way.

We subjoin our *Observations* upon *History* and *Experiments*, that the *Interpretation of Nature* may be the more in readiness and at hand.

Likewise we lay down *Canons* (but not such as are *fixed* and *determin'd*) and *Axioms* which are, as it were, in *Embrio*:

Such

Such as offer themselves to us in the quality of *Inquirers*, and not of *Judges*. Such *Canons* and *Axioms* are *profitable*, though they appear not yet *manifestly*, and upon all accounts *true*.

Lastly ; We meditate sometimes certain *Essays* of *Interpretation*, though such as are low and of small advance, and by no means to be honour'd (in our opinion) with the *very* name of *Interpretation*.

For what need have we of Arrogance or Imposture, seeing we have so often professed, that we have not such a supply of History and Experiments as is needful; and that without these, the Interpretation of Nature cannot be brought to perfection. Wherefore it is enough for us, if we are not wanting to the beginning of Things.

Now, for the sake of Perspicuity, and Order, we prepare our way by Avenues, which *are a kind of Prefaces to our Inquisitions*. Likewise we interpose *bonds of Connexion*, that our Inquisitions may not seem abrupt and dis-jointed.

Also we suggest for use, some *Hints of Practice*. Furthermore, we propose *wishes* of such things as are hitherto only desired and not had, together with those things which border on them, for the exciting the Industry of Man's Mind.

Neither

Neither are we ignorant, that thofe *Inquifitions* are fometimes mutually entangled; o that fome things of which we inquire (even the fame things) belong to feveral Tiles. But we will obferve fuch meafure, that (as far as may be) we may fhun both the *naufeoufnefs* of *Repetition*, and the trouble of *Rejection*, fubmitting notwithftanding to either of thefe, when in an Argument fo obfcure, there is neceffity of fo doing, in order to the more intelligible teaching of it.

This is the Form and Rule of our Alphabet.

May God, the Creator, Preferver, and Renewer of the Univerfe, protect and govern this Work, both in its *afcent* to his Glory, and in its *defcent* to the Good of Mankind, for the fake of his Mercy and good Will to Men, through his only Son [Immanuel] *God-with-us*,

Inqui-

Inquiſitions touching the Compounding of Metals, *by Sir* Francis Bacon, *Baron of* Verulam.

TO *make proof of the Incorporation of Iron with Flint, or other Stone.* For if it can be incorporated without over-great charge, or other incommodity, the cheapneſs of the Flint or Stone, doth make the Compound Stuff profitable for divers Uſes. The Doubts may be three in number.

Firſt ; Whether they will incorporate at all, otherwiſe than to a Body that will not hold well together but become brittle and uneven?

Secondly ; Although it ſhould incorporate well, yet whether the Stuff will not be ſo ſtubborn as it will not work well with a Hammer, whereby the charge in working will overthrow the cheapneſs of the material?

Thirdly ; Whether they will incorporate, except the Iron and Stone be firſt calcined into Pouder? And if not, Whether the charge of the Calcination will not eat out the cheapneſs of the material?

The *Uses* are most probable to be; *First* for the Implements of the Kitching; as Spits, Ranges, Cobirons, Pots, &c. then for the Wars, as Ordinance, Portcullasses, Grates, Chains, &c.

Note; The finer Works of Iron are not so probable to be served with such a Stuff; as Locks, Clocks, small Chains, &c. because the Stuff is not like to be tough enough.

For the better use in comparison of Iron, it is like the Stuff will be far *lighter*; for the weight of Iron to Flint, is double and a third part; and, secondly, it is like to rust not so easily, but to be *more clean*.

The ways of tryal are two. *First*; By the Iron and Stone of themselves, wherein it must be inquired, What are the Stones that do easiliest melt. *Secondly*; With an Additament, wherein Brimstone is approved to help to the melting of Iron or Steel. But then it must be considered, Whether the Charge of the Additament will not destroy the Profit.

It must be known also what proportion of the Stone the Iron will receive to incorporate well with it, and that with once melting; for if either the proportion be too small, or that it cannot be received but peece-meal by several meltings, the Work cannot be of value. *To*

To make proof of the incorp[oration]
and Brass. For the cheapnefs
in comparifon of the Brafs,
may be ferved, doth pr[o
The Doubt will be, touching
porating: for that it is approv[ed]
will not incorporate, neithe[r
nor other Metals of it felf b[e
So as the inquiry muft be up[on
nation, and the Additament, a[nd
of them.

The *Ufes* will be for fuch
now made of Brafs, and mig[ht
ferved by the compound Stu[ff
the Doubts will be chiefly of [
and of the beauty.

First; Therefore, if Bra[fs
could be made of the compo[
refpect of the cheapnefs of
would be of great ufe.

The Vantage which Brafs O[r
over Iron, is chiefly, as I fup[pofe
it will hold the blow, though
far thinner than the Iron can
it faveth both in the quantity
rial, and in the charge and c[
mounting & carriage, in regard
the thinnefs it beareth much
there may be alfo fomewhat in
eafily overheated.

Secondly; For the Beauty; those things wherein the beauty or luster are esteemed, are, Andirons, and all manner of Images, and Statues, and Columns, and Tombs, and the like. So as the *doubt* will be *double* for the Beauty; the *one* whether the colour will please so well, because it will not be so like Gold as Brass? the *other*, whether it will pollish so well? Wherein for the latter it is probable it will; for Steel glosses are more resplendant than the like Plates of Brass would be; and so is the glittering of a Blade. And besides, I take it, Andiron Brass, which they call White Brass, hath some mixture of Tin to help the luster. And for the Golden Colour, it may be by some small mixture of Orpiment, such as they use to Brass in the Yellow Alchymy, will easily recover that which the Iron loseth. Of this the Eye must be the Judg upon proof made.

But now for Pans, Pots, Curfues, Counters, and the like; the beauty will not be so much respected, so as the compound Stuff is like to pass.

For the better use of the compound Stuff, it will be sweeter and cleaner than Brass alone, which yieldeth a smell or soilness, and therefore may be better for the Vessels of the Kitchen and Brewing. It will also
be

be harder than Brass where hardness may be required.

For the tryal, the *Doubts* will be *two*: *First*; The over-weight of Brass towards Iron, which will make Iron float on the top in the melting. This perhaps will be holpen with the *Calaminar Stone*, which consenteth so well with Brass, and as I take it, is lighter than Iron. The *other Doubt* will be, the stiffness and driness of Iron to melt; which must be holpen either by *moistning* the Iron, or opening it. *For the first*, Perhaps some mixture of Lead will help. Which is as much more liquid than Brass, as Iron is less liquid. The *opening* may be holpen by some mixture of Sulphur, so as the trials would be with Brass, Iron, *Calaminar Stone*, and Sulphur; and then again with the same composition, and an addition of some Lead; and in all this the Charge must be considered, whether it eat not out the Profit of the cheapness of Iron?

There be *two Proofs* to be made of *incorporation of Metals for magnificence and delicacy*. The *one* for the *Eye*, and the *other* for the *Ear*. Statua Metal, and Bell Metal, and Trumpet Metal, and String Metal; in all these, though the mixture of Brass or Copper, should be dearer than the Brass

Brass it self, yet the pleasure will advance the price to profit.

First; Therefore for *Statua-Metal*, see *Pliny's* Mixtures, which are almost forgotten, and consider the charge.

Try likewise the mixture of Tin in large proportion with Copper, and observe the Colour and Beauty, it being polished. But chiefly let proof be made of the incorporating of Copper or Brass with Glass-Metal, for that is cheap, and is like to add a great glory and shining.

For *Bell-Metal*. *First*, It is to be known what is the Composition which is now in use. *Secondly*, It is probable that it is the driness of the Metal that doth help the clearness of the sound, and the moistness that dulleth it: and therefore the Mixtures that are probable are Steel, Tin, Glass-Metal.

For *String-Metal*, or *Trumpet-Metal*, it is the same reason; save that Glass-Metal may not be used, because it will make it too brittle; and trial may be made with mixture of Silver, it being but a delicacy with Iron or Brass.

To make proof of the Incorporation of Silver and Tin, in equal quantity, or with two parts Silver, and one part Tin, and to observe

serve whether it be of equal beauty and luster with pure Silver; and also whether it yield no soiliness more than Silver? And again, whether it will indure the ordinary Fire, which belongeth to Chafing-dishes, Posnets, and such other Silver Vessels? And if it do not endure the Fire, yet whether by some mixture of Iron it may not be made more fixt? For if it be in Beauty, and all the Uses aforesaid equal to Silver, it were a thing of singular profit to the State, and to all particular Persons, to change Silver Plate or Vessel into the Compound Stuff, being a kind of Silver *Electre*, and to turn the rest into Coin. It may be also questioned, Whether the Compound Stuff will receive gilding as well as Silver, and with equal luster? It is to be noted, That the common allay of Silver Coin is Brass, which doth discolour more, and is not so neat as Tin.

The Drownings of Metals within other Metals, in such sort as they can never rise again, is a thing of great profit. For if a quantity of Silver can be so buried in Gold, as it will never be reduced again, neither by Fire, nor parting Waters, nor otherways; and also that it serve all Uses as well as pure Gold, it is in effect all one, as if so much

much Silver were turned into Gold; only the weight will discover it: but that taketh off but half of the profit; for Gold is not fully double weight to Silver, but Gold is twelve times price to Silver.

The burial must be by one of these two ways, *either* by the smallness of the proportion, as perhaps fifty to one, which will be but six pence gains in fifty shillings: or it must be holpen by somewhat which may fix the Silver, never to be restored or vapour'd away, when it is incorporated into such a Mass of Gold; for the less quantity is ever the harder to sever; and for this purpose Iron is the likest, or Coppel Stuff, upon which the Fire hath no power of consumption.

The making of Gold seemeth a thing scarcely possible; because Gold is the heaviest of Metals, and to add Matter is impossible: and again, to drive Metals into a narrower room than their natural extent beareth, is a condensation hardly to be expected. But to make Silver seemeth more easy, because both Quick-silver and Lead are weightier than Silver; so as there needeth only fixing, and not condensing. The degree unto this that is already known, is infusing of Quick-silver in a Parchment, or otherwise in the midſt of molten Lead when it cooleth; for this ſtupifieth the Quick-ſilver that it runneth no more. This trial is to be advanced three ways. *First*, By iterating the melting of the Lead, to ſee whether it will not make the Quick-ſilver harder and harder. *Secondly*, To put *Realgar* hot into the midſt of the Quick-ſilver, whereby it may be condenſed, as well from within as without. *Thirdly*, To try it in the midſt of Molten Iron or Molten Steel, which is a Body more likely to fix the Quick-ſilver than Lead. It may be alſo tried, by incorporating Pouder of Steel, or Copple Duſt, by pouncing into the Quick-ſilver, and ſo to proceed to the ſtupifying.

Upon Glaſs, four things would be put in proof. The *first*, means to make the Glaſs more Cryſtalline. The *second*, to make it more ſtrong for falls, and for fire, though it come not to the degree to be malleable. The *third*, to make it coloured by Tinctures, comparable or exceeding pretious Stones. The *fourth*, To make a compound Body of Glaſs and Galletyle; that is, to have the colour milkey like a *Chalcedon*, being a Stuff between a Porcelane and a Glaſs.

For the *first*; It is good firſt to know exactly

exactly the several Materials, whereof the Glass in use is made ; Window-glass, *Normandy* and *Burgundy*, Alehouse-glass, English drinking-Glass: and then thereupon to consider what the reason is of the coarseness or clearness ; and from thence to rise to a consideration how to make some Additaments to the coarser Materials ; to raise them to the whiteness and crystalline splendour of the finest.

For the *second* ; We see Pebbles, and some other Stones will cut as fine as Crystal, which if they will melt, may be a mixture for Glass, and may make it more tough and more Crystalline. Besides, we see Metals will vitrify ; and perhaps some portion of the Glass of Metal vitrified, mixed in the Pot of ordinary Glass-Metal, will make the whole Mass more tough.

For the *third* ; It were good to have of coloured Window-Glass, such as is coloured in the Pot, and not by Colours——

* *Here something is wanting in the Copy.*

* * * * * * * * * * * *

It is to be known of what Stuff *Galletyle* is made, and how the Colours in it are varied; and thereupon to confider how to make the mixture of Glafs-Metal and them, whereof I have feen the Example.

Inquire what be the Stones that do eafilieft melt. Of them take half a pound, and of Iron a pound and a half, and an ounce of Brimftone, and fee whether they will incorporate, being whole, with a ftrong fire. If not, try the fame quantities calcined; and if they will incorporate, make a Plate of them, and burnifh it as they do Iron.

Take a pound and a half of Brafs, and half a pound of Iron; two ounces of the *Calaminar* Stone, an ounce and a half of Brimftone, an ounce of Lead; calcine them, and fee what body they make; and if they incorporate, make a Plate of it burnifhed.

Take of Copper an ounce and a half, of Tin an ounce, and melt them together, and make a Plate of them burnifhed.

Take of Copper an ounce and a half, of Tin an ounce, of Glafs-Metal half an ounce; ftir them well in the boiling, and if they incorporate, make a Plate of them burnifhed.

Take of Copper a pound and a half, Tin four ounces, Brafs two ounces; make a Plate of them burnished.

Take of Silver two ounces, Tin half an ounce; make a little Say-Cup of it, and burnish it.

To enquire of the Materials of every of the kind of Glasses, coarser and finer, and of the Proportions.

Take an equal quantity of Glass-Metal, of Stone calcined, and bring a Pattern.

Take an ounce of vitrified Metal, and a pound of ordinary Glass-Metal, and see whether they will incorporate; and bring a Pattern.

Bring Examples of all coloured Glasses, and learn the Ingredients whereby they are coloured.

Inquire of the substance of *Galletyle*.

Articles of Questions touching Minerals; written originally in English by the Lord *Bacon*, yet hitherto not published in that Language.

The Lord Bacon's *Questions and Solutions concerning the Compounding, Incorporating, or Union of Metals or Minerals; which Subject is the first Letter of his Lordships Alphabet.*

2. With what Metals Gold will Incorporate by simple Colliquefaction, and with what not? and in what quantity it will incorporate; and what kind of Body the Compound makes?

A. Gold with Silver, which was the Ancient Electrum.

Gold with Quicksilver.
Gold with Lead.
Gold with Copper.
Gold with Brass.
Gold with Iron.
Gold with Tin.

So

So likewise of Silver.

Silver with Quicksilver.
Silver with Lead.
Silver with Copper.
Silver with Brass.
Silver with Iron. (*Plinius Secund. lib.33. ix. miscuit denario Triumvir Antonius ferrum.*)
Silver with Tin.

So likewise of Quicksilver.

Quicksilver with Lead.
Quicksilver with Copper.
Quicksilver with Brass.
Quicksilver with Iron.
Quicksilver with Tin.

So of Lead.

Lead with Copper. ⎫
Lead with Brass. ⎬ *Pl.* 34. ix.
Lead with Iron.   ⎪
Lead with Tin.   ⎭

So of Copper.

Copper with Brass.

Copper with Iron.
Copper with Tin.

So of Brass.

Brass with Iron.
Brass with Tin.

So of Iron.

Iron with Tin.

What be the Compound Metals that are common and known? and what are the proportions of their Mixtures? As,

Latten of Brass, and the *Calaminar* Stone.
Pewter of Tin and Lead.
Bell-Metal of *&c.* and the counterfeit Plate, which they call *Alchimy.*

The Decompositees of three Metals or more, are too long to enquire of, except there be some Compositions of them already observed.

It is also to be observed, whether any two Metals which will not mingle of themselves, will mingle with the help of an other; and what. What

What Compounds will be made of Metal with Stone and other Fossiles; As Latten is made with Brass and the *Calaminar* Stone; As all the Metals incorporate with Vitriol; all with Iron poudered; all with Flint, &c.

Some few of these would be inquired of, to disclose the nature of the rest.

Whether Metals or other Fossiles will incorporate with molten Glass, and what Body it makes?

The quantity in the mixture would be well considered; for some small quantity perhaps will incorporate, as in the Allays of Gold and Silver Coin.

Upon the Compound Body, three things are chiefly to be observed; The Colour; the Fragility or Pliantness; the Volatility or Fixation, compared with the simple Bodies.

For present use or profit, this is the Rule: Consider the price of the two simple Bodies; consider again the dignity of the one above the other in use; then see if you can make a Compound that will save more in price than it will lose in dignity of the use.

As for Example; Consider the price of Brass-Ordnance; consider again the price of Iron-Ordnance, and then consider wherein the Brass-Ordnance doth excel the Iron-Ordnance

Ordnance in Use: Then if you can make a Compound of Brass and Iron that will be near as good in use, and much cheaper in price, then there is profit both to the Private, and the Common-wealth. So of Gold and Silver, the price is double of twelve: The dignity of Gold above Silver is not much, the splendor is a like, and more pleasing to some Eyes, as in Cloth of Silver, silvered Rapiers, &c. The main dignity is, That Gold bears the Fire, which Silver doth not, but that is an excellency in Nature, but it is nothing at all in use; for any dignity in use I know none, but that silvering will sully and canker more than gilding; which if it might be corrected with a little mixture of Gold, there is profit: And I do somewhat marvel that the latter Ages have lost the Ancient *Electrum*, which was a mixture of Silver with Gold: whereof I conceive there may be much use, both in Coin, Plate, and Gilding.

It is to be noted, That there is in the version of Metals impossibility, or at least great difficulty, as in making of Gold, Silver, Copper. On the other side, in the adulterating or counterfeiting of Metals, there is deceit and villany. But it should seem there is a middle way, and that is by new

new Compounds, if the ways of incorporating were well known.

What Incorporation or Inbibition Metals will receive from Vegetables, without being diffolved in their Subſtance: As when the Armorers make their Steel more tough and pliant, by afperfion of Water or Juice of Herbs; when Gold being grown fomewhat churlifh by recovering, is made more pliant by throwing in fhreds of tanned Leather, or any Leather oiled.

Note; That in thefe and the like fhews of Inbibition, it were good to try by the Weights whether the weight be increafed or no; for if it be not, it is to be doubted that there is no inbibition of Subſtance, but only that the application of that other Body, doth difpofe and invite the Metal to another pofture of parts than of it felf it would have taken.

After the Incorporation of Metals by fimple Colliquefaction, for the better difcovery of the Nature, and Confents, and Diffents of Metals, it would be likewife tried by incorporating of their Diffolutions.

There is to be obferved in thofe Diffolutions which will not eafily incorporate, what the Effects are: As the Bullition; the Precipitation to the bottom; the Ejaculation towards the top; the Sufpenfion in the midſt; and the like.   Note;

Note; That the diffents of the Menftrual or ftrong Waters, may hinder the incorporation, as well as the diffents of the Metals themfelves; Therefore where the *Menftrua* are the fame, and yet the Incorporation followeth not, you may conclude the Diffent is in the Metals; but where the *Menftrua* are feveral, not fo certain.

Dr. Meverell's *Anfwers to the Lord Bacon's Queftions, concerning the Compounding, Incorporating, or Union of Metals and Minerals.*

Gold will incorporate with Silver in any proportion. Plin. *lib.*33. *cap.* 4. *Omni Auro ineft Argentum vario pondere, alibi denâ, alibi nonâ, alibi octavâ parte——ubicunq; quinta Argenti portio invenitur, Electrum vocatur.* The Body remains fixt, folid, and coloured, according to the proportion of the two Metals.

Gold with Quickfilver eafily mixeth, but the product is imperfectly fixed; and fo are all other Metals incorporate with Mercury.

Gold incorporates with Lead in any proportion.

Gold incorporates with Copper in any proportion, the common Allay.

Gold incorporates with Brass in any proportion. And what is said of Copper, is true of Brass, in the union of other Metals.

Gold will not incorporate with Iron.

Gold incorporates with Tin, the ancient Allay, *Isa.* 1. 25.

What was said of Gold and Quicksilver, may be said of Quicksilver and the rest of Metals.

Silver with Lead in any proportion.

Silver incorporates with Copper. *Pliny* mentions such a mixture; for *triumphales Statuæ, lib.* 33. ix. *miscentur Argento, tertia pars æris Cyprii tenuissimi, quod coronarium vocant, & Sulphuris vivi quantum Argenti.* The same is true of Brass.

Silver incorporates not with Iron. Wherefore I wonder at that which *Pliny* hath *lib.*33.ix. *Miscuit denario Triumvir Antonius ferrum.* And what is said of this, is true in the rest, for Iron incorporateth with none of them.

Silver mixes with Tin.

Lead

Lead incorporates with Copper. Such a mixture was the Pot-Metal whereof *Pliny* speaks *lib. 34. ix. Ternis aut quaternis libris plumbi Argentarii in centenas æris additis.*

Lead incorporates with Tin. The mixture of these two in equal proportions, is that which was anciently called *Plumbum Argentarium,* Plin. 34. xvii.

Copper incorporates with Tin. Of such a mixture were the Mirrors of the Romans. Plin. *atque ut omnia de speculis peragantur hoc loco, optima apud Majores erant Brundisina, stanno & ære mistis. lib. 83. ix.*

Compounded Metals now in use.

1. Fine Tin. The mixture is thus; Pure Tin a 1000 pound, temper 50 pound, Glass of Tin 3 pound.
2. Course Pewter is made of fine Tin and Lead. Temper is thus made; The dross of pure Tin four pound and a half, Copper half a pound.
3. Brass is made of Copper and *Calaminaris.*
4. Bell-Metal. Copper 1000 pound, Tin from 300 to 200 pound, Brass 150 pound.
5. Pot-

5. Pot-Metal, Copper and Lead.

6. White Alkimie is made of Pan-Brass, 1 pound, and Arsenicum, 3 ounces.

7. Red Alkimie is made of Copper and Auripigmen.

There be divers imperfect Minerals, which will incorporate with the Metals. Being indeed Metals inwardly, but clothed with Earths and Stones. As Pyritis, Calaminaris, Mysi, Chalcyti, Sory, Vitriolum.

Metals incorporate not with Glass, except they be brought into the form of Glass.

Metals dissolved. The dissolution of Gold and Silver disagree, so that in their mixture, there is great Ebullition, Darkness, and in the end a precipitation of a black Pouder.

The mixture of Gold and Mercurie agree.

Gold agrees with Iron. In a word, the dissolution of Mercury and Iron agree with all the rest.

Silver and Copper disagree, and so do Silver and Lead. Silver and Tin agree.

The Lord Bacon's Articles of Inquiry concerning Minerals. The second Letter of the Cross-Row, touching the separation of Metals and Minerals.

SEparation is of three sorts; The *First*, is the separating of the pure Metal from the Ore, or Dross, which we call Refining. The *Second*, is the drawing one Metal or Mineral out of another, which we call Extracting. The *Third*, Is the separating of any Metal into his Original, or *Materia Prima*, or Element, or call them what you will; which Work we will call *Principiation*. For Refining, we are to enquire of it according to the several Metals; as Gold, Silver, &c. Incidently we are to inquire of the First Stone or Ore, or Marcasite of Metals severally, and what kind of Bodies they are, and of the degrees of Richness. Also we are to enquire of the means of Separating, whether by Fire, parting Waters, or otherwise. Also for the manner of Refining, you are to see how you can multiply the heat, ⅓ hasten the opening, and so save charge in the Fining.

The means of this in Three manners, that is to say, In the Blast of the Fire; In the manner of the Furnace, to multiply Heat by Union, and Reflection; and by some Additament, or Medicines which will help the bodies to open them the sooner.

Note the Quickning of the Blast, and the Multiplying of the Heat in the Furnace, may be the same for all Metals; but the Additaments must be several, according to the Nature of the Metals. Note again, That if you think that the multiplying of the Additaments in the same proportion, that you multiply the Ore, the Work will follow, you may be deceived: for quantity in the Passive will add more Resistance, than the same quantity in the Active will add force.

For Extracting, you are to enquire what Metals contain others, and likewise what not; As Lead, Silver; Copper, Silver, &c.

Note, Although the Charge of Extraction should excede the Worth, yet that is not the matter. For at least it will discover Nature and Possibility, the other may be thought on afterwards.

We are likewise to inquire what the differences are of those Metals which contain more or less other Metals, and how that agrees with the poorness or richness of the Metals or Ore in themselves. As the Lead that contains most Silver is accounted to be more brittle, and yet otherwise poorer in it self.

For *Principiation*, I cannot affirm whether there be any such thing or not; and I think the Chymists make too much ado about it, but howsoever it be, be it Solution, or Extraction, or a kind of Conversion by the Fire; it is diligently to be inquired what Salts, Sulphur, Vitriol, Mercury, or the like Simple Bodies are to be found in the several Metals, and in what quantity.

Doctor Meverel's *Answers to the Lord Bacon's Questions, touching the separations of Metals and Minerals.*

1. FOr the *means of Separating*. After that the Ore is washed, or cleansed from the Earth, there is nothing simply necessary, save only a Wind Furnace well framed, narrow above and at the Hearth, in shape Oval, sufficiently fed with Charcoal and Ore, in convenient proportions.

For

For Additions in this First Separation, I have observed none; the Dross, the Mineral brings, being sufficient. The Refiners of Iron observe, that that Iron-Stone is hardest to melt, which is fullest of Metal, and that easiest which hath most Dross. But in Lead, and Tin, the contrary is noted. Yet in melting of Metals, when they have been calcined formerly by Fire, or Strong-Waters, there is good use of Additaments, as of Borax, Tartar, Armoniac, and Salt-Peter.

2. *In Extracting of Metals.* Note, That Lead and Tin contain Silver. Lead and Silver contain Gold. Iron contains Brass. Silver is best separated from Lead, by the Test. So Gold from Silver. Yet the best way for that is *Aqua Regia*.

3. *For Principiation.* I can truly and boldly affirm, that there are no such principles as *Sal*, *Sulphur*, and *Mercury*, which can be separated from any perfect Metals. For every part so separated, may easily be reduced into perfect Metal without Substitution of that, or those principles which Chymists imagin to be wanting. As suppose you take the Salt of Lead; this Salt, or, as some name it Sulphur, may be turned into perfect Lead, by melting it with the like quantity of Lead which con-

tains principles only for it self.

I acknowledg that there is Quick-Silver and Brimstone found in the imperfect Minerals; but those are Nature's remote Materials, and not the Chymists Principles. As if you dissolve Antimony by *Aqua Regia*, there will be real Brimstone swimming upon the Water; as appears by the colour of the Fire when it is burnt, and by the smell.

The Lord Bacon's *Articles of Inquiry concerning Metals, and Minerals.*

THe Third Letter of the Cross-Row, touching the *Variation of Metals* into several Shapes, Bodies, or Natures, the particulars whereof follow,

  Tincture.
  Turning to Rust.
  Calcination.
  Sublimation.
  Precipitation.
  Amalgamatizing, or Turning into a soft body.
  Vitrification.
  Opening or Dissolving into Liquor.
          Sprout-

Sproutings, or Branchings, or Arbo-
   reſſents.
Induration and Mollification.
Making Tough or Brittle.
Volatility and Fixation.
Tranſmutation, or Verſion.

For *Tincture*; It is to be inquired how Metal may be tinged through and through, and with what, and into what Colours; As tinging Silver Yellow, tinging Copper White, and tinging Red, Green, Blew, eſpecially with keeping the Luſtre.

   Item, Tincture of Glaſſes.
   Item, Tincture of Marble, Flint, or other Stone.

For *turning into Ruſt*, two things are chiefly to be inquired; By what Coraſives it is done, and into what Colours it turns; As Lead into White, which they call *Cerus*; Iron into Yellow, which they call *Crocus Martis*; Quickſilver into Vermilion; Braſs into Green, which they call Verdigreaſe.

For *Calcination*, how every Metal is calcined, and into what kind of Body, and what is the exquiſiteſt way of Calcination.

For *Sublimation*; To enquire the manner of Subliming, and what Metals indure Subliming,

liming, and what body the Sublimate makes.

For *Precipitation* likewise; by what strong Water every Metal will precipitate, and with what Additaments, and in what time, and into what body.

So for *Amalgama*, what Metals will endure it, what are the means to do it, and what is the manner of the body.

For *Vitrification* likewise; what Metals will endure it, what are the means to do it, into what Colour it turns, and further where the whole Metal is turned into Glass, and where the Metal doth but hang in the Glassy parts; Also what weight the Vitrified body bears, compared with the Crude body; Also because Vitrification is accounted a kind of Death of Metals, what Vitrification will admit of turning back again, and what not.

For *Dissolution* into Liquour, we are to enquire what is the proper *Menstruum* to dissolve any Metal, and in the Negative, what will touch upon the one, and not upon the other, and what several *Menstrua* will dissolve any Metal, and which most exactly. *Item* the Process or Motion of the Dissolution, the manner of rising, boyling, vapouring more violent, or more gentle, causing much heat or less. *Item* the

the Quantity or Charge that the strong Water will bear, and then give over. *Item* the Colour into which the Liquor will turn. Above all it is to be enquired, whether there be any *Menstruum* to dissolve any Metal that is not Fretting, or Corroding, and openeth the Body by Sympathie, and not by Mordacity, or violent Penetration.

For *Sprouting or Branching*, though it be a thing but transitory, and a kind of Toy or Pleasure, yet there is a more serious use of it; for that it discovereth the delicate Motions of Spirits, when they put forth and cannot get forth, like unto that which is in Vegetables.

For *Induration*, or Mollification; It is to be enquired what will make Metals harder and harder, and what will make them softer and softer. And this enquiry tendeth to two ends: First, for Use; As to make Iron soft by the Fire makes it Malleable. Secondly, Because Induration is a degree towards Fixation, and Mollification towards Volatility, and therefore the Enquiry of them will give light towards the other.

For *Tough and Brittle*, they are much of the same kind, but yet worthy of an Enquiry apart, especially to joyn Hardness with

with Toughness, as making Glass malleable, &c. and making Blades strong, to resist and pierce, and yet not easie to break.

For *Volatility and Fixation.* It is a Principal Branch to be enquired: The utmost degree of Fixation is that whereon no Fire will work, nor strong Water joyned with Fire, if there be any such Fixation possible. The next is when Fire simply will not work without strong Waters. The next is by the Test. The next is when it will indure Fire not blown, or such a strength of Fire. The next is when it will not indure, but yet is malleable. The next is when it is not malleable, but yet is not fluent, but stupified. So of Volatility, the utmost degree is when it will flie away without returning. The next is when it will flie up, but with ease return. The next is when it will flie upwards over the Helm by a kind of Exufflation without Vapouring. The next is when it will melt, though not rise. The next is when it will soften, though not melt. Of all these diligent Enquiry is to be made in several Metals, especially of the more extreme degrees.

For *Transmutation*, or Version. If it be real and true, it is the furthest part of Art, and would be well distinguished,
from

from Extraction, from Restitution, and from Adulteration. I hear much of turning Iron into Copper; I hear also of the growth of Lead in weight, which cannot be without a Conversion of some body into Lead: but whatsoever is of this kind, and well expressed, is diligently to be inquired, and set down.

Doctor Meverel's Answers to the Lord Bacon's Questions, concerning the Variation of Metals and Minerals.

1. For *Tinctures*, there are none that I know, but that rich variety which springs from mixture of Metals with Metals, or imperfect Minerals.

2. The imperfect Metals are subject to *rust*, all of them except Mercury, which is made into Vermilion by Solution, or Calcination. The rest are rusted by any salt, sowr, or acid Water. Lead into a white body called *Cerussa*. Iron into a pale red called *Ferrugo*. Copper is turned into green, named *Ærugo*, *Æs Viride*. Tin into white. But this is not in use, neither hath it obtained a name.

The Scriptures mention the ruft of Gold, but that's in regard of the Allay.

3. *Calcination.* All Metals may be' calcined by ftrong Waters, or by admixtion of Salt, Sulphur, and Mercury. The imperfect Metals may be Calcined by continuance of fimple Fire; Iron thus calcined is called *Crocus Martis.*

And this is their beft way. Gold and Silver are beft calcined by Mercury. Their Colour is Gray. Lead calcined is very Red. Copper, duskie Red.

4. Metals are *sublimed* by joyning them with Mercury, or Salts. As Silver with Mercury, Gold with Sal Armoniac, Mercury with Vitriol.

5. *Precipitation,* is, when any Metal being diffolved into a ftrong Water, is beaten down into a Powder by falt Water. The chiefeft in this kind is Oyl of Tartar.

6. *Amalgamation,* is the joyning, or mixing of Mercury with any other of the Metals. The manner is this, in Gold, the reft are anfwerable: Take fix parts of Mercury, make them hot in a Crufible, and pour them to one part of Gold made red-hot in another Crufible, ftir thefe well together that they may incorporate; which done, caft the Mafs into cold Water and wafh it. This is called the Amalgama of Gold.

7. For

7. For *Vitrification.* All the imperfect Metals may be turned by strong Fire into Glass, except Mercury; Iron into Green; Lead into Yellow; Brass into Blew; Tin into pale Yellow. For Gold and Silver, I have not known them Vitrified, except joyned with Antimony. These Glassie bodies may be reduced into the form of Mineral bodies.

8. *Dissolution.* All Metals, without exception, may be dissolved.

1. Iron may be dissolved by any tart, salt, or vitriolated Water, yea, by common Water, if it be first calcined with Sulphur. It dissolves in *Aqua forti* with great ebullition and heat, into a red Liquor, so red as Blood.

2. Lead is fittiest dissolved in Vinegar, into a pale Yellow, making the Vinegar very sweet.

3. Tin is best dissolved with distilled Salt-water. It retains the colour of the *Menstruum.*

4. Copper dissolves as Iron doth, in the same Liquor, into a Blew.

5. Silver hath his proper *Menstruum,* which is *Aqua fortis.* The colour is Green, with great heat and ebullition.

6. Gold is dissolved with *Aqua Regia,* into a yellow Liquor, with little heat or ebullition. 7. Mercury

7. Mercury is diffolved with much heat and boyling, into the fame Liquors which Gold and Silver are. It alters not the colour of the *Menstruum*.

Note. Strong Waters may be charged with half their weight of fixed Metals, and equal of Mercury; if the Workman be skilful.

9. *Sprouting.* This is an accident of diffolution. For if the *Menstruum* be overcharged, then within fhort time the Metals will fhoot into certain Cryftals.

10. For *Induration*, or *Mollification*, they depend upon the quantity of fixed Mercury and Sulphur. I have obferved little of them, neither of Toughnefs nor Bitternefs.

11. The *degrees of Fixation* and *Volatility* I acknowledg, except the two utmoft, which never were obferved.

12. The Queftion of *Tranfmutation* is very doubtful. Wherefore I refer *your Honour* to the fourth Tome of *Theatrum Chymicum:* and there, to that Tract which is entituled *Difquifitio Heliana*; where you fhall find full fatisfaction.

The

The Lord Bacon's *Inquiries concerning Metals and Minerals. The fourth Letter of the* Cross-Row, *touching Restitution.*

First, Therefore it is to be inquired in the Negative, what Bodies will never return, either by their extreme Fixings; as in some Vitrifications, or by extreme Volatility.

It is also to be inquired of the two means of Reduction; and first by the Fire, which is but by congregation of Homogenial parts.

The second is, by drawing them down by some Body that hath consent with them. As Iron draweth down Copper in Water; Gold draweth Quick-Silver in vapour; whatsoever is of this kind, is very diligently to be inquired.

Also it is to be inquired what time, or age, will reduce without help of fire, or body.

Also it is to be inquired what gives impediment to Union, or Restitution, which is sometimes called Mortification; as when Quick-

Quick-Silver is mortified with Turpentine, Spittle, or Butter.

Lastly, It is to be inquired how the Metal restored, differeth in any thing from the Metal rare; as whether it become not more churlish, altered in colour, or the like.

Doctor Meverel's *Answers touching the Restitutions of* Metals *and* Minerals.

Reduction is chiefly effected by Fire, wherein if they stand and nele, the imperfect Metals vapour away, and so do all manner of Salts which separated them in *minimas partes* before.

Reduction is singularly holpen by joyning store of Metal of the same nature with it in the melting.

Metals reduced are somewhat churlish, but not altered in colour.

The Lord Verulam's Inquisition *concerning the Versions, Transmutations, Multiplications, and Effections of Bodies, written by him originally in English, but not hitherto published in that Language.*

EArth by Fire is turned into Brick, which is of the nature of a Stone, and serveth for Building as Stone doth: And the like of Tile.

Naphtha, which was the Bituminous Mortar, used in the Walls of *Babylon*, grows to an entire and very hard Matter like a Stone.

In Clay Countries, where there is Pebble and Gravel, you shall find great Stones, where you may see the Pebbles, or Gravel, and between them a Substance of Stone as hard, or harder than the Pebble it self.

There are some Springs of Water, wherein if you put Wood, it will turn into the nature of Stone: So as that within the Water shall be Stone, and that above the Water continue Wood.

K   The

The slime about the Reins and Bladder in Man's Body, turns into Stone: And Stone is likewise found often in the Gall; and sometimes, though rarely, in *Venâ Portâ*.

Quere what time the substance of Earth in Quarries, asketh to be turned into Stone?

Water, as it seems, turneth into Crystal, as is seen in divers Caves, where the Crystal hangs in *Stillicidiis*.

Try Wood, or the Stalk of Herbs, buried in Quicksilver, whether it will not grow hard and stony?

They speak of a Stone engendred in a Toad's head.

There was a Gentleman, digging in his Moat, found an Egg turned into Stone, the White and the Yolk keeping their Colour, and the Shell glistring, like a Stone cut with corners.

Try somethings put into the bottom of a Well; As Wood, or some soft Substance: but let it not touch the Water, because it may not putrify.

They speak, that the White of an Egg, with lying long in the Sun will turn Stone.

Mud in Water turns into shells of Fishes, as in Horse-Muscles, in fresh Ponds, old and

and overgrown. And the substance is a wondrous fine substance, light and shining.

A Speech touching the recovering of *Drowned Mineral Works*, prepared for the Parliament (as Mr. *Bushel* affirmed) by the Viscount of St. *Albans*, then Lord High Chancellor of *England*. (*a*)

(*a*) See Mr. Bee's *Extract.* p. 18, 19.

My Lords and Gentlemen,

THe King, *my Royal Master, was lately (graciously) pleased to move some Discourse to me concerning Mr.* Sutton's Hospital, *and such like worthy* Foundations *of memorable Piety: Which humbly seconded by my self, drew his Majesty into a serious consideration of the Mineral Treasures of his own Territories, and the practical discoveries of them by way of my Philosophical Theory: Which he then so well resented, that, afterwards, upon a mature digestion of my whole Design, he commanded me to let your Lordships understand, how great an inclination He hath to further so hopeful a Work, for the* Honour

The Lord Bacon's

Honour of his Dominions, as the most probable means to relieve all the Poor thereof without any other Stock or Benevolence, than that which Divine Bounty should confer on their own Industries and honest Labours, in recovering all such Drowned Mineral Works *as have been, or shall be,* therefore, *deserted.*

And, my Lords, All that is now desired of his Majesty and your Lordships, is no more than a gracious Act *of this present* Parliament *to authorize* Them *herein, adding a Mercy to a Munificence, which is, the Persons of such strong and able Petty-Felons, who, in true penitence for their Crimes, shall implore his Majesty's Mercy and Permission to expiate their Offences by their Assiduous Labours, in so innocent and hopeful a Work.*

For, by this unchangeable way (my Lords) have I proposed to erect the Academical Fabric of this Island's Salomon's House, modelled in my New Atlantis. *And I can hope (my Lords) that my Midnight Studies to make our Countries flourish and outvy European Neighbours in mysterious and beneficent Arts, have not so ingratefully affected the whole Intellects, that you will delay or resist his Majesty's desires, and my humble Petition in this Benevolent, yea, Magnificent Affair; Since your Honourable Posterities may be inriched*

riched thereby, *and my Ends are only, to make the World my Heir, and the learned Fathers of my* Salomon's House, *the successive and sworn Trustees in the dispensation of this great Service, for God's Glory, my Prince's Magnificence, this Parliaments Honour, our Countries general Good, and the propagation of my own Memory.*

And I may assure your Lordships, that all my Proposals in order to this great Architype, seemed so rational and feasable to my Royal Soveraign, our Christian Salomon, *that I, thereby, prevailed with his Majesty to call this Honourable Parliament, to Confirm and Impower me in my own way of Mining, by an Act of the same, after his Majesty's more weighty Affairs were considered in your Wisdoms; both which he desires your* Lordships, *and you* Gentlemen *that are chosen as the Patriots of your respective Countries, to take speedy care of: Which done, I shall not then doubt the happy Issue of my Undertakings in this Design, whereby concealed Treasures, which now seem utterly lost to Mankind, shall be confined to so universal a Piety, and brought into use by the industry of Converted Penitents, whose wretched Carcases the Impartial Laws have, or shall dedicate, as untimely Feasts, to the Worms of the Earth, in whose Womb those deserted mineral riches must ever*

K 3 *lie*

lie buried as lost *Abortments*, unless those be made the active Midwives to deliver them. For, my Lords, I humbly conceive Them to be the fittest of all Men to effect this great Work, for the Ends and Causes which I have before expressed.

All which, my Lords, I humbly refer to your Grave and Solid Judgments to conclude of, together with such other *Assistances* to this *Frame*, as your own Oraculous Wisdom shall intimate for the *Magnifying* our Creator, in his inscrutable Providence, and admirable Works of Nature.

Certain Experiments made, by the Lord Bacon, about Weight *in* Air *and* Water.

A New Soveraign of equal Weight in the Air to the piece in Brass, overweigheth in the Water 9 Grains. In three Soveraigns the difference in the Water is but 24 Grains.

The same Soveraign overweigheth an equal weight of Lead, 4 Grains in the Water, in Brass Grains for Gold. In three Soveraigns about 11 Grains.

The same Soveraign overweigheth an equal

qual weight of Stones in the Air, at least 65 Grains in the Water. The Grains being for the weight of Gold, in Brass Metal.

A Glass filled with Water weighing, in Troy Weights, 13 ounces and 5 drams, the Glass and the Water together, weigheth severally, *viz.* The Water 9 ounces and a half, and the Glass 4 ounces and a dram.

A Bladder weighing 2 ounces 7 drams and a half, a Pebble layed upon the top of the Bladder makes 3 ounces 6 drams and a half, the Stone weigheth 7 drams.

The Bladder (as above) blown, and the same fallen, weigheth equal.

A Spunge dry weigheth 1 ounce, 26 grains: The same Spunge being wet, weigheth 14 ounces, 6 drams, and 3 quarters: the Water weigheth in several 11 ounces, one dram, and a half; and the Spunge 3 ounces, and a half, and 3 quarters of a dram. *First Time.*

The Spunge and Water together weigh 15 ounces, and 7 drams: in several the Water weigheth 11 ounces, and 7 drams, and the Spunge 3 ounces, 7 drams and a half. *Second Time.*

Three Soveraigns made equal to a weight in Silver in the Air, differeth in the Water.

K 4   For

For false Weights, one Beam long, the other thick.

The Stick and Thread weigh half a dram, and 20 grains, being laid in the Ballance.

The Stick tied to reach within half an inch of the end of the Beam, and so much from the Tongue, weigheth 28 grains; the difference is 22 grains.

The same Stick being tied to hang over the end of the Beam an inch and a half, weigheth half a dram, and 24 grains; exceeding the weight of the said Stick in the Ballance by 4 grains.

The same Stick being hanged down beneath the Thread as near the Tongue as is possible, weigheth only 8 grains.

Two weights of Gold being made equal in the Air, and weighing severally 7 drams; the one Ballance being put into the Water, and the other hanging in the Air, the Ballance in the Water weigheth only 5 drams and 3 grains, and abateth of the weight in the Air 1 dram, and a half, and 27 grains.

The same trial being made the second time, and more truly and exactly betwixt Gold and Gold, weighing severally (as above) and making a just and equal weight in the Air, the one Ballance being put into to the Water, the depth of five inches, and the other hanging in the Air, the Ballance in the Water weigheth only 4 drams, and 55 grains, and abateth of the weight in the Air 2 drams, and 5 grains.

The trial being made betwixt Lead and Lead, weighing severally 7 drams in the Air, the Ballance in the Water weigheth only 4 drams, and 41 grains, and abateth of the weight in the Air 2 drams and 19 grains; the Ballance kept the same depth in the Water, as abovesaid.

The trial being made betwixt Silver and Silver, weighing severally 7 drams in the Air, the Ballance in the Water weigheth only 4 drams, and 25 grains. So it abateth 2 drams, and 35 grains; the same depth in the Water observed.

In Iron and Iron, weighing severally each Ballance, in the Air 7 drams, the Ballance in the Water weigheth only 4 drams and 18 grains; and abateth of the weight in the Air 2 drams, and 42 grains; the depth observe as above.

In Stone and Stone, the same weight of 7 drams, equally in the Air, the Ballance in the Water weigheth only 2 drams, and 22 grains, and abateth of the weight in the Air 4 drams, and 38 grains; the depth as above.

In

In Brass and Brass, the same weight of 7 drams, in each Ballance, equal in the Air, the Ballance in the Water weigheth only 4 drams, and 22 grains, and abateth in the Water 2 drams, and 38 grains; the depth observed.

The two Ballances being weighed in Air and Water, the Ballance in the Air overweigheth the other in the Water one dram, and 28 grains; the depth in the Water as aforesaid.

It is a profitable *Experiment* which sheweth the weights of several Bodies in comparison with Water. It is of use in lading of Ships, and other Bottoms, and may help to shew what Burthen, in the several kinds, they will bear.

Certain sudden Thoughts of the Lord Bacon's, set down, by him, under the Title of Experiments for Profit.

Muck of Leaves.
Muck of River, Earth, and Chalk.
Muck of Earth closed, both for Salt-Peter and Muck.
Setting of Wheat and Pease.
                              Mending

Mending of Crops by steeping of Seeds.
Making Pease, Cherries, and Strawberries come early.
Strengthening of Earth for often returns of Radishes, Parsnips, Turnips, &c.
Making great Roots of Onions, Radishes, and other Esculent roots.
Sowing of Seeds of Trefoil.
Setting of Woad.
Setting of Tobacco, and taking away the rawness.
Grafting upon Boughs of old Trees.
Making of a hasty Coppice.
Planting of Osiers in wet Grounds.
Making of Candles to last long.
Building of Chimneys, Furnaces, and Ovens, to give Heat with less Wood.
Fixing of Log-Wood.
Other means to make Yellow and Green fixed.
Conserving of Orenges, Limons, Citrons, Pomgranats, &c. all Summer.
Recovering of Pearl, Coral, Turchoise, Colour, by a Conservatory of Snow.
Sowing of Fennel.
Brewing with Hay, Haws, Trefoil, Broom, Heps, Bramble-Berries, Woodbines, wild Thime, instead of Hops, Thistles.
Multiplying and Dressing Artichokes.

Certain

Certain Experiments, *of the Lord* Bacon's, *about the* Commixture of Liquors *only,* not Solids, *without Heat or Agitation, but only by* simple Composition, *and Settling.*

Spirit of Wine mingled with common Water, although it be much lighter than Oyl, yet so, as if the first fall be broken, by means of a Sop, or otherwise, it stayeth above; and, if it be once mingled, it severeth not again, as Oyl doth. Tried with Water coloured with Saffron.

Spirit of Wine, mingled with common Water, hath a kind of clouding, and motion shewing no ready Commixture. Tried with Saffron.

A dram of Gold dissolved in *Aqua Regis*, with a dram of Copper in *Aqua forti* commixed, gave a Green Colour, but no visible motion in the parts. Note, That the dissolution of the Gold, was twelve parts Water, to one part Body: And of the Copper was six parts Water, to one part Body.

Oyl of Almonds commixed with Spirit of Wine, severeth, and the Spirit of Wine remaineth on the top, and the Oyl in the bottom.

Gold dissolved commixed with Spirit of Wine, a dram of each, doth commix, and no other apparent alteration.

Quick-silver dissolved with Gold dissolved, a dram of each, doth turn to a mouldy Liquor, black, and like Smith's water.

Note, The dissolution of the Gold was twelve parts Water, *ut supra*, and one part Metal: That of Water was two parts, and one part Metal.

Spirit of Wine, and Quick-silver commixed, a dram of each, at the first shewed a white Milky substance at the top, but soon after mingled.

Oyl of Vitriol commixed with Oyl of Cloves, a dram of each, turneth into a red dark Colour; and a substance thick, almost like Pitch: And upon the first motion gathereth an extream Heat, not to be endured by touch.

Dissolution of Gold, and Oyl of Vitriol commixed, a dram of each, gathereth a great Heat at the first, and darkneth the Gold, and maketh a thick Yellow.

Spirit of Wine, and Oyl of Vitriol, a dram of each, hardly mingle; the Oyl of Vitrriol going to the bottom, and the Spirit of Wine lying above in a Milky substance. It gathereth also a great Heat, and a sweetness in the Taste.

Oyl of Vitriol and dissolution of Quick-silver, a dram of each, maketh an extream strife, and casteth up a very gross fume, and after casteth down a white kind of Curds, or Sands; and on the top a slimish substance, and gathereth a great Heat.

Oyl of Sulphur, and Oyl of Cloves commixed, a dram of each, turn into a thick and red-coloured substance; but no such Heat, as appeared in the Commixture with the Oyl of Vitriol.

Oyl of Petroleum, and Spirit of Wine, a dram of each, intermingle otherwise than by Agitation, as Wine and Water do; and the Petroleum remaineth on the top.

Oyl of Vitriol, and Petroleum, a dram of each, turn into a mouldy Substance, and gathereth some warmth; there residing a black cloud in the bottom, and a monstrous thick Oyl on the top.

Spirit of Wine, and Red-wine Vinegar, one ounce of each, at the first fall, one of them remaineth above, but by Agitation they mingle.

Oyl of Vitriol, and Oyl of Almonds, one ounce of each, mingle not; but the
Oyl

Oyl of Almonds remaineth above.

Spirit of Wine, and Vinegar, an ounce of each, commixed, do mingle, without any apparent separation, which might be in respect of the Colour.

Dissolution of Iron, and Oyl of Vitriol, a dram of each, do first put a Milky substance into the bottom; and after incorporate into a mouldy Substance.

Spirit of Wine commixed with Milk, a third part Spirit of Wine, and two parts Milk, coagulateth little, but mingleth; and the Spirit swims not above.

Milk and Oyl of Almonds mingled, in equal portions, do hardly incorporate, but the Oyl cometh above, the Milk being poured in last; and the Milk appeareth in some drops, or bubbles.

Milk one ounce, Oyl of Vitriol a scruple, doth coagulate; the Milk at the bottom where the Vitriol goeth.

Dissolution of Gum *Tragacanth*, and Oyl of Sweet Almonds, do not commingle, the Oyl remaining on the top, till they be stirred, and make the Muselates somewhat more liquid.

Dissolution of Gum *Tragacanth*, one ounce and a half, with half an ounce of Spirit of Wine, being commixed by Agitation, make the Muselates more thick.

The

The White of an Egg with Spirit of Wine, doth bake the Egg into Clots, as if it began to Poch.

One ounce of Blood, one ounce of Milk, do easily incorporate.

Spirit of Wine doth curdle the Blood.

One ounce of Whey unclarified, one ounce of Oyl of Vitriol, make no apparent alteration.

One ounce of Blood, one ounce of Oyl of Almonds, incorporate not, but the Oyl swims above.

Three quarters of an ounce of Wax, being dissolved upon the Fire, and one ounce of Oyl of Almonds put together and stirred, do not so incorporate, but that when it is cold, the Wax gathereth and swims upon the top of the Oyl.

One ounce of Oyl of Almonds, cast into an ounce of Sugar seething, sever presently, the Sugar shooting towards the bottom.

A Catalogue of Bodies, *Attractive*, and not *Attractive*, made by the Lord *Bacon*, together with Experimental Observations about *Attraction*.

These following Bodies, *Draw*.

Amber, *Jeat*, *Diamond*, *Saphire*, *Carbuncle*, *Iris*, the *Gem*. *Opale*, *Amethist*, *Bristollina*, *Crystal*, *Clear Glass*, *Glass* of *Antimony*, divers *Flowers from Mines*, *Sulphur*, *Mastick*, *hard sealing Wax*, the harder *Rosin*, *Arsenic*.

These following Bodies, *do not Draw*.

Smaragd, *Achates*, *Corneolus*, *Pearl*, *Jaspis*, *Chalcedononius*, *Alablaster*, *Porphyric*, *Coral*, *Marble*, *Touch-Stone*, *Hæmatites*, or *Blood-stone*, *Smyris*, *Ivory*, *Bones*, *Eben-Tree*, *Cedar*, *Cypress*, *Pitch*, *softer Rosin*, *Camphire*, *Galbanum*, *Ammoniac*, *Storax*, *Benjoin*, *Load-stone*, * *Asphaltum*.

* The drawing of Iron excepted.

These Bodies, *Gold*, *Silver*, *Brass*, *Iron*, draw not, though never so finely polished.

In *Winter,* if the Air be sharp and clear, *Sal Gemmeum,* Rock *Alum,* and *Lapis Specularis* will draw.

These following Bodies are apt *to be Drawn,* if the Mass of them be small.

Chaff, Woods, Leaves, Stones, all Metals hewed, and in the Mine; Earth, Water, Oyl.

Si fiat versorium *ex* Metallo *aliquo, more Indicis* Magnetici, *& fini alteri apponatur succinum, leniter fricatum, versorium convertit se.*

Succinum calefactum *ab* Igne, *sive tepeat, sive ferveat, sive inflammetur, non trahit.*

Bacillum ferreum candens, Flamma, Candela ardens, Carbo ignitus, *admota festucis aut versoriis, non trahunt.*

Succinum *in majore mole, si fuerit politum, allicit, licèt non fricatum; si in minore, aut impurius, sine frictione non trahit.*

Crystallus, Lapis Specularis, Vitrum, Electrica cetera, *si urantur, aut torreantur, non trahunt.*

Pix

Pix.
Refina mollior.
Benjoin.
Afphaltum.   *Hæc cœlo calidiore*
Camphora.   *neutiquam prorſus tra-*
Galbanum.   *hunt; at tempore frigi-*
Ammoniacum.   *diore obſcurè & infirmè*
Storax.   *trahunt.*
Aſſa.

Vapidus **Aer** *ſuccino, &c. afflatus, vel ab ore, vel ab Aere humidiore, virtutem trahendi ſuffocat.*

Si charta *aut* linteum *interponatur inter ſuccinum & paleam, non fit motus aut At-tractio.*

Succinum *aut Electrica calefacta ex Radiis Solis, non expergefiunt ad trahendum, ſicut ex Frictione.*

Succinum *fricatum, & Radiis Solis expoſitum diutius vires trahendi retinet, nec tam citò eas deponit ac ſi in umbra poſitum eſſet.*

Fervor ex ſpeculo comburente *ſuccino, &c. conciliatus, non juvat ad trahendum.*

Sulphur accenſum, *& Cera dura inflammata, non trahunt.*

Succinum *cum citiſſimè à frictione, feſtucæ vel verſorio apponitur, optimè trahit.*

Virtus Electrica viget in retentione ad tem-
pus

pus, non minus quam in Attractione primâ.

Flamma *apposito succino intra orbem Activitatis non trahitur.*

Gutta Aquæ *admoto succino trahitur in* Conum. Electrica, *si durius affricentur, impeditur Attractio.*

Quæ ægrè alliciunt in claro cœlo, in crasso non movent.

Aqua imposita succino *virtutem trahendi suffocat, licet ipsum Aquam trahat.*

Sarca ità succino *circundatum, ut tangat, attractione tollit; sed interpositum ut non tangat, non omnino tollit.*

Oleum *succino appositum motum non impedit; nec succinum digito oleo madefacto fricatum, vires trahendi perdit.*

Firmius provocant, & diutius retinent Succinum, Gagates, *& hujusmodi, etiam minore cum frictione: Adamas Cryftallum,* Vitrum, *diutius teri debent, ut manifestò incalescant antequàm trahant.*

Quæ Flammæ approximant, licèt propinquâ distantiâ, à succino non trahuntur.

Fumum extincta lucerna *succinum,* &c. trahit. *Fumus ubi exit & crassus est, fortius trahit succinum; cum ascenderit, & rarior fit, debilius. Corpus ab Electricis attractum non manifestò alteratur, set tantùm incumbit.*

The

The same in English *by the Publisher.*

IF there be made a Turn-Pin of any Metal, after the fashion of a Magnetic Needle, and Amber be applied to one end of it, after having been gently rubbed, the Pin will turn.

Amber heated by the Fire, be it warmish, hot, or set on fire, it does not draw.

A little *Bar of Iron red hot, Flame, a lighted Candle, a hot Coal,* put nigh Sheaves (or Straws) or Turn-Pins (or Compass-Needles) do not draw.

Amber, in a greater Mass, if it be Polite, draws, though not rubbed: In a lesser quantity, and in a less polite Mass, it draws not without rubbing.

Crystal, Lapis Specularis, Glass, and other such Electric Bodies, if burnt, or scorch'd, draw not.

Pitch, the softer Rosin, Benjoin, Asphaltum, Camphire, Galbanum, Ammoniac, Storax, Assa, these draw not at all when the Air is hot: But when it is cooler, they draw weakly, and so that we can just perceive them to do so.

Reaking Air, blown upon Amber, &c.

from the Mouth, or from a moister Atmosphere; choaketh the attractive Virtue.

If a *Paper*, or *a piece of Linnen*, be put between *Amber* and *Chaff*, there is no Motion, or Attraction made.

Amber, or other Electrics, warmed *by the Sun-beams*, have not their attractive Virtue so awakened, *as by Rubbing*.

Amber rubb'd, and exposed to the Beams of the Sun, retains its attractive force the longer; and does not so soon lose it, as it would do in the shadow.

Heat deriv'd from a *Burning-Glass* to Amber, *&c.* does not help its Attraction.

Sulphur, and hard Wax, set on fire, do not draw.

Amber, when immediately after rubbing, it is applied to *a Shiver*, or a *Compass-Needle*, draws best of all.

The Electric Virtue is as vigorous, for a time, in its *Retention*, as it was in its first *Attraction*.

Flame (*Amber* being put within the sphere of its Activity) is not drawn by it.

A *drop of Water*, *Amber* being applied towards it, is drawn into a *Cone*.

If Electric Bodies be rubbed too hard, their attraction is, thereby, hindred.

Those Bodies, which in a clear Skie do scarce draw, in a thick Air move not at all.

Water

Water put upon *Amber* choaketh its attractive force, though it draweth the Water it self.

Fat * so encompassing *Amber*, that it toucheth it, takes away its attraction; but being so put betwixt it and the Object to be drawn, as not to touch it, it doth not take it away.

* For by *Sarca*, I suppose, he meaneth *Sarcia*.

Oyl put upon *Amber*, hinders not its motion: Neither doth *Amber*, rubb'd with the Finger moistned with Oyl, lose its attractive Virtue.

Amber, *Jeats*, *and the like*, do more strongly excite, and longer retain the Objects they draw, although the rubbing be but little. But *Diamonds, Crystal, Glass*, ought to be rubb'd longer, that they may appear hot, ere they be used for attraction.

Flames nigh to *Amber*, though the distance be very small, are not drawn by it.

Amber, &c. draw the *smoke of a Lamp* newly extinguish'd.

Amber draws Smoke *more strongly* when it comes forth, and is *more gross*; and *more weakly*, when it ascends and becomes *thinner*.

A Body drawn by Electric Bodies, is not manifestly alter'd, but only leans it self upon them.

Baconiana

Baconiana Medica.

OR,

REMAINS

OF

Sir Francis Bacon,

Baron of *Verulam*, and Viscount St. *Albans*;

Touching

Medical Matters.

LONDON,

Printed for R. C. at the Rose and Crown in St. *Paul's* Church-yard. 1679.

THE
Lord Bacon's
Medical Remains.

A Medical Paper of the Lord Bacon's, *to which he gave the Title of* Grains of Youth.

Grains of Youth.

TAke of Nitre 4 grains, of Amber-Greaſe 3 grains, of Orris-pouder 2 grains, of white Poppy-Seed the fourth part of a grain, of Saffron half a grain, with Water of Orenge Flowers, and a little Tragacanth ; make them into ſmall grains, four in number. To be taken at four a Clock, or going to Bed.

Preserving Oyntments

Take of Deers-suet 1 ounce, of Myrrh 6 grains, of Saffron 5 grains, of Bay-salt 12 grains, of Canary-Wine of two Years old, a Spoonful and a half:
Spread it on the inside of your Shirt, and let it dry, and then put it on.

A Purge familiar for opening the Liver.

Take Rubarb 2 drams, Agaric, Trochiscat 1 dram and a half, steep them in Claret Wine burnt with Mace: Take of Wormwood 1 dram, steep it with the rest, and make a mass of Pills, with *Syrup. Acetos. simplex.*
But drink an opening Broth before it, with Succory, Fennel, and Smallage Roots, and a little of an Onion.

Wine for the Spirits.

Take Gold perfectly refined 3 ounces, quench it six or seven times in good Claret Wine: Add of Nitre 6 grains, for two Draughts. Add of Saffron prepared 3 grains, of Amber-grease 4 grains, pass it through an Hippocras Bag, wherein there
is

is a dram of Cinamon groſs beaten, or to avoid the dimming of the Colour, of Ginger. Take two Spoonfuls of this to a Draught of freſh Claret Wine.

The Preparing of Saffron.

Take 6 grains of Saffron, ſteept in half parts of Wine and Roſe-water, and a quarter part Vinegar; then dry it in the Sun.

Wine againſt Adverſe Melancholy, preſerving the Senſes and the Reaſon.

Take the Roots of Bugloſs, well ſcraped, and cleanſed from their inner Pith, and cut them into ſmall ſlices; ſteep them in Wine of Gold extinguiſhed *ut ſuprà*, and add of Nitre 3 grains, and drink it *ut ſuprà*, mixed with freſh Wine: The Roots muſt not continue ſteeped above a quarter of an Hour; and they muſt be changed thrice.

Breakfaſt-Preſervative againſt the Gout and Rheumes.

To take once in the Month at leaſt, and for two Days together, one grain of *Caſtorei*, in my ordinary Broth.

The Preparation of Garlick.

Take Garlick 4 ounces, boyl it upon a soft Fire, in Claret Wine, for half an Hour. Take it out, and steep it in Vinegar; whereto add 2 drams of Cloves, then take it forth, and keep it in a Glass for use.

The Artificial Preparation of Damask-Roses, for Smell.

Take Roses, pull their Leaves, then dry them in a clear Day, in the hot Sun; then their smell will be as gone. Then cram them into an Earthen Bottle, very dry and sweet, and stop it very close; they will remain in Smell and Colour both fresher, than those that are otherwise dried. Note, The first drying, and close keeping upon it, preventeth all Putrefaction, and the second Spirit cometh forth, made of the remaining Moisture not dissipated.

Sometimes to add to the Maceration, 3 grains of Tartar, and 2 of Enula, to cut the more heavy and viscous Humours; lest Rubarb work only upon the lightest.

To take sometimes the Oxymel before it, and sometimes the Spanish Hony simple.

A Restorative Drink.

Take of *Indian Maiz* half a pound, grind it not too small, but to the fineness of ordinary Meal, and then bolt and ferce it, that all the husky part may be taken away. Take of Eringium Roots 3 ounces, of Dates as much, of Enula 2 drams, of Mace 3 drams, and brew them with Ten-shilling Beer, to the quantity of four Gallons: And this do, either by decocting them in a Pottle of Wort, to be after mingled with the Beer, being new tapped, or otherwise infuse it in the New Beer in a Bag.

Use this familiarly at Meals.

Against the waste of the Body by Heat.

Take sweet Pomgranates, and strain them lightly, not pressing the Kernel, into a Glass; where put some little of the Peel of a Citron, and two or three Cloves, and three grains of Amber-grease, and a pretty deal of fine Sugar. It is to be drunk every Morning whilst Pomgranates last.

Methusalem

Methusalem Water.

Against all Asperity and Torrefaction of Inward parts, and all Adustion of the Blood, and generally against the Driness of Age.

Take Crevises very new, *q. s.* boyl them well in Claret Wine; of them take only the shells, and rub them very clean, especially on the inside, that they may be throughly cleansed from the Meat. Then wash them three or four times in fresh Claret Wine, heated, still changing the Wine, till all the Fish-taste be quite taken away. But in the Wine wherein they are washed, steep some tops of green Rosemary; then dry the pure shell throughly, and bring them to an exquisite Pouder. Of this Pouder take 3 drams. Take also Pearl, and steep them in Vinegar twelve Hours, and dry off the Vinegar; of this Pouder also 3 drams. Then put the Shell Pouder, and Pearl Pouder together, and add to them of Ginger one scruple, and of white Poppy Seed half a scruple, and steep them in Spirit of Wine (wherein six grains of Saffron hath been dissolved) seven Hours. Then upon a gentle heat, vapour away all the he Spirit of Wine, and dry the Pouder against the Sun without Fire. Add to it of Nitre one dram, of Amber-greafe one scruple and a half; and so keep this Pouder for use, in a clean Glass. Then take a Pottle of Milk, and slice in it of fresh Cucumers, the inner Pith only (the Rind being pared off) four ounces, and draw forth a Water by Distillation. Take of Claret Wine a Pint, and quench Gold in it four times.

Of the Wine, and of the water of Milk, take of each three ounces, of the Pouder one scruple, and drink it in the Morning; stir up the Pouder when you drink, and walk upon it.

A Catalogue *of* Astringents, Openers, *and* Cordials, *instrumental to Health. Collected by* Sir Francis Bacon, *Baron of* Verulam.

Astringents.

RED Rose, Blackberry, Myrtle, Plantane, Flower of Pomegranate, Mint, Aloes well washed, Mirabolanes, Sloes, Agresta,

Agresta, Fraga, Mastich, Myrrh, Saffron, Leaves of Rosemary, Rubarb received by Infusion, Cloves, Service-Berries, Corna, Wormwood, Bole Armeniac, Sealed Earth, Cinque-foil, Tincture of Steel, *Sanguis Draconis*, Coral, Amber, Quinces, Spikenard, Galls, Allum, Bloodstone, Mummy, Amomum, Galangal, Cypress, Ivy, Psyllum, Houseleek, Sallow, Mulleni, Vine, Oak-leaves, Lign-Aloes, Red Sanders, Mulberrie, Medlers, Flowers of Peach-Trees, Pomegranates, Pears, Palmule, Pith of Kernels, Purslain, Acacia, *Laudanum, Tragacanth, Thus Olibani,* Comfrey, Shepherds-purse, *Polygonium.*

Astringents (both hot and cold) which corroborate the Parts, and which confirm, and refresh such of them as are loose, or languishing.

Rosemary, Mint, especially with Vinegar, Cloves, Cinamon, Cardamom, Lign-Aloes, Rose, Myrtle, Red Sanders, Cotonea, Red-Wine, Chalybeat-Wine, Five-finger-Grass, Plantane, Apples of Cypress, Barberries, Fraga, Service-Berries, Corneille's, Ribes, Sowr-Pears, Rambesia.

Astrin-

Aſtringents Styptic, *which, by their* Styptic Virtue, *may ſtay* Fluxes.

Sloes, Acacia, Rind of Pomegranates infuſed, at leaſt three Hours, the Styptic Virtue not coming forth in leſſer time. *Alum, Galls, Juice of Sallow, Syrup of unripe Quinces, Balauſtia, the Whites of Eggs* boyled hard in Vinegar.

Aſtringents *which, by their* cold *and* earthy Nature, *may ſtay the motion of the Humours tending to a Flux.*

Sealed Earth, Sanguis Draconis, Coral, Pearls, the *ſhell* of the Fiſh *Dactylus.*

Aſtringents *which, by the* thickneſs *of their ſubſtance,* ſtuff *as it were the* thin Humours, *and thereby ſtay* Fluxes.

Rice, Beans, Millet, *Cauls,* dry *Cheeſe,* freſh *Goats-Milk.*

Aſtringents *which, by virtue of their* Glutinous ſubſtance, *reſtrain a* Flux, *and ſtrengthen the* looſer Parts.

Karabe *, *Maſtich, Spodium, Harts-horn,* Frank-

* Perhaps he meant the fruit of *Ka ole.*

Frankincense, dried *Bulls Pistle*, *Gum Tragacanth*.

Astringents Purgative, *which, having by their purgative, or expulsive Power, thrust out the Humours, leave behind them of Astrictive Virtue.*

Rubarb, especially that which is tosted against the Fire; Mirabolanes, Tartar, Tamarinds, [an *Indian* Fruit like Green Damasens].

Astringents *which do very much suck and dry up the Humours, and thereby stay Fluxes.*

Rust of Iron, *Crocus Martis*, Ashes of Spices.

Astringents, *which by their Nature, do dull the Spirits, and lay asleep the Expulsive virtue, and take away the acrimony of all Humours.*

Laudanum, *Mithridate*; *Diascordium*, *Diacodium*.

Astringents, *which by cherishing the strength of the parts, do comfort and confirm their Retentive power.*

A Stomacher of Scarlet Cloth.
Whelps, or young healthy Boys, appli- to the Stomach.
Hypocratic Wines, so they be made of austere Materials.

Openers.

Succhory, Endive, Betony, Liverwort, Petroselinum, Smallage, Asparagus, Roots of Grass, Dodder, Tamarisk, Juncus Odoratus, Lacca, Copparus, Wormwood, Chamæpitis, Fumaria, Scurvy-grass, Eringo, Nettle, Ireos, Elder, Hyssop, Aristolochia, Gentian, Costus, Fennel-root, Maidenhair, Harts-tongue, Daffodilly, Asarum, Sarsaparilla, Sassafras, Acorns, Abretonium, Aloes, Agaric, Rubarb infused, Onions, Garlick, Bother, Squilla, Sowbread, Indian Nard, Celtic Nard, Bark of Laurel-Tree, Bitter Almonds, Holy Thistle, Camomile, Gun-powder, Sows (Millipedes)

des) Ammoniac, Man's Urine, Rue, Park-Leaves (Vitex) Centaury, Lupines, Chamædris, Coſtum, Ammeas, Biſtort, Camphire, Daucus Seed, Indian Balſam, Scordium, Sweet Cane, Galingal, Agrimony.

Cordials.

Flowers of Baſil Royal, *Flores Caryophillati*, Flowers of Bugloſs and Borage, Rind of Citron, Orenge-Flowers, Roſemary, and its Flowers, Saffron, Musk, Amber, Folium, [*i. e.* Nardi Folium,] Balm-Gentle, Pimpernel, Gems, Gold, Generous Wines, Fragrant Apples, Roſe, *Roſa Moſchata*, Cloves, Lign-Aloes, Mace, Cinamon, Nutmeg, Cardamom, Galingal, Vinegar, Kermes-berry, *Herba Moſchata*, Betony, White Sanders, Camphire, Flowers of Heliotrope, Penny-royal, Scordium, Opium corrected, White Pepper, Naſturtium, white and red Bean, Caſtum Dulce, Dactylus, Pine, Fig, Egg-ſhell, *Vinum Malvaticum*, Ginger, Kidneys, Oyſters, Creviſes (or River-Crabs) Seed of Nettle, Oyl of Sweet Almonds, *Seſamium Oleum*, Aſparagus, Bulbous Roots, Onions, Garlick, Eruca, Daucus Seed, Eringo, *Siler Mon-*

Montanus, the smell of Musk, *Cynethi Odor*, Caraway Seed, Flower of Pules, Anniseed, Pellitory, anointing of the Testicles with Oyl of Elder, in which Pellitory hath been boyl'd, Cloves with Goats-Milk, Olibanum.

An Extract by the Lord Bacon, for his own use, out of the Book of the Prolongation of Life, together with some new Advices in order to Health.

1. ONce in the Week, or at least in the Fornight, to take the Water of *Mithridate distilled*, with three parts to one, or Strawberry-water to allay it; and some grains of *Nitre* and *Saffron*, in the Morning between sleeps.

2. To continue my Broth with *Nitre*; but to interchange it every other two Days, with the Juyce of Pomgranates expressed, with a little Cloves, and Rind of Citron.

3. To order the taking of the *Maceration*, * as followeth.

To add to the *Maceration*, six grains of *Cremor Tartari*, and as much Enula.

* Viz. Of *Rubarb infused into a draught of white Wine and Beer, mingled together, for the space of half an Hour, once in six or seven Days.* See the Lord *Bacon's* Life by Dr. *Rawley*, towards the end.

To add to the *Oxymel*, some Infusion of Fennel-roots in the Vinegar, and four grains of Angelica-seed, and Juyce of Limons, a third part to the Vinegar.

To take it not so immediately before Supper; and to have the Broath specially made with *Barley*, *Rosemary*, *Thyme*, and *Cresses*.

4. To take once in the Month at least, and for two Days together, a grain and a half of Castor in my Broath, and Breakfast.

5. A Cooling Clyster to be used once a Month, after the working of the Maceration is settled.

> Take of Barley-water, in which the Roots of Bugloss are boyled, three ounces, with two drams of Red-Sanders, and two ounces of Raisins of the Sun, and one ounce of Dactyles, and an ounce and a half of Fat Carycks; let it be strained, and add to it an ounce and a half of Syrup of Violets: Let a Clyster be made.
>
> Let this be taken (with Veal) in the aforesaid Decoction.

6. To take every Morning, the Fume of Lign-Aloes, Rosemary and Bays dried, with Juyce; but once in a Week to add a little Tobacco, without otherwise taking it in a Pipe.

7. To appoint every Day an Hour, *ad Affectus Intentionales & sanos. Qu. de particulari.*

8. To remember Mastichatories for the Mouth.

9. And Orenge-flower Water to be smelt to, or snuffed up.

10. In the third Hour after the Sun is risen, to take in Air from some high and open Place, with a ventilation of *Rosæ Moschatæ,* and fresh Violets; and to stir the Earth, with infusion of Wine and Mint.

11. To use Ale with a little Enula Campana, Carduus, Germander, Sage, Angelica Seed, Cresses of a middle age, to beget a robust heat.

12. Mithridate thrice a Year.

13. A bit of Bread dipt in *Vino Odorato,* with Syrup of dry Roses, and a little Amber, at going to Bed.

14. Never to keep the Body in the same posture above half an Hour at a time.

15. Four Precepts. To break off Custom. To shake off Spirits ill disposed. To meditate on Youth. To do nothing against a Man's Genius.

16. Syrup of Quinces for the Mouth of the Stomach. Enquire concerning other things useful in that kind.

17. To

17. To use once during Supper time, Wine in which Gold is quenched.

18. To use anointing in the Morning lightly with Oyl of Almonds, with Salt and Saffron, and a gentle rubbing.

19. Ale of the second Infusion of the Vine of Oak.

20. Methusalem Water, of Pearls and Shells, of Crabs, and a little Chalk.

21. Ale of Raisins, Dactyles, Potatoes, Pistachios, Hony, Tragacanth, Mastich.

22. Wine with Swines-flesh, or Harts-flesh.

23. To drink the first Cup at Supper hot, and half an Hour before Supper, something hot and Aromatiz'd.

24. Chalybeats, four times a Year.

25. *Pilulæ ex tribus*, once in two Months, but after the Mass has been macerated in Oyl of Almonds.

26. Heroic Desires.

27. Bathing of the Feet once in a Month, with Lie *ex Sale nigro*, Camomile, sweet Marjoram, Fennel, Sage, and a little *Aqua Vitæ*.

28. To provide always an apt Breakfast.

29. To beat the Flesh before Rosting of it.

30. Macerations in Pickles.

31. Agi-

31. Agitation of Beer by Ropes, or in Wheel-Barrows.

32. That Diet is good which makes Lean, and then Renews. Consider of the ways to effect it.

Medical Receipts of the Lord *Bacon*'s.

The First Receipt, or his Lordship's Broath and Fomentation for the Stone.

The Broath.

TAke one dram of Eryngium Roots, cleansed and sliced; and boyl them together with a Chicken. In the end, add of Elder-Flowers, and Marigold-Flowers together, one pugil, of Angelica-Seed half a dram, of Raisins of the Sun stoned fifteen, of Rosemary, Thyme, Mace, together, a little.

In six ounces of this Broath, or thereabouts, let there be dissolved of white *Cremor Tartari* three grains.

Every

Every third or fourth Day, take a small Toast of Manchet, dipped in Oyl of Sweet Almonds new drawn, and sprinkled with a little Loaf-Sugar.

You may make the Broath for two Days, and take the one half every Day.

If you find the Stone to stir, forbear the Toast for a Course or two.

The Intention of this Broath, is, not to Void, but to Undermine the Quarry of the Stones in the Kidneys.

The Fomentation.

Take of Leaves of Violets, Mallows, Pellitory of the Wall, together, one Handful. Of Flowers of Camomile and Mellilot, together one Pugil. The Root of Marsh-Mallows one ounce; of Annis and Fennel-seeds, together one ounce and a half, of Flax-seed two drams. Make a Decoction in Spring-water.

The Second Receipt, shewing the way of making a certain Oyntment, which h s Lordship called, Unguentum Fragrans sive Romanum; *The Fragrant, or Roman Unguent.*

TAke of the Fat of a Deer, half a pound; of Oyl of Sweet Almonds two ounces. Let them be set upon a very gentle Fire, and stirr'd with a stick of Juniper, till they are melted.

Add of

 Root of Flower de Luce poudered, Damask Roses poudered, together, one dram; of Myrrh dissolved in Rosewater, half a dram; of Cloves, half a scruple; of Civet, four grains; of Musk, six grains; of Oyl of Mace expressed, one drop; as much of Rosewater as sufficeth to keep the Unguent from being too thick.

Let all these be put together in a Glass, and set upon the Embers, for the space of an Hour; and stirred with a stick of Juniper.

Note,

Note, That in the Confection of this Oyntment, there was not used above a quarter of a pound, and a tenth part of a quarter of Deers Suet: And that all the Ingredients, except the Oyl of Almonds, were doubled, when the Oyntment was half made, because the Fat things seemed to be too Predominant.

The Third Receipt.

A Manus Christi *for the Stomack.*

TAke of the best Pearls very finely pulveriz'd, one dram; of *Sal Nitre,* one scruple; of Tartar, two Scruples; of Ginger and Gallingal, together, one ounce and a half; of Calamus, Root of Enula Campana, Nutmeg, together, one scruple and a half; of Amber, sixteen grains; of the best Musk, ten grains; with Rose-water, and the finest Sugar, let there be made a *Manus Christi.*

The Fourth Receipt.

A Secret for the Stomack.

Take *Lignum Aloes* in grofs shavings, steep them in Sack, or Alacant, changed twice, half an Hour at a time, till the bitternefs be drawn forth. Then take the Shavings forth and dry them in the fhade, and beat them to an Excellent Pouder. Of that Pouder, with the Syrup of Citrons, make a fmall Pill, to be taken before Supper.

Baconiana Theologica:
OR A FEW
REMAINS
OF THE
Lord Bacon,
Relating To
Divine Matters.

LONDON,
Printed for *R. C.* at the Rose and Crown in St. *Paul's* Church-yard. 1679.

THE Lord Bacon's *Theological Remains.*

The Lord Bacon's Questions about *the Lawfulness of a* War *for the Propagating of* Religion.

Questions wherein I desire Opinion, joyned with Arguments and Authorities.

Whether a War be lawful against Infidels, only for the Propagation of the Christian Faith, without other cause of Hostility?

Whether a War be lawful, to recover to the Church, Countries, which formerly have been

been Christian, though now Alienate, and Christians utterly extirped?

Whether a War be lawful, to free and deliver Christians that yet remain in Servitude, and subjection to Infidels?

Whether a War be lawful in Revenge, or Vindication, of Blasphemy and Reproaches against the Deity and our Saviour? or for the ancient effusion of Christian Blood, and Cruelties upon Christians?

Whether a War be lawful for the Restoring, and purging of the Holy Land, the Sepulchre, and other principal places of Adoration and Devotion?

Whether in the Cases aforesaid, it be not Obligatory to Christian Princes, to make such a War, and not permissive only?

Whether the making of a War against the Infidels, be not first in order of Dignity, and to be preferr'd before extirpations of Heresies, reconcilements of Schisms, reformation of Manners, pursuits of just Temporal Quarrels, and the like Actions for the Publick Good, except there be either a more urgent Necessity, or a more evident Facility in those Inferior Actions, or except they may both go on together in some Degree?

Two

Two Prayers compos'd by Sir Francis Bacon, Baron of Verulam, and Viscount of St. Albans.

The First Prayer, called by his Lordship, The Student's Prayer.

TO God the Father, God the Word, God the Spirit, we pour forth most humble and hearty Supplications; that He, remembring the Calamities of Mankind, and the Pilgrimage of this our Life, in which we wear out Days few and evil; would please to open to us new Refreshments out of the Fountains of his Goodness, for the alleviating of our Miseries. This also, we humbly and earnestly beg, that *Humane* things, may not prejudice such as are *Divine*; neither that from the unlocking of the Gates of Sense, and the kindling of a greater Natural Light, any thing of Incredulity, or Intellectual Night, may arise in our Minds towards Divine Mysteries. But rather that by our Mind, throughly cleansed and purged from Phancy and Vanities; and yet subject, and perfectly given up to the *Divine Oracles*, there may be *given unto Faith, the things that are Faith's.* Amen.

The Second Prayer, called by his Lordship, The Writer's Prayer.

THou, O Father! who gavest the *Visible Light* as the First-born of thy Creatures, and didst pour into Man the *Intellectual Light*, as the top and consummation of thy Workmanship; be pleased to protect and govern this Work, which, coming from thy *Goodness*, returneth to thy *Glory*. Thou, after Thou hadst review'd the Works which thy Hands had made, beheldest that *every Thing was very Good*; and Thou didst rest with Complacencie in them. But Man, reflecting on the Works, which he had made, saw that *all was Vanity and vexation of Spirit*, and could, by no means, acquiesce in them. Wherefore, if we labour in thy Works with the sweat of our Brows, Thou wilt make us partakers of *thy Vision*, and *thy Sabbath*. We humbly beg that this Mind may be stedfastly in us; and that Thou, by our Hands, and also by the Hands of others, on whom Thou shalt bestow *the same Spirit*,

rit, wilt please to conveigh a largeness of new *Alms* to thy *Family* of Mankind. These things we commend to Thy everlasting Love, by *our Jesus, thy Christ*, God *with us*. Amen.

Baconiana Bibliographica:

OR CERTAIN

REMAINS

OF THE

LORD BACON

Concerning His

Writings.

To thefe are added Letters and Difcourfes by others, upon the fame Argument; In which alfo are contained fome Remarks concerning his Life.

LONDON,

Printed for *R. C.* at the Rofe and Crown in St. *Paul*'s Church-yard. 1679.

REMAIN
LORD A...
Concerning his
Writings.

Remains Bibliographical,

Written by the

Lord Bacon

HIMSELF.

The Lord Chancellor Bacon's *Letter to the Queen of* Bohemia * *in Answer to one from her Majesty, and upon sending to her his Book about a* War with Spain.

*In the year 1625.

It may please your Majesty,

I Have received your Majesties Gracious Letter from Mr. Secretary *Morton*, who is now a Saint in Heaven. It was at a time, when the great Desolation of the Plague was in the City, and when my self
was

was ill of a dangerous and tedious Sickneſs. The firſt time that I found any degree of Health, nothing came ſooner to my Mind, than to acknowledg your Majeſties great Favour, by my moſt humble Thanks: And becauſe I ſee your Majeſty taketh delight in my Writings, (and to ſay truth, they are the beſt Fruits I now yield) I preſume to ſend your Majeſty a little Diſcourſe of mine, touching a War with *Spain*, which I writ about two Years ſince; which the King your Brother liked well. It is written without Bitterneſs, or Invective, as Kings Affairs ought to be carried: But if I be not deceived, it hath Edge enough. I have yet ſome Spirits left, and remnant of Experience, which I conſecrate to the King's Service, and your Majeſtie's; for whom I pour out my daily Prayers to God, that he would give your Majeſty a Fortune worthy your rare Vertues: Which ſome good Spirit tells me, will be in the end. I do in all reverence kiſs your Majeſtie's Hands, ever reſting

Your Majeſtie's moſt humble

and devoted Servant.

Francis St. *Alban*.

A

A Letter of the Lord *Bacon's* to the University of *Cambridg*, upon his sending to their Public Library, his Book of the *Advancement of Learning*.

Franciscus Baro de *Verulamio*, Vicecomes Sancti *Albani*, Almæ Matri inclytæ Academiæ *Cantabrigiensi*, Salutem.

Debita Filii, qualia possum, persolvo. Quod verò facio, idem & vos hortor; ut Augmentis Scientiarum strenuè incumbatis, & in Animi modestiâ libertatem ingenii retineatis, neque Talentum à veteribus concreditum in sudario reponatis. Affuerit proculdubiò & Affulserit divini Luminis Gratia, si humiliatâ, & submissâ Religioni Philosophiâ, Clavibus sensûs ligitimè, & dextrè utamini, & amoto omni contradictionis studio, quisque cum Alio, ac si ipse secum, disputet, Valete.

The

The same in English *by the Publisher.*

Francis, *Baron of* Verulam, *and Viscount of* St. Albans, *to the Indulgent Mother, the famous University of* Cambridg, *Health.*

I Here repay you, according to my Ability, the Debts of a Son. I exhort you also, to do the same thing with my self: That is, to bend your whole might towards the Advancement of the Sciences, and to retain freedom of Thought, together with humility of Mind; and not to suffer the Talent which the Ancients have deposited with you, to lie dead in a Napkin. Doubtless, the favour of the Divine Light will be present and shine amongst you, if Philosophy being submitted to Religion, you lawfully and dextrously use the Keys of Sense; and if all study of Opposition being laid aside, every one of you so dispute with another, as if he were arguing with himself.

Fare ye well.

A Letter of the Lord *Bacon*'s, to the University of *Cambridg*, upon his sending to their public Library, his *Novum Organum*.

Almæ Matri Academiæ Cantabrigiensi.

Cum vester filius sim & Alumnus, voluptati mihi erit, Partum meum nuper editum vobis in gremium dare: Aliter enim velut pro exposito eum haberem. Nec vos moveat, quòd via nova sit. Necesse est enim talia per Ætatum, & seculorum circuitus evenire. Antiquis tamen suus constat honos; ingenij scilicet: Nam Fides verbo Dei, & experientiæ tantùm debetur. Scientias autem, ad Experientiam retrahere, non conceditur: At easdem ab Experientiâ de integro excitare, operosum certè sed pervium. Deus vobis, & studiis vestris faveat.

Filius vester Amantissimus,

Franc. Verulam, Cancel.

The

The same in English *by the Publisher.*

SEeing I am your Son, and your Disciple, it will much please me to repose in your Bosom, the Issue which I have lately brought forth into the World; for otherwise I should look upon it as an exposed Child. Let it not trouble you, that the Way in which I go is new: Such things will of necessity, happen in the Revolutions of several Ages. However, the Honour of the Ancients is secured: That, I mean, which is due to their Wit. For Faith is only due to the Word of God, and to Experience. Now, for bringing back the Sciences to Experience, is not a thing to be done: But to raise them a-new from Experience, is indeed, a very difficult and laborious, but not a hopeless Undertaking. God prosper you and your Studies.

Your most loving Son,

Francis Verulam, *Chancel.*

A Letter of the Lord *Bacon's*, written to *Trinity College* in *Cambridg*, upon his sending to them his Book of the *Advancement of Learning*.

Franc. Baro de *Verulamio*, Vice-comes Sancti *Albani* percelebri Collegio Sanctæ & Individuæ *Trinitatis* in *Cantabrigia*, Salutem.

R*Es omnes carúmque progressus initiis suis debentur. Itaque cùm initia Scientiarum, è fontibus vestris hauserim; incrementa ipsarum vobis rependenda existimavi. Spero itidem fore, ut hæc nostra apud vos, tanquam in solio nativo, felicius succrescant. Quamobrem & vos hortor, ut salvâ animi modestiâ, & ergà Veteres reverentiâ, ipsi quoque scientiarum augmentis non desitis: Verùm ut post volumina sacra verbi Dei & Scripturarum, secundo loco volumen illud magnum Operum Dei & Creaturarum, strenuè & præ omnibus Libris (qui pro Commentariis tantùm haberi debent) evolvatis.*

Valete.

The same in English *by the Publisher.*

Francis, *Baron of* Verulam, *Viscount of St.* Albans, *to the most Famous College of the holy and undivided* Trinity *in* Cambridg, *Health.*

THe progresses of Things, together with themselves, are to be ascribed to their Originals. Wherefore, seeing I have derived from your Fountains, my first beginnings in the Sciences, I thought it fit to repay to you the Increases of them. I hope also, it may so happen, that these Things of ours may the more prosperously thrive among you, being replanted in their native Soil. Therefore, I likewise exhort you, that ye your selves, so far as is consistent with all due Modesty, and Reverence to the Ancients, be not wanting to the Advancement of the Sciences: But that, next to the study of those sacred *Volumns of God,* the *holy Scriptures,* ye turn over that *great Volume of the Works of God, his Creatures,* with the utmost diligence, and before all other Books, which ought to be looked on only as Commentaries on those Texts. *Farewel.*

The Lord Chancellour Bacon's *Letter to Dr.* Williams, *then Lord Bishop of* Lincoln, *concerning his Speeches,* &c.

MY very good Lord, I am much bound to your Lordship, for your Honourable Promise to Dr. *Rawley:* He chuseth rather to depend upon the same in general, than to pitch upon any particular; which modesty of Choice I commend.

I find that the Ancients (as *Cicero*, *Domesthenes*, *Plinius Secundus*, and others) have preserved both their Orations and their Epistles. In imatation of whom, I have done the like to my own: Which nevertheless, I will not publish while I live: But I have been bold to bequeath them to your Lordship, and Mr. Chancellor of the Dutchy. My Speeches (perhaps) you will think fit to publish: The Letters, many of them, touch too much upon late Matters of State, to be published; yet I was willing, they should not be lost. I have also by my Will, erected two Lectures in Perpetuity, in either University one; with an Endowment of 200 *l.*

per Annum apiece. They to be for *Natural Phylosophie*, and the Sciences thereupon depending; which Foundations I have required my Executors to order, by the advice and direction of your Lordship, and my Lord Bishop of *Coventry* and *Lichfield*. These be my thoughts now. I rest

Your Lordships most

Affectionate to do

you Service.

A Letter written in Latine, *by the Lord* Verulam, *to Father* Fulgentio, *the* Venetian, *concerning his Writings and now Translated into* English *by by the Publisher.*

Most Reverend Father,

I Must confess my self to be a Letter in your Debt; but the Excuse which I have, is too too just. For I was kept from doing you right by a very sore Disease, from which I am not yet perfectly delivered.

I am now defirous to communicate to your Fatherhood, the Defigns I have touching thofe Writings which I form in my Head, and begin; not with hope of bringing them to Perfection, but out of defire to make Experiment, and becaufe I am a Servant to Pofterity: (For thefe things require fome Ages for the ripening of them.)

I judg'd it moft convenient to have them Tranflated in the *Latine* Tongue, and to divide them into certain Tomes.

The firft Tome confifteth of the Books of the *Advancement of Learning*, which (as you underftand) are already finifh'd, and publifh'd; and contain the *Partition of Sciences*, which is the *Firft part of my Inftauration*.

The *Novum Organum* fhould have immediately follow'd. But I interpos'd my *Moral and Political Writings*, becaufe they were more in Readinefs.

And for them, they are thefe following. The firft is, *The Hiftory of* Henry *the* 7th, *King of England*. Then follows that Book which you have call'd in your Tongue, *Saggi Morali*. But I give a graver name to that Book; and it is to go under the Title of *Sermones Fideles*, [Faithful Sayings,] or *Interiora Rerum*, [The Infide of Things.] Thofe *Effayes* will be increafed in their number, and enlarged in the handling of them.

Also that *Tome* will contain the Book of the *Wisdom of the Ancients*. And this Tome (as I said) doth, as it were, interlope, and doth not stand in the Order of the *Instauration*.

After these, shall follow the *Organum Novum*, to which a second part is yet to be added, which I have already compriz'd and measur'd in the Idea of it. And thus, the *Second Part* of my *Instauration*, will be finished.

As for the *Third Part* of the *Instauration*, that is to say, the *Natural History*, it is plainly a Work for a *King*, or a *Pope*; or for some *College*, or *Order*; and cannot be, by Personal Industry, performed as it ought.

Those Portions of it, which have already seen the Light (to wit, concerning *Winds*, and touching *Life and Death*). They are not *pure History*, by reason of the *Axioms*, and larger *Observations*, which are interposed. But they are a kind of *mixed Writings*, composed of *Natural History*, and a rude and imperfect *Instrument* [or Help] of the Understanding.

And this is the *Fourth Part* of the *Instauration*. Wherefore that Fourth Part shall

shall follow, and shall contain many Examples of that *Instrument*, more exact, and much more fitted to *Rules of Induction*.

Fifthly, There shall follow a Book, to be entitled by us, *Prodromus Philosophiæ Secundæ*, [*The Fore-runner of Secondary Philosophy*]. This shall contain our Inventions about *new Axioms*, to be raised from the Experiments themselves, that they, which were before as Pillars lying [uselessly] along, may be raised up. And this we resolve on for the *Fifth Part* of our *Instauration*.

Lastly, There is yet behind, the *Secondary Philosophy it self*, which is the *Sixth Part* of the *Instauration*. Of the perfecting this, I have cast away all hopes; but in future Ages, perhaps, the Design may bud again. Notwithstanding, in our *Prodromie*, [or *Prefatory Works*,] (such I mean only, which touch, almost, the *Universals of Nature*) there will be laid no inconsiderable foundations of *this Matter*.

Our *Meanness* (you see) attempteth great *Things*; placing our hopes only in this, that they seem to proceed from the *Providence* and *Immense Goodness* of God.

And I am, by two Arguments, thus persuaded.

First, I think thus from that *zeal* and

constancy of my Mind, which has not waxed old in this Design, nor after so many Years, grown cold and indifferent. I remember, that about *Forty Years ago*, I compos'd a *Juvenile Work* about these things, which with great Confidence, and a *Pompous Title*, I called *Temporis Partum Maximum*,* [or the most considerable Birth of Time.]

* Or, it may be Masculum, as I find it read elsewhere.

Secondly, I am thus persuaded, because of its *infinite Usefulness*; for which reason it may be ascribed to *Divine Encouragement*.

I pray your *Fatherhood*, to commend me to that most Excellent Man, *Signior Molines*, to whose most delightful and prudent Letters I will return answer shortly, if God permit. *Farewel, most Reverend Father.*

Your

Most assured Friend,

Francis St. Alban.

A Letter of the Lord Bacon's, in French, to the Marquess Fiat, relating to his Essays.

Monsieur l' Ambassadeur mon Fils,

VOyant que vostre Excellence faict et traite Mariages, non seulement entre les Princes d' *Angleterre* et de *France*, mais aussi entre les Langues (puis que faictes traduire non Liure de l' Advancement des Sciences en Francois) i' ai bien voulu vous envoyer mon Liure dernierement imprimé, que i' avois pourveu pour vous, mais i' estois en doubte, de le vous envoyer, pour ce qu' il estoit escrit en Anglois. Mais a' cest' Heure pour la raison susdicte ie le vous envoye. C' est *un Recompilement de mes Essayes Morales et Civiles*; mais tellement enlargiés et enrichiés, tant de Nombre que de Poix, que c' est de fait un Oeuvre nouveau. Ie vous baise les Mains, et reste,

Vostre tres Affectionée Ami,

ex tres humble Serviteur.

The same in English, by the Publisher.

My Lord Embassador, My Son,

SEeing that your Excellency makes, and treats of Marriages, not only betwixt the Princes of France and England, but also betwixt their Languages (for you have caus'd my Book *of the Advancement of Learning,* to be Translated into *French*) I was much inclin'd to make you a Present of the last Book which I published, and which I had in readiness for you.

I was sometimes in doubt, whether I ought to have sent it to you, because it was written in the *English Tongue.* But now, *for that very Reason,* I send it to you. It is a Recompilement of my Essaies Moral, and Civil; but in such manner enlarged and enriched both in Number and Weight, that it is in effect, a new Work. I kiss your Hands, and remain

Your most Affectionate and

most humble Servant, &c.

A Transcript (by the Publisher) out of the Lord Bacon's *last* Will, *relating especially, to his* Writings.

First, I bequeath my Soul and Body, into the Hand of God, by the blessed Oblation of my Saviour; the one at the time of my Dissolution, the other at the time of my Resurrection.

For my Burial, I desire it may be at St. *Michael's* Church, near St. *Albans*. There was my Mother buried; and it is the Parish Church of my Mansion-House of *Gorhambury*; and it is the only Christian Church within the Walls of Old *Verulam*. I would have the Charge of my Funeral not to exceed 300 *l*. at most.

For my Name and Memory, I leave it to Foreign Nations, and to mine own Country-Men, after some Time be passed over.

But towards that durable part of Memory, which consisteth in my Writings, I require my Servant, *Henry Percy*, to deliver to my Brother *Constable*, all my Manuscript-Compositions, and the Fragments also of such as are not Finished; to the end that, if any of them be fit to be Publiſhed, he may accordingly diſpoſe of them. And herein I deſire him, to take the advice of Mr. *Selden,* and Mr. *Herbert,* of the *Inner Temple,* and to publiſh or ſuppreſs what ſhall be thought fit. In particular, I wiſh the Elegie, which I writ in *felicem Memoriam Elizabethæ,* may be Publiſhed.——

Papers written by *others,* concerning the *Writings* of the Lord *Bacon.*

A Letter from the *Univerſity of Oxford,* to the Lord *Bacon,* upon his ſending to them his Book *De Augmentis Scientiarum.*

Prænóbilis, & (quod in Nobilitate pænè miraculum eſt) Scientiſſime Vicecomes!

N*Ihil concinnius tribuere,* Amplitudo veſtra, *nihil gratius accipere potuit* Academia, *quàm* Scientias: Scientias, *quas prius inopes, exiguas, incultas emiſerat, accepit tandem nitidas, proceras,* Ingenii tui copiis *(quibus*

bus unicè augeri potuerant) uberrimè dotatas.
Grande ducit munus illud sibi à peregrino (si
tamen peregrinus sit, tam propè consanguineus)
auctius redire, quod Filiolis suis instar Patri-
monii impendit; & libentèr agnoscit hic nasci
Musas, alibi tamen quam domi suæ crescere.
Creverunt quidem, & sub Calamo tuo, qui
tanquam strenuus literarum Alcides, Columnas
tuas, Mundo immobiles, propriâ Manu in
Orbe Scientiarum, plus ultrà statuisti. Euge
exercitatissimum Athletam, qui in aliorum
patrocinandis virtutibus occupatissimus, alios;
in scriptis propriis, teipsum superâsti. Quippe
in illo Honorum tuorum fastigio, viros tantùm literatos promovisti, nunc tandem (ô
dulce prodigium!) etiam & literas. Onerat
Clientes beneficii hujus augustior Munificentia;
cujus in accipiendo Honor apud nos manet, in
fruendo emolumentum transit usq; in Posteros.
Quin ergo si Gratiarum talioni impares sumus,
juncto robore alterius sæculi Nepotes succur-
rant, qui reliquum illud, quod tibi non possunt, saltem nomini tuo persolvent. Felices
illi, nos tamen quàm longè feliciores, quibus
honorificè conscriptam tuâ manu Epistolam,
quibus oculatissima lectitandi præcepta, &
Studiorum Concordiam, in fronte voluminis
demandâsti: Quasi parum esset Musas de tuâ
pennu locupletare, nisi ostenderes quo modo &
ipsæ discerent. Solenniori itaq; Osculo acerrimum
judicij

The Lord Bacon's

judicij tui Depositum excepit frequentissimus Purpuratorum Senatus; exceperunt pariter minoris ordinis Gentes; & quod omnes in publico Librorum Thesaurario, in Memoriâ singuli deposuerunt.

Dominationis vestræ Studiosissima

Academia Oxoniensis.

E Domo nostrâ Congregationis, 20. Decem. 1623.

The Superscription was thus;

To the Right Honourable *Francis,* Baron of V*erulam,* and Vicount of St *Alban,* our very good Lord.

The same Letter in English, *by the Publisher.*

Most Noble, and—— *most learned Viscount.*

YOur *Honour* could have given nothing more agreeable, and the *University* could have received nothing more acceptable, than the *Sciences.* And those *Sciences* which

which *She* formerly sent forth, Poor, of low Stature, Unpolished; she hath received Elegant, Tall; and by the supplies of your *Wit* (by which alone they could have been Advanced) most rich in Dowry. She esteemeth it an extraordinary favour to have a return with Usury, made of *that* by a *Stranger* (if so near a Relation may be call'd a Stranger) which *She* bestows as a Patrimony, upon her Children: And *She* readily acknowledgeth, that though the *Muses* are *born* in *Oxford*, they *grow* elsewhere. Grown they are, and under *your* Pen, *who*, like some mighty *Hercules* in Learning, have by your own Hand, further *advanced those Pillars* in the Learned World, which by the rest of that World, were supposed immoveable.

We congratulate you, you most accomplish'd *Combatant*, who by your most diligent Patronage of the Vertues of others, have overcome other Patrons, and, by *your own Writings*, your self. For by the eminent heighth of your Honour, you advanced only *Learned Men*; now at last (O ravishing Prodigie!) you have also advanced *Learning it self*.

The ample Munificence of this Gift, lays a *Burthen* upon your *Clients*, in the receiving of *which*, *We* have the Honour; but in the

the *enjoying* of it, the Emolument will descend to late *Posterity*. If therefore we are not able of *our selves*, to return sufficient and suitable Thanks, our *Nephews* of the next Age ought to give their Assistance, and pay the Remainder, if not to your *Self*, to the Honour of your *Name*. Happy *they*; but *we* how much more happy, *&c*. To *whom* you have pleas'd to do the honour of sending a Letter, written by no other than by your own Hand: To whom you have pleas'd to send the clearest Instructions, for reading [your Work] and for concord in our Studies, in the Front of your Book. As if it were a small thing for your *Lordship* to inrich the *Muses* out of your own Stock, unless you taught them also a Method of getting Wealth. Wherefore this most accurate Pledg of your Understanding, has been with the most solemn Reverence, received in a very full *Congregation*, both by the *Doctors* and *Masters*; and that which the *common Vote* hath placed in our *Public Library*, every *single Person* has gratefully deposited in his *Memory*.

Your Lordships most devoted Servant,

The University of Oxford.

From our Convocation-house December. 20. 1623.

A

A Letter written by Dr. Roger Mayn-waring, *to Dr.* Rawley, *concerning the Lord* Bacon's Confession of Faith.

SIR,

I Have at your Command, furveigh'd this deep and devout *Tract* of your deceafed *Lord*; and fend back a few Notes upon it.

In the firft Page, Line 7, (*a*) are thefe words:

"I *believe*, that God is fo Holy, Pure,
"and Jealous, that it is impoffible for Him
"to be pleafed in any *Creature*, though the
"Work of his own Hands: So that nei-
"ther *Angel*, *Man*, nor *World*, could
"ftand, or can ftand, one moment in his
"Eyes, without beholding the fame in the
"Face of a *Mediator*: And therefore, that
"before Him, with whom all things are
"prefent, the *Lamb of God* was flain be-
"fore *all Worlds*: Without which eternal
"Counfel of his, it was impoffible for *Him*
"to have defcended to any work of Crea-
"tion; but he fhould have enjoyed the
"bleffed

(*a*) *That is, in* Refufcit. p. 117. l. 8. *to, for* ever, *in p!* 118.

P

"blessed and individual Society of *Three* "*Persons in Godhead, only,* for ever.

This Point I have heard some Divines question, *Whether God, without Christ, did pour his Love upon the Creature?* And I had, sometimes, a Dispute with Dr. *Sharp,* * of your University, who held, that the *Emanation of the Father's Love to the Creature, was Immediate.* His Reason, amongst others, was taken from that Text, *So God loved the World, that he gave his only begotten Son.* Something of that Point, I have written amongst my Papers, which on the suddain, I cannot light upon. But I remember that I held the Point in the *Negative,* and that St. *Austin,* in his Comment on the Fifth Chapter to the *Romans,* gather'd by *Beda,* is strong that way.

* *The same (I think) who was committed to the Tower, having taught Hoskins his Allusion to the Sicilian Vespers.* See Reliqu. Wotton. p. 434.

In Page 2, line the 9th to the 13th, (b) are these words:

(b) *That is, in Refuse. c. p. 118 l. 9. to refer.*

——"God, by the Reconcilement of the "*Mediator,* turning his Countenance to- "wards his *Creatures,* (though not in equal "Light, and Degree) made way unto the "Dispensation of his most holy and *secret* "Will; whereby some of his Creatures might "*stand* and keep their State; others might "(possibly) fall, and be restored; and "others

"others might *fall, and not be restored* in "their Estate, but yet *remain in Being,* "though *under Wrath* and Corruption; "all with respect to the *Mediator:* Which "is the great *Mystery,* and perfect *Center* "of all God's Ways with his Creatures; "and unto which all his other Works and "Wonders do but serve and refer.

Here *absolute Reprobation* seems to be defended, in that the *Will of God* is made the Reason of the *Not-restitution* of some: At least-wise his Lordship seems to say, that *'twas God's will that some should fall:* Unless that may be meant of *Voluntas Permissiva* [his will of Permission.]

In Page the 2d, at the end, (c) where he saith, [Amongst the *Generations of Men,* he Elected a small Flock,] if that were added [*of fallen Men,*] it would not be amiss; lest any should conceive that his Lordship had meant, the Decree had passed on *Massa incorrupta,* [on Mankind considered before the Fall.]

(c) *That is, in* Re- fuse. p. 118. l. 24. *&c.*

In Page the 4th, lines the 13th and 14th, (d) are these words.

"Man made a total defection from God, "presuming to imagine, that the Com- "mandments and Prohibitions of God, "were not the *Rules of Good and Evil,* but

(d) *That is, in* Re- fuse. p. 119. l. 36. *&c.*

"that

" that *Good* and *Evil* had their own principles
" and beginnings.

Consider whether this be a *Rule Universal*, that the *Commands and Prohibitions of God are the Rules of Good and Evil*. For, as St. *Austin* saith, many things are *Prohibita quia mala*, [For that reason forbidden, because they are Evil:] As those Sins which the Schools call *Specifical*.

(e) *That is, in p. 120. l. 40, 41, &c.*

In Page 7, lines the 23*d* and 24*th*, (e) are these words.

" The three Heavenly Unities——— ex-
" ceed all Natural Unities. That is to say,
" The Unity of the Three Persons in God-
" head; the Unity of God and Man in
" Christ; and the Unity of Christ and the
" Church; the *Holy Ghost being the Worker*
" *of both these latter Unities:* For by the
" *Holy Ghost*, was *Christ Incarnate*, and
"*quickened in Flesh*; and by the Holy
"Ghost is *Man Regenerate*, and *quickened*
" *in Spirit*.

Here two of the Unities are ascribed to the Holy Ghost. The First seems excluded; yet Divines say, that *Spiritus Sanctus est Amor, & vinculum Patris & Filii*, [The Holy Ghost is the Love, and the Bond of the Father and the Son.]

In

In Page 8, line the 13*th*, (*f*) are these words. ^{(f) *That is, in* Refuse. p. 121. l. 8, & 9.}

"Christ— accomplish'd the whole Work "of the Redemption, and Restitution of "Man, to *a state Superiour to the Angels.*

This [Superiour] seems to hit upon that place, ἰσάγγελοι *, which argues but Equality. Suarez (*De Angelis lib.* 1. *cap.* 1.) saith, that Angels are Superiour to Men, *Quoad gradum Intellectualem, & quoad immediatam habitationem ad Deum:* [Both in respect of the degree of their Intellectual Nature, and of the nearness of their habitation to God.] Yet St. *Austin* affirmeth, *Naturam humanam in Christo perfectiorem esse Angelicâ.* [That the Humane Nature in Christ, is more perfect than the Angelical.] Consider of this. And thus far, not as a *Critick*, or Corrector, but as a Learner. For ^{* Luke 20, 36.}

Corrigere, Res est tantò magis ardua, quantò Magnus, Aristarcho, Major, Homerus erat.

In haste,

Your Servant,

Roger *Maynwaring.*

A Letter written by Dr. *Rawley*, to *Monsieur Deodate*, concerning his publishing of the Lord *Bacon's* Works.

Generosissime & Amicissime Domine,

RUri nunc demùm ago, Vere & Jejunio ineunte: Mæstus, defuisse mihi facultatem teipsum invisendi, ante discessum: At Certus, nunquam defuturum me occasioni cuicunq;, teipsum demerendi, & omni Officio, sive Amoris sive Observantiæ, prosequendi. Curabo, prout vires suppetent, Impressionem Librorum Illustrissimi Herois, Cui olim inserviisse, atq; etiamnum inservire, præcipuum mihi duco. Ne qua suspicio Fidei meæ suboriatur; quàm primùm commodum erit, præstabo. Cupio, Amicitiam, & Notitiam hanc inter Nos initam, perpetuam fore: Ac Literis, ejusdem Tesseris & Fotricibus (si velis) subinde reflorescere, te vel Parisiis, Agente; Quas, si unquam mihi Felicitas tanta contingere possit, tui gratiâ etiam invisere sperabo. Neu credas me Verbis tantùm opulentum, Factis inopem; Quin potiùs negotia molestissima obfuisse, dum in Urbe præsens fueram.

Re-

Reliquum erit, ut Te *unicè colat, & redamet, &* Tibi *semer optima precetur;*

Generosissime, Dominationi tuæ

Servus addictimus & Amicus perpetuus,

Martii 9.
1632.

Guil. Rawley.

The same in English *by the* Publisher.

Most noble and dear Sir,

I Am now, at last, in the Country, the *Spring* and *Lent* coming on. I am sorry that I had not the opportunity of waiting on you before I left the Town: But, I am sure, I shall never be wanting in serving you upon all Occasions, and in performing towards you all Offices, either of Friendship, or Observance.

I will (to the utmost of my Power) take care to publish the [remaining] Labours of that *Illustrious Heroe,* [the Lord *Verulam;*] esteeming it my greatest happiness, to have *formerly* serv'd him, and *still* to do so. And that I may avoid all suspicion of being worse than my Word, I will perform my Promise with all convenient speed. I desire that this *Friendship*, and mutual *Inwardness* begun betwixt us, may always continue, and (if you please) live and flourish by *Letters*, the Badges and Nourishers of it, even when you are at *Paris*: A place, which (if ever I be so happy) I will see for your sake, as well as for other Reasons. Pray, think not that I am *free of my Words*, and *frugal of my Deeds*, but rather that my thick and very troublesome Occasions, whilst I was in the *City*, would not suffer me to kiss your Hands. It remains, that I heartily Honour you, and retaliate your Love, and wish you all the good in the World, as being

Sir,

Your most faithful Servant,

and constant Friend,

William Rawley.

March the
9th. 1632.

A Letter written by Monsieur *Ælius Deodate*, to Dr. *Rawley*, in answer to his of *March* the 9th, 1632. touching his publishing the Lord *Bacon*'s Works.

Reverendo Viro Domino *Gulielmo Rawley*, sacræ Theologiæ *Doctori*, & *Regiæ Majestatis Capellano*, Amico colendissimo.

 Reverende Vir, & Amicissime Domine,
PAucis abhinc diebus redditæ sunt mihi gratissimæ & exoptatissimæ tuæ literæ, quibus pro solatio suavissimæ tuæ consuetudinis, per improvisum tuum ex urbe discessum mihi ereptæ, novam, arctæ, & in perpetuum duraturæ amicitiæ tuæ fiduciam mihi spondes. Hoc munere (quod quidem omni mutui amoris & observantiæ officio pro viribus demereri sedulò sutagam) vix quicquam potuit mihi obtingere charius ; adeò tua *Virtus*, & *Illustrissimi Herois nostri* (cujus afflatus Divinos in sinu foves) æternùm colenda Memoria, mihi in precio est. Promptam ejus Operum
           Edi-

Editionem, quam polliceris, tam avidè expecto, ut spe eam jam totam penè continuerim: Ne patere, quæso, quovis casu, ullam huic desiderio meo, moram injici: Cùm etiam (quod & agnoscis) multis nominibus, maximè tua intersit, eam quantò citius promoveri. Parum fœliciter mihi cessit votum, pro versione Libri Experimentorum, ut percipies ex ejus specimine, quod ad te mitto: Ea propter illum, qui id laboris fuerat aggressus, rogavi, ut ab eo desisteret, cujus id solùm quod videbis paucis foliis exaratum, hactenus præstitit, cùm ante duos annos, perficiendum suscepisset. De tempore mei in Galliam reditûs, nondum statui: Ejus te, ante discessum, faciam certiorem, & tibi futuræ nostræ, per literas, communicationis internuncios indicabo. Vale.

Reverentiæ tuæ Obser-

vantissimus Servus,

Ælius Deodatus.

Londini, Aprilis 4. 1633.

The same in English *by the Publisher.*

To the Reverend, his most Honoured Friend, William Rawley, *Doctor of Divinity, and Chaplain to the King's Majesty.*

Reverend and most dear Sir,

A Few Days ago, I received your most acceptable and most desired Letter, in which, to comfort me for the loss of your most agreeable Company (of which I was depriv'd by your sudden leaving the Town) you make me a new promise of a near and lasting Friendship. Nothing could have happened to me more pleasing, than this Kindness (which I shall diligently endeavour, to the utmost of my Power, by all ways of Love and Observance, to deserve); so much I value your own Worth, and the ever estimable Memory, of our most *Illustrious Heroe,* a portion of whose *Spirit,* resides in your Brest.

I so greedily expect the speedy *Edition* of his *Works,* which you have promised; that I have already almost devour'd the whole

whole of it in my Hopes. Suffer not (I beseech you) any delay by any means, to obstruct this my earnest desire: Seeing, especially, it much concerns your self (as you confess) upon many accounts, to promote it with all Expedition.

My design of a *Translation* of the *Natural History*, has not succeeded so happily as I could wish, as you will perceive by the *Specimen* which I send to you. Wherefore I desired him, who had undertaken the Work, to desist from it, he having done only that little which you will see in a few Leaves; whereas he undertook the doing of the whole, two Years ago. I am not yet resolv'd about the time of my returning into *France*. I will let you know it e're I go, and tell you by whom our Letters may be convey'd to one another. *Farewel.*

Reverend Sir,

Your most humble Servant,

Ælius Deodate, *Advocate.*

London, April
4. 1633.

The

The First Letter of Mr. *Isaac Gruter,* to Dr. *Rawley,* concerning the MSS of the Lord *Bacon.*

Reverendo Doctissimoq; viro *Gulielmo Rawleio,* S. P. D. *Isaacus Gruterus.*

Vir Reverende,

*F*Ratris mei cruda mors, cui latinam Naturalis Historiæ Verulamianæ versionem debemus, perdiu me subsistere coegit in natali nobis Zelandia, dum mortualis familiæ negotia expedio. Domum reversus ad Batavos invenio literas tuas sane quàm gratissimas; sed quod dolebam, serô responso ob sonticam ab Haganis absentiæ causam, excipiendas. Veniam meretur qui peccat invitus, tarditatísq; à fortuna impositam necessitatem pensare conabitur affectûs studiô, nunquam post hac indormituro amicitiæ obsequiis & offerenti se occasioni. Viri istius institutum, qui Baconi Historiam Naturalem, ut eam priores meæ designarunt, Gallicè dedit, paucis verbis comprehensum exhibent fratris mei prolegomena; quæ velim videas, & judicium de iis censoriámq;, ubi laborat

borat fides, notam transmittas proximis literis. Editio ille Germani mei, quam cum voluptate summa inspexisse te scribis, mox emendatior prodibit ex secundis defuncti curis, cum auctuario ejusdem argumenti, expungendæ Atlantidi substituendo. Quod non aliud futurum ab ista hominis Galli interpretatione, Latiô donandâ, cum Anglice reperiri non queat unde sua vertit; nisi tu hæc ut spuria & adulterina damnaveris, ubi videre contigerit librum. Observationes tuas in male intellecta perperamq; versa ex Anglico Historiæ Naturalis quod à te evulgatus legitur (qualia in primis conatibus interpretis non indigenæ, & indies tunc cum adolesceret ætate proficientis haud pauca occurrere nemo mirabitur, qui noverit Physiologicam argumenti latè patentis varietatem, perplexi ex tot rerum congerie, sua non ubiq; vocabula apud Antiquos habentium, & præsenti nota signandas appellationes requirentium) velim mihi non invideas, conferendas cum τȣ μακαρίτȣ emendationibus solicitè elaboratis; an & feliciter, tum cùm paucis istarum elegantiarum intelligentibus displices. Mitto indicem eorum, quæ ex Boswelliani Musei scriniis chartaceis penes me exstant vel propria manu descripta, vel alterius apud vos, sed Baconi manum & limam experta; ut Boswellus olim mihi, admisso ad interiores familiaritatis aditus, commemoravit

Horat.

In

In apographis meis (ut testabitur index hisce literis comes) reperies historiam Densi & Rari, *sed imperfectam, opusculo licet longiusculè producto.* De Gravi & Levi *in manibus habui integrum & grande volumen, sed quod præter nudam delineatæ fabricæ compagem ex titulis, materiam, prout eam conceperat illustris* Baconus, *absolventibus, nihil descriptionis continebat. Includitur hisce exemplar contextûs, sola capitum lemmata complexi, & plenam ex ista* σκιαγραφία *tractationem nunc frustra requirentis.* De Denso & Raro *quæ asservas ab extrema Authoris incude, quæq; in appendicem venient fragmenta, utinam cum ineditis* Physiologicis Virulamei, *in apographa per me redactis ex legato* Boswelliano, *subjicere liceat prelo Batavo, sibi invicem commendationem, si junctius prodeant, præstitura. Agere jam cæpi cum Typographo magnæ in istis industriæ & curiositatis; faxo nihil justè queri possis de fide nostra & candore, si editionem illam mihi permiseris, consummandam non sine honorifica tui mentione. Sed utcunq; constitues, nihil detractum volo amicitiæ officiis, ulterius ab hoc ingressu quacunq; occasione provehendæ.* Ludovicus Elsevirius Amstelodamo *nuper ad me scripsit meditari se, fore brevi inchoandam, in quarto editionem eorum omnium, quæ* Bacono *circumferuntur Authore, vel Latinè vel Anglicè, sed*

hæc

hæc in Romanum Sermonem vertenda, petiitq;
à me eatenus consilium, & si quid è manu-
scriptis & interpretatione conferre possem ad-
miniculi, quo auctiora & quantum pote, or-
natiora prodeant opera, diu faventissimis Eru-
diti mundi præconiis & applausu confestatissi-
mo excepta. Tu si quid in mente aut manu
habes unde affulgeat adjumenti spes in moli-
tione tam celebri, & plurimum conciliatura exi-
stimationis istam editionem procurantibus, fac
intelligam, & habe me porro inter devotissi-
mos Baconiani nominis & virtutum tuarum
cultores. Vale. Exspecto quæ tibi cognita
de Verulamij majoribus, Nicolao Patre im-
primis, de adolescentia nostri, studiis apud
Cantabrigienses, peregrinationibus, honori-
bus, Cancellariatu & exauthoratione, Parla-
mentariæ authoritatis decreto. Ista floridè
& liberaliori. in laudes meritissimas stylo,
hoc ultimum cauto pertractando, suscipiam, ne
hominibus calumniari aut probra serere natis
præbeatur noxiæ garrulitatis è mea Commenta-
tione de viri longè Doctissimi vita & morte,
materies.

Hagæ Comitis, Maii 29. 1652.

The same, in English, by the Publisher.

To the Reverend, and most Learned, William Rawley, Isaac Gruter wisheth much Health.

Reverend Sir,

BY reason of the immature Death of my Brother, to whom we owe the *Latine* Translation of the *Lord Bacon's Natural History*, I have been forced to stay a long while in our Native Country of *Zealand*, in order to the settling of the Domestick Affairs of the Person deceased. Returning home to *Holland*, I found your Letter, which, I assure you, was most acceptable to me; yet at this I was concern'd, that my necessary absence from the *Hague* had occasioned so late an Answer to it. He deserves pardon who offends against his will: And who will endeavour to make amends for this involuntary delay, by the study of such kindness as shall be vigilant in Offices of Friendship, as often as occasion shall be offer'd.

The Design of him, who translated into *French*, the *Natural History* of the *Lord Bacon*, (of which I gave account in my former Letters) is briefly exhibited in my Brother's Preface, which I desire you to peruse; as also, in your next Letter, to send me your Judgment concerning such Errors as may have been committed by him.

That *Edition* of my Brother's, of which you write, that you read it with a great deal of Pleasure, shall shortly be set forth with his Amendments, together with some *Additions* of the like Argument to be substituted in the place of the *New Atlantis*, which shall be there omitted. These *Additions* will be the same with those in the *Version* of the formentioned *Frenchman*, put into *Latine*; seeing we could not find the English Originals from which he translates them: Unless you, when you see the Book, shall condemn those Additions as adulterate.

For your Observations on those Places, either not rightly understood, or not accurately turned out of the *English* by you published, (which, from one not a Native, in his first Essay, and growing in Knowledg together with his Years, if they be many, no Man needs wonder at it, who understands the Physiological variety of an

Argu-

Argument of such extent, and rendred difficult by such an heap of things of which it consists, and for the expressing of which there is not a supply of words from the Ancients, *but some of a new stamp, and such as may serve for present use,* are required) I intreat you not to deny me the sight of them: That so I may compare them with the Corrections which my Brother (now with God) did make with a very great deal of pains. But, whether the *truth* of them answers his diligence, will be best understood by your self, and those few others by whom such Elegancies can be rightly judged of.

I send you here a Catalogue of those writings (a) which I had, in *MS*. out of the study of Sir *William Boswel*, and which I now have by me, either written by the *Lord Bacon* himself, or by some *English Amanuensis*, but by him revised; as the same Sir *Willam Boswel* (who was pleased to admit me to a most intimate familiarity with him) did himself tell me. Among my Copies (as the Catalogue which comes with this Letter shews) you will find the History of *rare and dense Bodies*, but imperfect, though carried on to some length.

(a) *These were the Papers which* J. Gruter, *afterwards publish'd, under the title of* Scripta Philosophica.

I had once in my hands, an entire and thick Volume concerning *Heavy and Light Bodies*, but confisting only of a naked delineation of the *Model*, which the Lord *Bacon* had framed in his Head, in *titles of Matters*, without any defcription of the Matters themfelves. There is here enclofed, a Copy of that Contexture (*b*) containing only the Heads of the Chapters, and wanting a full handling from that rude Draught; which fupplement I difpair of

(*b*) *This Letter came to my hands without that Copy. See, in lieu of it,* Topica de Gravi & Levi, *in lib.* 5. *cap.* 3. de Augm. Scien.

For the Book of *Denfe and Rare Bodies*, which you have by you, perfected by the Author's laft Hand, as likewife the *Fragments* which are an *Appendix* to it, I could wifh that they might be here publifh'd in *Holland*, together with thofe hitherto unpublifh'd *Philofophical Papers* copied by me, out of M S S. of Sir *William Bofwel*; feeing, if they come out together, they will fet off, and commend one another.

I have begun to deal with a *Printer*, who is a Man of great Diligence and Curiofity. I will fo order the matter, that you fhall have no reafon to complain of my Fidelity and Candor, if you leave that Edition to me. Care fhall be taken by me, that it be not done without honourable mention

tion of your felf. But be it what it will you fhall refolve upon, it fhall abate nothing of the offices of our Friendfhip, which, from this beginning of it, fhall ftill further be promoted upon all occafions.

Lewis Elzevir, wrote me word lately, from *Amfterdam*, that he was defigned to begin fhortly, an *Edition in Quarto*, of all the Works of the *Lord Bacon*, in *Latine*, or *Englifh:* But not of the *Englifh*, without the *Tranflation* of them into *Latine*. And he defir'd my advice, and any affiftance I could give him by *Manufcripts*, or *Tranflations*; to the end that, as far as poffible, thofe *Works* might come abroad with advantage, which have been long receiv'd with the kindeft *Elogies*, and with the moft attefted Applaufe of the *Learned World*. If you have any thing in your *Mind*, or your *Hands*, whence we may hope for affiftance in fo famous a Defign, and conducing fo much to the Honour of thofe who are Inftrumental in it, pray let me know it, and reckon me henceforth amongft the devout Honourers of the name of the *Lord Bacon*, and of your own Vertues.

Farewel.

I expect from you what you know, about the Ancestors of the *Lord Bacon*, especially concerning his *Father*, *Nicholas Bacon*; concerning his Youth, his Studies in *Cambridg*, his Travels, his Honours, his Office of *Chancellour*, and his deposal from it by *Sentence of Parliament*. The former I will undertake in a more florid and free Style, expatiating in his just Praises; the latter, with a wary Pen, lest out of my *Commentary* of the Life of this most Learned Man, matter be offered of pernicious Prating, to Slanderers, and Men of dishonest Tempers.

From the Hague,

May, 29. 1652.

The second Letter of Mr. *Isaac Gruter*, to Dr. *Rawley*, concerning the Writings of the *Lord Bacon*.

V. R. *Gulielmo Rawlejo*, S. S. Theologiæ Doctori S. P. D. *Isaacus Gruterus*.

Vir Reverende,

DE *responsi tui tarditate queri non licet, cùm & difficultas trajectûs facile moram injiciat ex anno in hiemem declivi dum tuas dares, atq; abunde in iis inveniat quo se pascat desiderium; tantò uberiori accessione, quantò cunctantius ad manus nostras fortassis pervenisse dici potest. Et quamvis pauxillum erat quod præter gratias pro indiculo reponerem, ejus tamen id momenti visum est, ut supprimere diutius noluerim;præsertim cùm nefas mihi haberetur* Smithum *responso carere, virum amicissimum, & cujus in Res nostras studio quicquid in me est curæ debetur affectúsque, nihil imminuti parte, in quam sane non levem,* Rawleius *venit, ut in Trigam, coäluisse dici queat optimè consentientes animos. Illustrissimi Herois* Verulamii *quàm sancta apud me sit ex-*

isti-

æstimatio, etsi perquam sollicitè ostendisse me putabam, faciam tamen ut in posterum religiosius me operam dedisse quo hoc literato orbi innotesceret negari haud possit. Neq; enim procedet ista contrahendi omnia Baconiana in unum volumen molitio, nisi te consulto, & ad symbolas tam insigni editione dignas invitato; ut lectoris jam pridem ex prævio eorum quæ circumferuntur gustu, cupidi concilietur gratia ex illibatâ auctarii non pœnitendi novitate. Gallo interpreti, & qui sua nescio unde consarcinavit centonésq; consuit, locus non dabitur in magno Syngrammate. Ut autem separatim cum Historia Naturali excudatur exoticum opus per excerpta hinc inde corrogatum, & latinitate meâ donatum, spero à te impetrari patieris. Interesse enim puto cum Verulamiana genuina Gallici Sermonis induta cultu passim prostent, ut sciat transmarinus lector è quibus filis contexta sit istius libri tela, & quàm verum sit quod Anonymus iste in prefatione ad Lectorem de te innominato scribit. Verba ejus frater meus B. M. Latinè versit in primâ editione Historiæ Naturalis, cùm de fide Authoris ignoti dubitaret. Ego in secundâ dabo, repetita & justis confossa notis, ut moneantur in quorum manus perventurum sit istud opus, suppostitium esse, aut potius ex avulsis sparsim laciniis consutum, quicquid specioso Verulamii titulo munitum venditat Author.

Nisi

Nisi forte speciatim tuo nomine suggerere libet, isti loco inserenda in cautelam, & ne quid Gloriæ celeberimi viri detrahat vel malignitas, vel inconsideratum studium. Si me fata meis ^{Virgil.} paterentur ducere vitam auspiciis, *in Angliam evolarem, ut quicquid Verulamianæ officinæ servas in scriniis tuis ineditum, coram inspicerem, & oculos saltem haberem arbitros, si possessio negetur mercis nondum publicæ. Nunc vota impatientis desiderii sustentabo spe aliquando videndi, quæ fidis mandata latebris occasionem exspectant ut tuto in lucem educantur, non enecentur suffocato partu. Utinam interim videre liceat Apographum* epistolæ ad *Henricum Savilium* circa adjumenta facultatum intellectualium; *cætera enim Latinæ monetæ persuadeor statione sua moveri non posse in temporarium usum.* Vale.

Trajecti ad Mosam,

Martii 20. S. N. CIƆ IƆC LV.

The

The same in English, *by the Publisher.*

To the Reverend William Rawley, *D.D.* Isaac Gruter *wisheth much health.*

Reverend Sir,

IT is not just to complain of the slowness of your Answer, seeing that the difficulty of the Passage, in the season in which you wrote, which was towards Winter, might easily cause it to come no faster: Seeing likewise, there is so much to be found in it which may gratifie Desire, and perhaps, so much the more, the longer it was e're it came to my Hands. And although I had little to send back, besides my Thanks for the *little Index*, (*a*) yet that seemed to me of such moment, that I would no longer suppress them; especially because I accounted it a Crime to have suffer'd Mr. *Smith* (*b*) to have been without an Answer: Mr. *Smith*, my most kind Friend, and to whose care in my Matters, I owe all Regard

(*a*) *A Note of some Papers of the Lord Bacon's in D. R's. hands.*

(*b*) *Of Christ's Colledg in Cambridg, and Keeper of the publick Library there.*

gard and Affection, yet without diminution of that part (and that no small one neither) in which Dr. *Rawley* hath place: So that the *Souls* of *us Three* so throughly agreeing, may be aptly said to have united in a *Triga*.

Though I thought that I had already, sufficiently shew'd, what Veneration I had for the *Illustrious Lord Verulam*, yet I shall take such care for the future, that it may not possibly be deny'd, that I endeavour'd most zealously to make this thing known to the learned World.

But neither shall this Design, of setting forth in one Volume, all the *Lord Bacon*'s Works, proceed without consulting you, and without inviting you to cast in your Symbol, worthy such an excellent Edition: That so the Appetite of the Reader, provoked already by his publish'd Works, may be further gratifi'd by the pure novelty of so considerable an Appendage.

For the *French Interpreter*, who patch'd together his Things I know not whence (*c*), and tack'd that motley piece to him; they shall not have place in this *great Collection*. But yet, I hope, to obtain your leave to publish apart, as an Appendix to the *Natural History*,

(c) *Certain spurious Papers added to his Translation of the* Advancement of Learning.

History, that *Exotick Work*, gather'd together from this and the other place [of his Lordships Writings] and by me translated into *Latine*. For seeing the genuine Pieces of the Lord *Bacon* are already Extant, and in many Hands, it is necessary that the Forreign Reader be given to understand, of what Threds the Texture of that Book consists, and how much of Truth there is in that, which that shameless person does in his Preface to the Reader, so stupidly write of you.

My Brother, *of blessed Memory*, turn'd his words into *Latine*, in the *first Edition* of the *Natural History*, having some suspition of the Fidelity of an unknown Author. I will, in the *second Edition*, repeat them, and with just severity, animadvert upon them: That they, into whose hands that Work comes, may know it to be suppositious, or rather patch'd up of many distinct Pieces; how much soever the Authour bears himself upon the specious Title of *Verulam*.

Unless, perhaps, I should particularly suggest in your Name, that these words were there inserted, by way of Caution; and lest Malignity and Rashness should any way blemish the Fame of so eminent a Person.

Si me, Fata, meis, paterentur ducere vitam Auspiciis——— (to use the words of *Virgil.*) If my Fate would permit me to live according to my Wishes, I wolud flie over into *England*, that I might behold whatsoever remaineth, in your Cabinet, of the *Verulamian* Workmanship, and at least make my Eyes witnesses of it, if the possession of the Merchandize be yet denied to the Publick.

At present I will support the Wishes of my impatient desire, with hope of seeing, one Day, those [Issues] which being committed to faithful Privacie, wait the time 'till they may safely see the Light, and not be stifled in their Birth.

I wish, in the mean time, I could have a sight of the Copy of the Epistle to Sir *Henry Savil*, concerning the *Helps of the Intellectual Powers:* For I am persuaded, as to the other *Latine Remains*, that I shall not obtain, for present use, the removal of them from the place in which they now are. *Farewel.*

Maestricht, March 20.

New Style, 1655.

The

The Third Letter written by Mr. *Isaac Gruter*, to Dr. *Rawley*, concerning the Writings of the Lord *Bacon*.

Reverendo, Doctissimoq; viro *Gulielmo Rawleio*, S. Theologiæ Doctori S. P. D. *Isaacus Gruterus*.

Vir Reverende & amicissime,

Quanta in parte honoris deputarem missa Verulamii *posthuma, quæ è tuo non ita pridem Museo Latina prodiere, actæ protinus Gratiæ significarunt, si curam amici, qui hic operam suam non frustra requiri passus est, haud luserit fortuna trajectus, varia è causa sæpe dubij. Nunc tantò majus mihi istud beneficium est, quantò insigniorem frugem præstitit lectio non ignava, & par cum quibusdam ex officina* Baconiana *à me editis collatio; auctiorem enim tibi debemus Historiam* densi & rari, *sed & alia isto contenta Volumine priusquam non conspecta. Unum mirabar, non exstare ibi cæteris aggregatam* Verulamii Epistolam *ad* Henricum Savilium, *de adjumentis facultatum Intellectualium, si ex literis olim tuis*

tuis non vanè mihi recordanti subjicit Titulum appellata memoria, saltem inscriptione non longè dissimili. Si *per oblivionem ibi forte non comparet, scriniis tamen vestris inerrat, optem videre Apographum, in cujus usu bonam fidem non desiderabis;* nisi *Anglicano Sermone scripta locum invenerit in majori opere, quod vernacula duntaxat complectitur. Id si nos scire patiaris, & an obtinendi Libri, in quo & Oratoria, fors & Epistolica, digeruntur, maternæ Linguæ partus, spes ex promisso fuerit non immodesta, animo meo consecraris tui memoriam, in cujus veneratione nunquam defatigabitur segnescere alacritas obstrictissimi affectus.* Vale.

Trajecti *ad* Mosam, *unde post duos trésve menses* Novomagum *migro,* Batavis *futurus propior. Per* Smithæum *tamen transmittere ad me perges, si quid volueris.*

Kal. Julii,

St. N. CIƆ IƆC LIX.

The

The same in English, *by the Publisher.*

To the Reverend, and most Learned, William Rawley, *D. D.* Isaac Gruter *wisheth much Health.*

Reverend Sir, and my most dear Friend,

HOw much I hold my self honour'd by your *Present* of the Lord *Bacon's Posthumous Works*, published lately by you in *Latine*, my thanks immediately return'd, had let you understand, if ill Fortune in the Passage (which is, for divers causes, uncertain) had not deluded the care of a Friend, who did here with much readiness, undertake the Conveyance of them.

Now, the Gift is by so much the greater, by how much the more benefit I reap'd by diligent reading of those Papers, and by comparing them with some of the Lord *Bacon's* Works, which I my self had formerly published. For to you we owe the more enlarged *History de Denso & Raro*, as also many other things, contain'd in that Volume, which saw not the Light before.

One

One Paper I wonder I saw not amongst them, the *Epistle* of the Lord *Bacon* to Sir *Henry Savil*, about the Helps of the Intellectual Powers, spoken of long ago in your Letters, under that, or some such Title, if my Memory does not deceive me. If it was not forgotten, and remains among your private Papers, I should be glad to see a *Copy* of it, in the use of which, my Faithfulness shall not be wanting. But, perhaps, it is written in the *English Tongue*, and is a part of that greater *Volume*, which contains only his *English Works*. If you will please to let me understand so much, and likewise give me assurance of obtaining that Book, in which the *Speeches*, and it may be the *Letters* of the Lord *Bacon*, written by him in *English*, are digested; you will render your Memory sacred in my Mind, in the veneration of which, the chearfulness of a most devoted affection shall never be weary. *Farewel.*

From *Maestricht*, from whence, after two or three Months, I remove to *Nimmeghen* nigher to *Holland*. But you may convey to me, any thing you desire, by Mr. *Smith*.

July, 1st. *New Style*, 1659.

A brief Account of the Life, and particularly of the Writings of the Lord Bacon, written by that learned Antiquarie, Sir William Dugdale, *Norroy King of Arms, in the second Tome of his Book entituled,* The Baronage of England *; together with divers Insertions by the Publisher.*

* Pag. 437. 438, 439.

Francis, *Lord* Verulam, *Vicount* St. Alban.

[16 *Jac.*]

COnsidering that this Person was so Eminent for his Learning, and other great Abilities, as his Excellent Works will sufficiently manifest; though a short Narrative *a* of his Life, is already set forth by Doctor *William Rawley*, his domestique Chaplain, I am not willing to omit the taking notice of such particulars, as are most memorable of him; and therefore shall briefly recount; partly from that Narrative,

a *Impr. Lond. an. 1670.*

tive, and partly from other Authorities, what I have obſerved in order thereto.

As to his Parentage, he was *b* the youn- ᵇ *Ibid.*
geſt of thoſe two Male Children, which Sir *Nicholas Bacon* of *Redgrave, in Com. Suff.* Knight, had by *Anne* his Wife, one of the ſix Daughters of Sir *Anthony Cook*, of *Giddy-Hall, in Com. Eſſex.* Knight, (a perſon much honoured for his Learning, and being Tutor to King *Edward* the Sixth) all thoſe Daughters being exquiſitely skilled *c* in the *Greek* and *Latine* Tongues.   ᶜ *Annal. Eliz. per Cambd. in*

Which *Nicholas*, having been a diligent *an. 1576.*
Student of the Laws in *d Grays-Inn*, was ᵈ *Life of, &c. by Dr. Rawley.*
made *e* the King's Attorney in the Court of Wards, in 38 *H.* 8. and upon the death of that King, (which ſoon after happened) ᵉ *Pat.* 38 *H.* 8. *p.* 6.
had his Patent for the ſame truſt, renewed by his Son and Succeſſor, King *Edward* ᶠ *Pat.* 1 E. *p.* 3. *m.* 36.
the Sixth. In the ſixth year of whoſe Reign, he was conſtituted *g* Treaſurer for ᵍ *Orig. Jurid. p.* 298.
that Noble Society of *Grays-Inn*, whereof he had been ſo long a Member. And being grown famous for his Knowledg, was ſhortly after, *viz.* in 1 *Eliz.* made *h* Lord ʰ *Pat.* 1 E. *p.* 3.
Keeper of the great Seal of *England*, and Knighted, *i* which Office in his time, was ⁱ *M.* 6. *in offic. Arm. f. ib.* 67. *b.*
by Act of Parliament made equal in Authority with the Chancellours.

What I have otherwiſe obſerved of this

^{k l} *Annal.*
Eliz. ut
supra in
an. 1564.

Sir *Nicholas Bacon,* is, *k* that being no friend to the Queen of *Scots,* (then Prisoner in *England*) he was *l* privy, and assenting to what *Hales* had publisht, in derogation to her Title, as next and lawful Successor to Queen *Elizabeth*; asserting that of the House of *Suffolk* before it, for

^{m n} *Ibid.*

which, *Hales* suffered *m* Imprisonment, and had not *Cecil* stood his faithful friend, *n* so might he; nothing being more distastful to Queen *Elizabeth,* than a dispute upon that point. Next, that in 14 *Eliz.* up-

^{o p} *Ibid. in*
an. 1571.

on those Proposals made by the Nobility of *Scotland,* for her enlargement, he opposed *o* it; alleadging, *p* that no security could ballance the danger thereof. Lastly, That upon his death, which happened in April, *An.* 1579. (21 *Eliz.*) this Chara-

^q *Ib. in*
an. 1579.

cter *q* is given of him by the learned *Cambden, viz.* that he was *Vir præpinguis, ingenio acerrimo, singulari prudentia, summâ eloquentia, tenaci memoriâ, & sacris consiliis alterum columen:* Of person very corpulent, most quick Wit, singular Prudence, admirable Eloquence, special Memory, and another Pillar to the Privy-Council.

* This Account is inserted by the Publisher, who took it out of a Paper of the Lord *Bacon's.*

Of his Death, this is said *to be the occasion. "He had " his Barber rubbing and com- " bing his Head. And, because it " was

"was very hot, the Window was open to let in a
"fresh Wind. He fell asleep, and awaked all
"distemper'd, and in a great sweat, Said
"he to the Barber, Why did you let me sleep?
"Why, my Lord, said he, I durst not wake
"your Lordship. Why then, saith my Lord
"Keeper, you have killed me with Kindness.
"So he removed into his Bed-Chamber, and
"within a few days died.]

Whereupon, being Interred on the South-side of the Quire in St. *Paul's* Cathedral, within the City of *London*, he had a noble Monument, *r* there erected to his Memory, with this Epitaph:

^r *Hist. of St. Paul's Cath. p. 74.*

Hic Nicolaum *ne* Baconem *conditum existima illum, tam diu* Britannici *Regni secundum columen; Exitium malis, Bonis Asylum; cæca quem non extulit ad hunc honorem sors; sed Æquitas, Fides, Doctrina, Pietas, unica & Prudentia. Neu fortè raptum crede, qui unica brevi, vitâ perenni emerit duas, agit vitam secundam cælites inter animas. Fama implet orbem, vita quæ illi tertia est. Hac positum in arâ est Corpus, olim animi Domus, Ara dicata sempiternæ Memoriæ.*

*This Translation is done by the Publisher, for the benefit of the English Reader.

That is, * Think not that this Shrine contains that *Nicholas Bacon*, who was so long the second Pillar of *Great Britain*; the Scourge of the Vicious, and the Sanctuary of the Good: Whom blind Fortune did not exalt to that height of Honour; but his Equity, Fidelity, Learning, Piety, singular Prudence. Neither believe him to be by chance snatch'd away, who, by one short Life, purchased two in Life Eternal. He lives his second Life among the Heavenly Spirits. His Fame filleth the World, which is his third Life. In this Altar is reposed his Body, sometime the House of his Soul; an Altar dedicated to his perpetual Memory.

[† Life of, &c. by Dr. Rawley.]

Thus much touching the Parentage of this *Francis*; his Birth ſ being at *York-House* in the *Strand*, upon the twenty second day of *January*, *Anno* 1560. (2 *Eliz.*) It is observed, † that in his tender Years, his Pregnancy was such, as gave great indication of his future high Accomplishments; in so much, as Queen *Elizabeth* took notice of him, and called him *The young Lord-Keeper*; also, that asking him, how old he was, though but a Boy, he answered, that he *was two years younger than her Majesties most happy Reign*.

A6

As to his Education, he was *u* of *Trinity* [u Ibid.]
College, in *Cambridg*, under the tuition of
Doctor *John Whitgift*, then Master there,
but afterwards the renowned Arch-Bishop
of *Canterbury*. Where having with great
proficiency, spent some time, he was sent
x into *France*, with Sir *Amias Paulet*, her [x y Ibid.]
Majestie's Leiger Ambassador, and thence
intrusted with a Message *y* to the Queen,
which he performed with much approbation; and so returned.

After this, coming from Travail, and
applying himself to the study of the Common Law, he was seated *z* in *Grays-Inn*. [z Ibid.]
Where in short time, he became so highly
esteemed for his Abilities, as that in 30
Eliz. (being then but 28 years of Age)
that honourable Society, chose *a* him for [a Orig. Jurid. p. 295. a.]
their *Lent* Reader: And in 32 *Eliz.* was
made *b* one of the Clerks of the Council. [b Pat. 32 Eliz. p. 11.]

In 42 *Eliz.* being *c* double Reader in [c Orig. Ju. 295 b.]
that House, and affecting much the Ornament thereof, he caused *d* that beautiful [d Ib. 272. b.]
Grove of Elms, to be planted in the Walks,
which yet remain. And upon the 23 of
July, 1 *Jac.* was Knighted *e* at *White-Hall*. [e MS. in offic. Arm.]
Shortly after which, *viz.* in 2 *Jac.* he was
made *f* one of the King's Council learned, [f g Pat. 2 Jac. p. 12.]
having therewith a grant *g* of forty Pounds
per

per annum Fee; and in 5 *Jac.* conftituted *h* his Majeftie's Solicitor General. In 9 *Jac.* he was made *i* joynt Judge with Sir *Thomas Vavafor*, then Knight Marfhal, of the Knight Marfhal's Court, then newly erected within the Verge of the King's Houfe, and in 11 *Jac.* (27 *Octob.*) being made *k* Attorney General, was fworn *l* of the Privy Council.

In 14 *Jac.* he was conftituted *m* Lord Keeper of the Great Seal, (7 *Martii*) being then fifty four years of Age.

k Pat. 5 Jac. p. 14. i Pat. 9 Jac. p.

h Pat. 11 Jac. p. 5. l Annal. R. Jac. per Cambd. m n Ib. in An. 1617.

‖ *An Infertion by the Publifher.*

* *The Court of King James, p. 115, 116.*

‖ " It is faid in a * Libel,
" (in which are many o-
" ther notorious Slanders,)
" that the Duke of *Bucking-*
" *ham*, to vex the very Soul
" of the Lord Chancellour *Egerton*, in his
" laft Agony, did fend Sir *Francis Bacon*
" to him for the Seals; and likewife that
" the dying Chancellor, did hate that *Ba-*
" *con* fhould be his Succeffor, and that his
" Spirit not brooking this ufage, he fent
" the Seals by his Servant to the King, and
" fhortly after, yielded his Soul to his Ma-
" ker. In which few words there are two
palpable Untruths.

For firft, The King himfelf fent for the Seal, not the Duke of *Buckingham*: And he fent for it, not by Sir *Francis Ba-*
con,

con, (a) but by Secretary *Winwood*, with this Meſſage, that himſelf would be his Under-Keeper, and not diſpoſe of the Place of Chancellour while he lived: Nor did any receive the Seal out of the King's ſight, till the Lord *Egerton* died; which ſoon fell out.

(a) *Aulicus Cœquinariæ.* p. 171.

Next, The Lord Chancellour *Egerton* was willing that Maſter Attorney *Bacon*, ſhould be his Succeſſor; and ready to forward his Succeſſion: So far was he from conceiving hatred againſt him, either upon that, or any other Account.

The Lord *Egerton* was his Friend in the Queen's time; and I find Mr. *Bacon* making his acknowledgements in a Letter to him, in theſe words, which I once tranſcribed from the unpubliſh'd Original. "For my placing, your Lordſhip beſt "knoweth, that when I was moſt dejected "with her Majeſtie's ſtrange dealing to "wards me, it pleaſed you of your ſingu "lar favour, ſo far to comfort, and encou "rage me, as to hold me worthy to be ex "cited, to think of ſucceeding your Lord "ſhip in your ſecond Place: Signifying, "in your plainneſs, that no Man ſhould "better content your ſelf. Which your "exceeding favour you have not ſince car "ried from; both in pleading the like ſig
"nifica-

"nification into the hands of some of my "best Friends; and also in an honourable "and answerable Commendation of me, "to her Majesty. Wherein I hope, your "Lordship (if it please you call to mind) "did find me, neither overweening, in "presuming too much upon it, nor much "deceived in my opinion of the Event, for "the continuing of it still in your self; nor "sleepy in doing some good Offices to the "same purpose.

This favour of the Lord *Egerton*'s, which began so early, continued to the last. And thus much Sir *Francis Bacon* testified in a Letter to Sir *George Villiers*, of which this is a part. (b) "My Lord Chancellor told "me, yesterday, in plain terms, that if the "King would ask his opinion, touching the "Person that he would commend to suc- "ceed him, upon Death, or Disability; "he would name me, for the fittest Man. "You may advise, whether use may not be "made of this Offer. And the like appears by what Master Attorney wrote to King *James*, during the sickness of my Lord Chancellor. Amongst other things, he wrote this to the King. * "It pleased my "Lord Chancellor, out of his ancient and "great Love to me, which many times, in "Sickness, appeareth most; to admit me
"to

(b) Refuscit. p. 65. of the Collect. of Letters.

* Ibid. p. 50.

"to a great deal of Speech with him this
"Afternoon; which, during these three
"Days, he hath scarcely done to any.

In the same * Libel, my Lord *Bacon* is reproach'd as a very necessitous Man, and one, for that Reason, made Keeper by the Duke, to serve such Turns, as Men of better Fortunes would never condescend to. And this, also, is a groundless and uncharitable Insinuation. He had now enjoy'd, a good while, many profitable Places, which preserv'd him from Indigence, though his great Mind did not permit him to swell his Purse by them, to any extraordinary Bigness. And, in the Queen's time, when he was in meaner Circumstances, he did not look upon himself as in that estate of Necessity, which tempteth generous Minds to vile things. Hear himself representing his Condition; no Man knew it better, or could better express it. Thus he states his Case in the aforesaid unpublish'd Letter to the Lord Chancellor *Egerton*, of the whole of which, I sometime had the perusal, though now much of it is lost, and, as I believe, beyond all recovery.
"My Estate (said he) I confess a truth to
"your Lordship, is weak, and Indebted,
"and needeth Comfort. For both my Fa-
"ther (though, I think, I had greatest
"part

* *Court of K. James*, p. 119.

"part in his Love of all his Children)
"in his Wisdom served me in, as a last
"Comer: And my self, in mine own In-
"dustry, have rather referred, and aspired
"to *Vertue*, than to *Gain*; whereof I am
"not yet wise enough to repent me. But
"the while, whereas *Salomon* speaketh, *That*
"*Want cometh first as a Wayfaring Man, and*
"*after as an Armed Man*; I must acknow-
"ledg my self to be in *primo gradu*; for it
"stealeth upon me. But, for the second, that
"it should not be able to be resisted; *I hope*
"*in God, I am not in that case.* For the
"preventing whereof, as I do depend up-
"on God's Providence all in all; so in the
"same, his Providence I see, opened unto
"me, three not unlikely expectations of
"Help. The one, my Practice; the other,
"some proceeding in the Queen's Service;
"the third, the Place I have in Reversion,
"which as it standeth now unto me, is but
"like another Man's Ground buttalling
"upon my House, which may mend my
"Prospect, but it doth not fill my Barn.

This Place he meaneth, was the Registers Office in the Star-Chamber, which fell to him in the time of King *James*, and was worth about 1600 *l.* by the Year.

But to return from this Digression. When Sir *Francis Bacon* was constituted
Lord-

Lord-Keeper, the King admonisht him, that he should Seal nothing rashly; as also that he should Judg uprightly, and not extend the Royal Prerogative too high. After which, *viz.* upon the seventh Day of *May*, (which was the first Day of *Easter Term* next ensuing) he made his solemn proceeding *c* to *Westminster-Hall*, in this order. First, The Writing Clerks and inferiour Officers belonging to the Court of Chancery. Next the Students of the Law. Then the Gentlemen of his own Family. After them, the Sergeant at Arms, and bearer of the Great Seal, on foot. Then himself on Horsback, in a Gown of Purple Satin, riding betwixt the Lord-Treasurer, and Lord Privy-Seal. Next divers Earls, Barons, and Privy-Councellors. Then the Judges of the Court at *Westminster*, whose place in that proceeding, was assigned after the Privy-Councellors. And when he came into the Court, the Lord-Treasurer, and Lord Privy-Seal, gave him his Oath, the Clerk of the Crown reading it.

c Ibid.

Upon the fourth of *January*, 16 *Jac.* he was made Lord Chancellor *d* of *England*. On the eleventh of *July* next ensuing, created *e* Lord *Verulam*, and on the 27th of *January*, 18 *Jac.* advanced *f* to the

d Clauf. 16 Jac. in dorso. p. 15.
e Pat. 16 Jac. p. 11.
f Pat. 18 Jac. p. 4.

the dignity of Vicount *St. Alban*; his solemn Inveſtiture *g* being then performed at *Theobalds*; his Robe carried before him by the Lord *Carew*, and his Coronet by the Lord *Wentworth*. Whereupon he gave the King ſevenfold thanks; *h* firſt, for making him his Solicitor; ſecondly, his Attorney; thirdly, one of his Privy Council; fourthly, Lord-Keeper of the Great Seal; fifthly, Lord-Chancellor; ſixthly, Baron *Verulam*; and laſtly, Vicount *St. Alban*.

But long he enjoyed not that great Office of Lord-Chancellor: for in *Lent*, 18 *Jac.* Corruption in the exerciſe thereof being objected *i* againſt him, (of which 'tis believed, his Servants were moſt guilty, and he himſelf not much acceſſory) the Great Seal was taken *k* from him.

This Fall *l* he foreſaw, yet he made no ſhew of that baſe and mean Spirit, with which the Libel before remembred, does unworthily charge him *m*. The late King, of bleſſed Memory (then Prince) made a very differing obſervation upon him. "Returning from Hunting, *n* he eſpied a "Coach attended with a goodly Troop of "Horſemen, who, it ſeems, were gather-"ed together to wait upon the Chancellor "to his Houſe at *Gorhambury*, at the time "of his Declenſion. The Prince ſmiling, "ſaid,

g h *Annal. R. Jac. in an.* 1621.

i *Orig. Jurid. in Chr.* p. 102.
k *This is inſerted by the Publiſher.*
l *Ibid.*

m *Court of K. James,* 122, 123.

n *Aul. Coqu.* p. 174.

"said, *Well! Do we what we can, this Man
"scorns to go out like a Snuff.* And he com-
"mended his undaunted Spirit, and excel-
"lent Parts, not without some Regret, that
"such a Man should be falling off.

It is true, that after the Seal was taken from him, he became a great example of Penitence and Submission. But it was a Submission which both manifested his just sense of his Fault, and the more Venial Nature of it, as arising from Negligence, rather than Avarice and Malice.

He shewed by it, that there was not in his Heart that stiffness of Pride, which openly denies or justifies those Crimes of which it self is secretly convinced: But it appeared not by any thing, during all the time of his Eclipse of Fortune, that there was any abjectness of Spirit in him. The many and great Works which he wrote, shew a mind in him, not distracted with Anxiety, nor depressed with Shame, nor slow for want of Encouragement, nor broken with Discontent. Such a Temper is inconsistent with such noble Thoughts and Designs, such strict Attention, such vigour of Conceit, such a Masculine Style, such quickness in Composition, as appeared in his learned Labours.

When

The Lord Bacon's

When the Great Seal was taken from him, it was committed to the Custody of *Henry* Vicount *Mandevil*, (at that time President of the Council) and certain other Lords Commissioners: And upon the tenth of *July* after, to *o* Doctor *John Williams*, Dean of *Westminster*, afterwards Bishop of *Lincoln*.

_{o *Ib. p.* 104.}

Towards his rising years, he married *p* *Alice*, one of the Daughters and Co-heirs to *Benedict Barnham*, Alderman of *London*, with whom he had an ample Portion; but by her had no Children, to perpetuate his Memory, which his learned Works, being for the most part composed in the five last years of his Life, will amply supply, being then totally retired from all Civil Affairs, and applying himself daily to Contemplation and Study; the particulars were these, *q viz.*

_{p *Life of, &c. by Dr. Rawley.*}

_{q *Ibid.*}

¶ *The History of the Reign of King* Henry *the Seventh.*

Abcedarium Naturæ; or a Metaphysical piece now lost. *

Historia Ventorum.

Historia Vitæ & Mortis.

Historia Densi & Rari, not yet Printed. ‖

Historia Gravis & Levis, which is also lost.

A Discourse of a War with Spain.

_{* *Part of it is here retriev'd by the Publisher.*}

_{‖ *'Twas Publisht at London, An.* 1658.}

A

A Dialogue touching an Holy War.
The Fable of the New Atlantis.
A Preface to a Digest of the Laws of England.
The beginning of the History of the Reign of King Henry *the Eighth.*
¶ *De Augmentis Scientiarum; or the Advancement of Learning, put into Latine, with several Enrichments and Enlargements.*
¶ *Councils Civil and Moral; Or his Book of Essays, likewise enriched and enlarged.*
¶ *The Conversion of certain* Psalms *into English Verse.*
The Translation of the History of King Henry *the Seventh, into Latine; as also of the Councils, Civil and Moral, and Dialogue of the Holy War.*
¶ *His Book de Sapientiâ Veterum, revised.*
¶ *Inquisitio de Magnete.*
¶ *Topica Inquisitionis de Luce & Lumine.* } Not Printed. * * *'Twas Printed with the Book de Denso & Raro, 1658.*
¶ *Sylva Sylvarum; or his Natural History.*

He departed *r* this Life, upon the ninth day of *April*, 1626, (being *Easter-Day*) in the sixty sixth year of his Age, at the Earl of *Arundel's* House in *High-Gate*, near *London*, to which place he casually repaired about a Week before; and was Buried *ſ* in the North-side of the Chancel in St. *Michael's*

r Ibid.

ſ Ibid.

Michael's Church at St. *Albans*, according to the appointment by his last Will and Testament; because *t* the Body of his Mother lay there Interred, it being the only Church remaining within the Precinct of Old *Verulam*, where he hath a Monument of White Marble, representing his full Body in a contemplative posture, sitting in a Chair; erected by Sir *Thomas Meautys*, Knight, formerly his Secretary, but afterwards Clerk of the Council to King *James*, and King *Charles* the First. On which is this following Epitaph, Composed by the Learned Sir *Henry Wotton*, Knight.

t Ibid.

Franciscus Bacon, Baro de Verulam, S. Albani Vicecomes: Seu, notioribus titulis
Scientiarum Lumen, facundiæ Lex, sic sedebat.
Qui, postquam omnia Naturalis sapientiæ, & Civilis Arcana evolvisset, Naturæ decretum explevit. Composita solvantur, Anno. Dom. MDCXXVI. *Ætatis* Lxvi.
Tanti viri memoriæ Thomas Meautus *superstitis cultor; defuncti Admirator.*

H. P.

That

That is, *Francis Bacon*, Baron of *Veru-* [*This is a Transla-tion of the Publishers.*]
lam, Vicount of St. *Albans* : Or in more
conspicuous Titles;
The Light of the Sciences, the Law of Eloquence, sate on this manner.
Who, after he had unfolded all the Mysteries of Natural and Civil Wisdom, obeyed the Decree of Nature.
Let the *Companions* be parted ||, in the Year [|| *i. e. Soul and Body.*]
of our Lord 1626, and the sixty sixth
year of his Age.

Thomas Meautys, a Reverencer of him whilst Alive, and an Admirer of him now Dead, hath set up this to the Memory of so great a Man.

CHARACTERS
OF THE
Lord Bacon.

LONDON,
Printed for *R. C.* at the Rose and Crown
in St. *Paul's* Church-yard, 1679.

A CHARACTER OF THE Lord Bacon,

Given by Dr. *Peter Heylin*, in his Life of Arch-Bishop *Laud*, Part 1. Pag. 64. Anno 1620.

The Lord Chancellor *Bacon*, was a Man—— of a most strong Brain, and a Chymical Head; designing his Endeavours to the perfecting of the *Works of Nature*; or rather improving *Nature* to the best Advantages of Life, and the common Benefit of Mankind. Pity it was, he was not entertain'd with some liberal Salary, abstracted from all Affairs both of Court and Judicature, and furnished with Sufficiency, both of Means and Helps, for the going on in his Design: Which had it been, he might have given us such a body of *Natural Philosophy*, and made it so subservient to the Publick Good, that neither *Aristotle*, nor *Theophrastus*, amongst the Ancients; nor *Paracelsus*, or the rest of our latter Chymists, would have been considerable.

A Character of the Lord Bacon, *given by Dr.* Sprat, *in his* History *of the* Royal Society, *Part* 1. *Sect.* 16. *Pag.* 35, 36.

—— "The Third sort of *New Philosophers* have been those, who have not only disagreed from the *Ancients*, but have also propos'd to themselves the right Course of slow and sure *Experimenting:* And have prosecuted it as far as the shortness of their own Lives, or the multiplicity of their other Affairs, or the narrowness of their Fortunes, have given them leave. Such as these, we are to expect to be but few: For they must devest themselves of many vain Conceptions, and overcome a thousand false "Images,

"Images, which lie like Monsters in their
"way, before they can get as far this. And
"of these, I shall only mention one Great
"Man, who had the true Imagination of
"the whole extent of this *Enterprize*, as
"it is now set on foot; and that is, the
"Lord *Bacon*. In whose Books there are,
"every where scattered, the best Argu-
"ments that can be produc'd for the de-
"fence of *Experimental Philosophy*; and
"the best directions that are needful to
"promote it. All which he has, already
"adorn'd with so much Art; that if my
"desires could have prevail'd with some
"excellent Friends of mine, who engag'd
"me to this Work, there should have been
"no other Preface to the *History* of the *Royal*
"*Society*, but some of *his Writings*. But,
"methinks, in this one Man, I do at once
"find enough occasion, to admire the
"strength of Humane Wit, and to bewail
"the weakness of a Mortal Condition. For,
"is it not Wonderful, that he, who had
"run through all the degrees of that *Pro-*
"*fession*, which usually takes up Mens whole
"time; who had Studied, and Practised,
"and Governed the *Common Law*: Who
"had always liv'd in the Crowd, and born
"the greatest burden of Civil Business;
"Should yet find leisure enough for these
                                   "retir'd

"retird Studies, to excel all those Men,
"who separate themselves for this very pur-
"pose? He was a Man of strong, clear,
"and powerful Imaginations: His *Genius*
"was searching, and inimitable: And of
"this I need give no other Proof, than his
"Style it self; which as, for the most part,
"it describes Men's minds, as well as Pi-
"ctures do their Bodies: So it did *His*,
"above all Men living. The *Course* of it
"Vigorous, and Majestical: The *Wit* bold
"and familiar: The *Comparisons* fetch'd out
"of the way, and yet the most easie: In
"all, expressing a Soul equally skill'd in
"*Men*, and *Nature*. All this, and much
more, is true of him: But yet his *Philosophical* Works do shew, that a single and
busie Hand, can never grasp all this whole
Design, of which we treat. His *Rules*
were admirable: Yet his *History* not so
faithful as might have been wish'd in many
places: He seems rather to *take all that comes*,
than to choose; and to *heap* rather than
to *register*. But I hope this Accusation of
mine, can be no great injury to his Memory; seeing, at the same time, that I say he
had not the strength of *a thousand Men*, I
do also allow him to have had as much as
Twenty.

A Character of the Lord Bacon's Philosophy, by Mr. Abraham Cowley, in his Poem to the Royal Society.

—Some few exalted Spirits this latter Age has shown,
That labour'd to assert the Liberty
(From Guardians, who were now Usurpers Grown)
Of this Old Minor * still, Captiv'd Philosophy;
But 'twas Rebellion call'd, to Fight
For such a long oppressed Right.
Bacon at last, a mighty Man, arose,
Whom a Wise King and Nature chose
Lord-Chancellor of both their Laws,
And boldly undertook the injur'd Pupils Cause.

* Herbert in Auctorem Instaurationis — Scientiarum, sub-pupillari statu Degentium olim, Emancipator.

3.

Authority, which did a Body boast,
Though 'twas but Air condens'd and stalk'd about,
Like some old Giant's more Gigantic Ghost,
To terrifie the learned Rout

With

With the plain Magic of true Reason's light,
   He chac'd out of our sight,
Nor suffer'd Living Men to be misled
   By the vain shadows of the Dead:
To Graves, from whence it rose, the conquer'd Phantom fled;
   He broke that Monstrous God, which stood
In midst of th' Orchard, and the whole did claim,
   Which with a useless Sithe of Wood,
   And something else not worth a Name,
     (Both vast for shew, yet neither fit
     Or to defend, or to beget;
     Ridiculous and senseless Terror!) made
Children and superstitious Men afraid.
   The Orchards open now, and free;
Bacon has broke that Scar-crow Deitie;
   Come, enter, all that will,
Behold the rip'ned Fruit, come gather now your fill.
   Yet still, methinks, we fain would be
   Catching at the forbidden Tree,
     We would be like the Deitie;
When Truth and Falshood, Good and Evil we,
Without the Senses aid within our selves would see:
   For 'tis God only who can find
   All Nature in his Mind.

4.

From Words, which are but Pictures of the Thought,
(Though we our Thoughts from them perversly drew)
To Things, the Minds right Object, he it brought,
Like foolish Birds to painted Grapes we flew;
He sought and gather'd for our use the true;
And when, on heaps, the chosen Bunches lay,
He prest them wisely the Mechanic way,
'Till all their Juice did, in one Vessel joyn,
Ferment into a nourishment Divine,
   The thirsty Soul's refreshing Wine.
Who to the Life an exact Piece would make,
Must not from others Work a Copy take;
   No, not from *Reubens*, or *Vandike*;
Much less content himself to make it like
Th' Ideas, and the Images which lie
   In his own Fancy, or his Memory.
     No, He, before his sight, must place
     The natural and living Face;
     The real Object must command
Each judgment of his Eye, and motion of his Hand.

5.

From these, and all long Errors of the way,
In which our wandring Predecessors went,
And like th' old *Hebrews*, many years did
    stray
  In Deserts but of small extent,
Bacon, like *Moses*, led us forth at last,
  The barren Wilderness he past,
  Did on the very Border stand
  Of the blest promis'd Land,
And, from the Mountains top of his exal-
    ted Wit,
  Saw it himself, and shew'd us it.
But Life did never to one Man allow
Time to discover Worlds, and conquer too;
Nor can so short a Line sufficient be,
To fadom the vast depths of Nature's Sea.
  The work he did we ought t' admire,
And were unjust if we should more require
From his few years, divided 'twixt th' excess
Of low Affliction, and high Happiness:
For who on things remote can fix his sight,
  That's always in a Triumph, or a Fight?

FINIS.

www.ingramcontent.com/pod-product-compliance
Lightning Source LLC
Chambersburg PA
CBHW030349230426
43664CB00007BB/589